Chickasaw Chief George Colbert: His Family and His Country

Chickasaw Chief George Colbert: His Family and His Country

Rickey Butch Walker

Published by:
Bluewater Publications
1812 CR 111
Killen, Alabama 35645
www.BluewaterPublications.com

Table of Content

Introduction

George Colbert was born about 1744 in the Chickasaw Nation in northeastern Mississippi. George was raised and lived most of his life in the original eastern Chickasaw homelands which included north Mississippi, western Tennessee, southwestern Kentucky, and into north Alabama as far east as Flint River near present-day Huntsville, Alabama. The Chickasaws were the first tribe that occupied the Tennessee Valley to make peace with the United States Government; and the Colbert boys distinguished themselves as military leaders while fighting with the Americans in various campaigns. George Colbert was commissioned to the rank of Colonel by President George Washington, and his older half-brother William Colbert was promoted to the rank of General.

Hernando De Soto
1496-1542

Even though the Chickasaws were considered a small tribe of some 5,000 people, they were some of the fiercest warriors in the Southeastern United States. In the 1541 Spanish expedition through the Chickasaw Nation, the Chickasaws inflicted great loss of equipment when they burned Hernando De Soto's army camp because he tried to enslave some 200 Chickasaw warriors to serve as load bearers. Shortly after the fight with the Chickasaws, Hernando De Soto died and his body was dumped into the Mississippi River; then, the straggling remains of his army made their way south to Spanish territory.

On three occasions from the 1720's through the 1750's, the French tried to defeat the

Chickasaws but failed miserably. George was born prior to the third French-Chickasaw War; and his father James Logan Colbert fought against the French. The Chickasaws were never defeated by the French or any other group; therefore, because of never being defeated in war, the Chickasaws became known as the "Unconquered, Unconquerable". It was in this rich and noble tradition of the Chickasaws that George Colbert was born to a full-blood Chickasaw mother and a full-blood Scots father. For all intents and purposes, George Colbert was Chickasaw and he reared in the lifestyles of the Chickasaws. George Colbert became a great Chickasaw warrior, leader, and chief.

George Colbert's Chickasaw people were said to be the cleanest and neatest group of natives on any continent at any time. Since the Chickasaws bathed every day in the summer and winter, no other people were considered cleaner. During the depth of winter, they were known to break the ice at the river bank so they could enter the water to bathe. Many historians believe that this high regard for cleanliness was one of the reasons the Chickasaws sided with the Celtic traders of the English as opposed to the French and the Spanish. Even though the English sold much better goods at half the price of both the French and Spanish just to undermine their influence with the Chickasaws and Cherokees, George Colbert was very cautious and oversaw much of the trade of his people.

Horatio Cushman who lived among the Choctaws and Chickasaws gives his description of the Chickasaw people as follows: *"The Chickasaws, in common with all the Indians of the South, possessed many fine orators whose orations were eloquent, persuasive and full of animation; and it is a question of great doubt if the White Race ever found among their uneducated citizens a single orator who could respectably compare with hundreds of unlettered orators among the Indians of the South, or even of any of the North American Indians. As a race of people the Chickasaws were tall, elegantly proportioned, erect and muscular, with a square forehead, high cheek bones, compressed lips and dark penetrating eyes. In their councils (like all other Indians) grave and dignified, and never indulged, under any circumstances, in noisy harangues; they spoke slowly, distinctly and to the point. It is, and has always been, the universal declaration and belief of the Whites that the North American Indians are taciturn, grave, and never smiled or indulged in merriment or laughter under any circumstances. This is a great error, and but a repetition of the same old edition of the same old story, which, like all else said and written and published about the North American Indians, was begotten by ignorance, conceived in duplicity and brought forth in prejudice—to say the least of it. Never did a more jovial, good natured and light hearted race of people exist upon earth than the North American Indians. True, they were grave and taciturn in the presence of strangers, and the reason is obvious. The white people*

2

(excepting the old missionaries of the long ago), in all their actions among them, and in all their conduct toward them, have ever and everywhere assumed an air of superiority over them, which the Indians have ever justly denied; and which justly created in their minds pity for the foolish self-conceit and egotism of the Whites, which seemed to them a lamentable weakness unknown and unseen before, in the human race; and also created equal contempt for such a display of presumption and evident want of sound judgment, or rather of common sense; the natural consequences of which were taciturnity and gravity when in the presence of such self-imagined august specimens of humanity" (Cushman, 1899).

Some of the best known Chickasaw chiefs during the years of European and American occupation were the half Scots sons of James Logan Colbert. One of those sons, Chickasaw Chief George Colbert, became a famous operator of the ferry that crossed the Tennessee River at Natchez Trace which became known as Colbert's Ferry.

General Mad Anthony Wayne
1/1/1745-12/15/1796

Earlier his ferry was located at the mouth of Bear Creek; however by the treaty of December 1801 with the United States and the Chickasaws, the ferry was moved up the Tennessee River to higher ground that was not subject to flooding. This crossing became the famed trade route the Natchez Trace, a former buffalo trail coming from the Big Lick or French Salt Lick at present-day Nashville, Tennessee south into Alabama and Mississippi.

George Colbert served not only as the chief of the Chickasaws for 12 years, but he also served in the United States military in different campaigns under General Mad Anthony Wayne, General George Washington, and General Andrew Jackson. George attained the rank of colonel in the United States Army and was highly esteemed by his white counterparts. Although Colonel George Colbert was presented a sword by President Andrew Jackson for his military service, the Chickasaws trust and admiration of Andrew Jackson was dashed. The Chickasaws were betrayed by Jackson who rewarded their loyalty by seeing to it that they were removed from their ancestral homelands in Alabama and Mississippi.

Today, many people in the northwestern portion of Alabama and northeastern Mississippi are tied to George Colbert and other members of his family, not only by history, but by blood. They admirably speak of their Colbert ancestors in very favorable words and are proud of their association with George Colbert, a person considered by many to be the greatest Celtic-Indian legend and hero of this area. George Colbert was half Chickasaw and half Scots and was known as Tootemastubbe or The Ferryman by his Indian friends and relatives. He was born close to the Tennessee River about 1744 near the mouth of Bear Creek in the present-day corner of northeast Mississippi and died January 7, 1839, near Fort Towson, Arkansas in Indian Territory.

George Colbert's Father

James Logan Colbert's Origin

George Colbert's father was James Logan Colbert, who historians agree was of Scots ancestry and came to Chickasaw country with traders of the British. The hub of British trade was located in Olde Charles Town, South Carolina where many pack horsemen would bring goods of English merchants along the High Town Path into north Alabama and northeastern Mississippi to trade with the Cherokees and Chickasaws. It was from this eastern colonial town that James Logan Colbert first came into the Chickasaw Nation of the southeastern Indian Territory at a young age. According to James Adair, Colbert had lived among the Chickasaws from childhood as seen in the following statement, *"The deputies treatment of Captain James Colbert, who has lived among the Chikkasah from his childhood, and speaks their language even with more propriety than the English, deserves to be recorded -- but I hope the gentleman will soon do it himself, to show the higher powers the consequences of appointing improper, mercenary, and haughty persons to such offices"* (Adair, 1775). Notice that Adair recognizes that James Logan Colbert had a military rank of Captain probably given him by the British commanders.

Some historians disagree on the origin of James Logan Colbert saying he was born in Scotland and came to the colonies during the Jacobite Rebellion in the early 1700's. Another source states that James Logan Colbert came to America aboard the Prince of Whales, which landed at Darien, Georgia on January 10, 1736. Also on board were John McIntosh, Lachlan McGillivray, and John's older brother, Lachlan McIntosh. All these men played significant roles in the history of the "Five Civilized Tribes" (Martini, 1986). According to family member Linda Catoe who posted on Rootsweb on April 10, 2000, *"he (James Logan Colbert) apparently was a stowaway on a vessel called "The Prince of Wales" which departed from Dornach on October 10, 1725, and arrived at Darion, Georgia on January 10, 1736. Family archives indicate he was 15 years old and originated from Inverness, Scotland"*.

Prince of Whales

Scots Irish—During the early 1700's, approximately one million Celtic people of Scots Irish origin came to America seeking freedom they were unable to find in their homelands. Many Celts came as indentured servants of the English and were seeking a

5

new life away from bloodshed and hardships in Northern Ireland. The Scots emigrated from Scotland to Ireland and then to America and were neither pure Scots nor Irish. Some considered themselves as Scots, and others were thought of as Irish; therefore, they became known as the Scots Irish.

The mass migration of Scots to Ulster in Northern Ireland did not come about as a natural urge to seek new or better lands or homes. The move from Scotland to Ireland was a plan developed by James I of England and was responsible for violence that still lingers in the region of Northern Ireland today. It took England many years to defeat the fierce descendants of the ancient Celtic leaders and to control their lands in Northern Ireland. Finally, in 1602, England gained a toehold in Northern Ireland and took possession of the land ruled by Irish chieftains Tyrone and Tyconnel.

Therefore, England and Ireland became divided by years of bloody conflict; but, after the Protestant Reformation from 1517-1648, religion was another factor that separated the two countries. King James planned to populate the area with Protestant Scots settlers who would outnumber and defeat the Catholic Irish. Although holding the title "King of Scots," James had no love for his northern subjects, whom he called barbarous; however, these Celtic people of Scots and Irish ancestry became somewhat assimilated causing great difficulty in determining whether a person was truly Scotch or Irish; therefore, to escape bloodshed many Scots Irish migrated to America. These first Scots Irish emigrants were usually young indentured kids; and, they were in Southeastern United States

King James I of England
6/19/1566-3/27/1625

some 100 years prior to the four million that migrated to the northeastern cities of America during the Irish potato famine of the middle 1840's. Many of the first indentured Scots Irish youth came to America to serve English merchants until they were 21 years of age; they came on English ships they boarded at various seaports including Cork, Ireland. Very quickly many of these young Scots Irish men worked with traders to the Indian nations, took Indian wives, and moved out of the British colonies to live their lives of freedom within their Indian families.

According to the Chronicles of Oklahoma, James Logan Colbert came to America from Scotland during the upheaval as follows: *The collapse of the Jacobite Uprising in Scotland, fomented by the Scottish adherents of James the Pretender, in 1715, and the ensuing years of reprisal exacted by the English, influenced the emigration to America of many of the grim Highlanders. The inflow continued for many years. The first contingent of these people to settle in Georgia arrived at Savannah, in January 1736, and among these earliest arrivals was young Logan Colbert. He doubtless came with the party led by John Mohr McIntosh which sailed from Inverness, Scotland, on October 18, 1735, on the ship "Prince of Wales" commanded by Captain George Dunbar. Soon after landing at Savannah, courageous young Colbert abandoned the white settlement, ventured to the far West and settled among the militant Chickasaw Indians who then ranged along the eastern banks of the Mississippi from the mouth of the Ohio to the vast stretches of the lower river. It was an adventurous undertaking and his life story, if known, doubtless would be one of dramatic interest. He seems to have cultivated a sympathetic understanding with the Indians, married into the tribe and became a character of much prominence among them and a renowned leader in their wars against the French. The descendants of Logan Colbert in Oklahoma today, recall with much pride, the emigrant Scotch lad of the early days of the eighteenth century. He met a tragic death at the hands of a negro slave who was accompanying him on a trip back to Georgia* (Meserve, 1937).

Most widely accepted by historians is that James Logan Colbert was born in the Carolinas in the colonies and came to the Chickasaws with Indian traders. The most convincing evidence points to James Logan Colbert's birth in the Carolinas around 1721. According to Chickasaw interpreter Malcolm McGee from an interview with Lyman Draper in 1841, stated that Colbert was, *"a native of the Carolinas, probably South Carolina and came to the Chickasaw Nation prior to 1750."* It is highly probably that James fell in love with the beautiful Chickasaw maidens and chose to stay among them. Another historic version claims that James Logan Colbert was born in the colonies about 1721 and traveled west to the area of the Muscle Shoals of the Great Bend of the Tennessee River in Alabama. He came from the Carolinas with a band of

Scots Irish traders of the British merchants, traveled with them into Chickasaw Nation, stayed among the Chickasaw as a youth, and was eventually adopted by a Chickasaw family. His contemporary, fellow trader James Adair wrote that Colbert *"...lived among the Chikkasaw from his childhood, and speaks their language even with more propriety than the English. He married three Chickasaw wives and had nine children: seven sons and 2 daughters. He led his life as an Indian trader, interpreter, and leader of men during a time in history which was a turbulent struggle for land and new opportunity"* (Adair, 1775).

On July 5, 1782, a declaration was made by Spanish merchant Silbestre Labadie who had been a captive of Colbert in the spring of 1782 when his boat and goods were captured at Chickasaw Bluff on the Mississippi River. Labadie stated that James Logan Colbert, *"was about 60 years old, possessed of good health, and a strong constitution. An active man, despite his years, he had a violent temper, and was capable of enduring the greatest hardship. He had lived among the Chickasaws for 40 years and boasted that he was owner of a fine house and some hundred and fifty blacks. He said he had several sons by Chickasaw women, who were very important chiefs in that nation."* If the statement made by Labadie in 1782 is correct on Colbert's age of 60, it appears that James Logan Colbert was born about 1722. If Labadie's statement of Colbert living with the Chickasaws for 40 years is correct, then James Logan Colbert had been living with the Chickasaws since 1742.

At one time, Colbert stated, *"I was born in the Carolinas and about 1740, moved to the Chickasaw Nation and married into the tribe"*. Apparently, in a letter dictated to Governor Harrison of Virginia on July 25, 1783, James Logan Colbert stated he wished to, *"serve the country in which he lives and was born"*.

James Logan Colbert's Family—It appears that James Logan Colbert was named after his maternal grandfather James Logan. If Joseph Calvert was his father, his last name eventually got changed to Colbert. Name changes were very common in the early days of this country, because many people wrote names like they sounded to them. William Lindsey McDonald (2007) said that, James Logan Colbert *"may have been born in North Carolina between 1722 and 1727. These sources indicate, too, that he was related to Joseph Calvert, who may have been his father or grandfather or perhaps a close relative. One family genealogist suspects that James' maternal grandfather was James Logan, a woodsman who traded with the Indians"* (McDonald, 2007).

In addition, Richard A. Colbert (1994) in *James Logan Colbert of the Chickasaws: The Man and the Myth* show a strong relationship between inter-related families associated with the Logan family and Calvert family which suggests that the two families were acquainted with each other; therefore, children from the Logan and Calvert families could have easily married and had a son they named James Logan Calvert (Colbert). In addition, Colbert (1994) also shows another interesting relationship of both the Logan and Calvert families to their neighbors who were Indian traders that did business with the Chickasaws. All these families were living in the same area where a lot of the Chickasaw traders were also living which indicates that James Logan Colbert could have initially been a pack horseman of a local family; therefore, he had the means to travel into the Chickasaw Nation at a young age. The relationships identified by Colbert (1994) suggest that James Logan Colbert was very probable the son of Joseph Calvert and maternal grandson of James Logan as seen in the following:

James Logan—*According to Colbert family tradition, a man named "James Logan" was the grandfather of James Logan Colbert. Given the similarity of names, plus the fact that Chickasaw traders lived at Quankey Creek, Occoneechee Neck, and on Plumb Tree Island, circumstantial evidence strongly suggests that this James Logan was indeed the grandfather of James Logan Colbert.*

In 1732 James Logan, Joseph Sims and James Moore witnessed the selling of land from Thomas Matthews to Joseph Brewer from Albermarle County, North Carolina, at Quankey Creek..."200 acres in north west parish on the south side of the Morratuck River and the south side of Great Quankey Creek whereon the said Matthews now lives, joining Peter Jones, other lands of said Matthews, the land formerly owned by Robert Wood and the creek part of a tract granted to William Williams for 340 acres May 17, 1730, Witnesses: Joseph Sims, James Logan, James Moore..." William Williams, a former owner mentioned in the above sale, had traded with the Chickasaw Nations since the early 1720s.

Additional information on James Logan comes from F.B. Kegley...he describes some of the earliest settlers on "the southwest frontier below the mountains" in Virginia..."On the South eastern creeks were... the highest inhabitant on Roanoke River, about six miles above the fork. Among the first to become settled on Cub Creek were John and William Caldwell, James Logan..."The Caldwells and Logans had originally come from Pennsylvania before migrating to Virginia and North Carolina. In addition to settling a Presbyterian colony, several of the Caldwells were also Chickasaw traders. When Bernard Romans visited the Chickasaw and Choctaw Indians in 1775, he wrote of his accounts of an Indian trader named Caldwell...

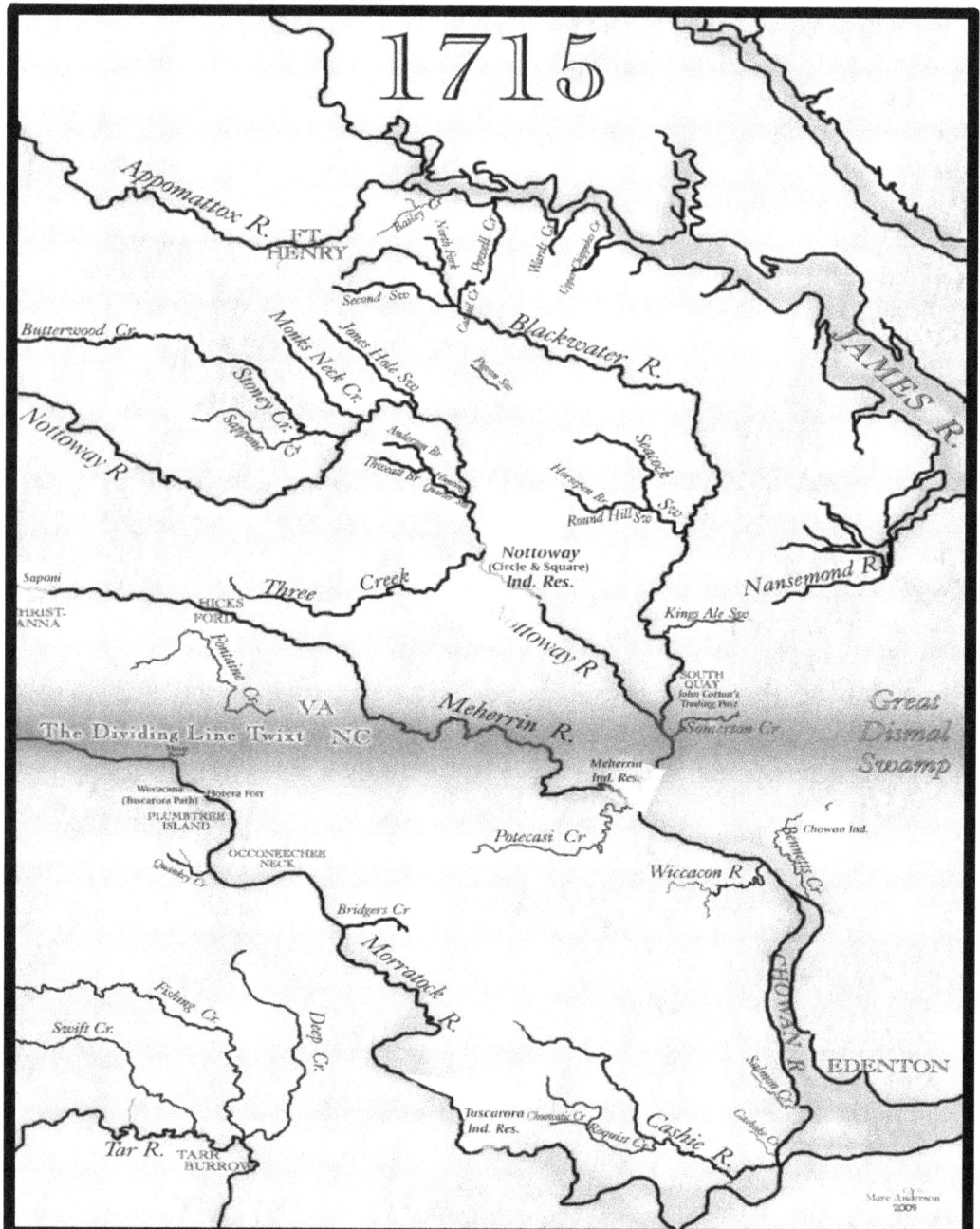

Plum Tree Island Map by Marc Anderson, 2009

Joseph Calvert—*The family of* <u>Joseph Calvert</u> *(pronounced kahl/vert) also lived on Plumb Tree Island and owned property on the Occoneechee Neck. Deed records* *strongly suggest that <u>Joseph Calvert</u> and Joseph Colson were either partners and/or related to one another. On March 20, 1721, both bought property on the Morratuck River from Thomas Whitmell, an Indian trader..."<u>Joseph Calvert</u> bought 385 acres of land on Plumb Tree Island from Thomas Whitmell...on June 24, 1724, <u>Joseph Calvert</u> bought an additional 250 acres from John Gray on Morratuck River and Plumb Tree Island adjacent to William Green near Foltera Fort.*

The lands bought by Colson and <u>Calvert</u>, and Turbeville on the north side of the Morratuck (Roanoke) River were near an Indian path leading to the courthouse in Brunswick County, Virginia, and to the plantation of Major Robert Mumford. The Turbevilles, Colsons, and <u>Calverts</u> worked for Major Robert Mumford of Brunswick County, Virginia, and with Thomas Whitmell.

Major Mumford was a large land speculator and the descendant of an Indian trading family...since the late 1600s. The Turbevilles learned of the Occoneechee Neck on the Roanoke through their association with Arthur Kavanaugh and Major Robert Mumford, who were large landowners in Virginia and North Carolina by 1712...Thomas Whitmell, the Indian trader, bought six hundred acres from Kavanaugh on the north side of the Morattuck River in 1715. Before moving to North Carolina, the Turbevilles sold land they owned in Prince George County, Virginia, to Peter Mitchell, an Indian trader and land speculator that lived high on the Roanoke River near the Caldwells and <u>James Logan</u>. Major Mumford acted as Mary Turbeville's power of attorney and it was witnessed by Arthur Kavanaugh and John Anderson, who was also an Indian trader and land speculator who worked with Mumford...When Richard Turbeville and his family moved to North Carolina, they lived on the Occoneechee with other Chickasaw traders and next to Anderson, Colson, Pace, Mason, Gibson, Lang (Long), and Thomas Whitmell. On March 1, 1720, the Lords Proprietors of North Carolina issued patents to Plumb Tree Island and on the south side of Plumb Tree Swamp abutting the island. These patents went to Thomas Whitmell, William Green, John Cotton, John Geddes, William Reeves, Barnaby Milton, and Robert Lang (Long). Shortly after Thomas Whitmell obtained his patent on Plumb Tree Island, <u>Joseph Calvert</u> and his family moved on the island and were later joined by the Turbevilles and Colsons (Colbert, 1994).

On April 4, 2009, Richard A. Colbert confirmed on a post on WorldFamilies.net that indeed, James Logan Colbert's father was Joseph Calvert in the following: *I am a descendant of Christopher Calvert. He arrived in Accomack County, VA in the summer of 1636 from Northampton Shire, England. <u>My 5th great-grandfather, Joseph Calvert, was the father of James Logan Colbert of the Chickasaws. James Logan Colbert was</u>*

born ca. 1722 on Plum Tree Island in the Roanoke River and near the NC/VA border. James' mother was Amy Beeson. She married four times; First to Francis Vernon, and then to Joseph Calvert. They were married approximately 25 years. After Joseph died she married Phillip Smith, then a man named Catlin. She moved to London and was alive in 1775 when she came back to Halifax County, NC to settle estate problem re: Plum Tree Island. James' twin brother, Thomas, was my 4th great-grandfather. He was indentured to be a blacksmith and lived in the town of Halifax (8 miles south of Plum Tree Island) for over twenty years. He and his family later moved to Bute (Franklin County), NC. James was indentured to Abraham Colson to be a tanner and Indian trader. Abe Colson was a registered Chickasaw trader. His brother, Joseph Colson, lived on Plum Tree Island and bought land on the island the same day as Joseph Calvert. In 1736 Abraham Colson, William Turbeville, Gideon Gibson, and the Mulkey family moved to Sandy Bluff, S.C. The Turbeville and Mulkey family also lived on Plumtree Island and all of the above families were related by marriage. Gideon Gibson was also a Chickasaw Indian trader. Before moving to Sandy Bluff he lived on land near Plum Tree Island. This land he bought from Robert Lang/Long/Longo who also lived on Plum Tree Island. Robert Long was a descendant of Anthony Longo of Accomack County, VA and lived there the same time as Christopher Calvert. (The Colson's also lived in Accomack County, VA during the mid-1600's). In 1750 James Logan Colbert, James Adair, Abraham Colson, and Johnathan Mulkey all bought land in Bladen County, NC (now Robeson County) on the same day. Abe Colson later died in 1750. He had been scalped by Indians in 1745 and never recovered from his injuries. Christopher Calvert II and his wife Elinor had five children: Christopher III, Charles, John, George, and Mary. Mary married Garrett Sipple in 1675. I am trying to track down the brothers of Christopher II. Christopher III married Ann _____. They had son Reuben b. Nov. 5, 1682 in Richmond County, VA. Christopher III is believed the father of Joseph Calvert of Plum Tree Island (Colbert, 2009).

When James Logan Colbert was listed in English records as a trader to the Chickasaw Nation his name is spelled James Calbert. Notice that James' name written by the English is spelled very similar to his father, and also note that James Logan Colbert named his last two sons Joseph and James probably after his father and grandfather! The preponderance of evidence leads one to believe that James Logan Colbert's father was Joseph Calvert and his maternal grandfather was James Logan.

James Logan Colbert's Occupation

Pirate—As some other Celtic people who lived among the Indians prior to their lands being taken for white settlements, James Logan Colbert was a pirate taking from the French and Spanish on the Mississippi River. Colbert fought with Chickasaws and also led their warriors into battle against the French and Spanish along the Mississippi River where valuable slaves and cargo were confiscated. During his days as a pirate, James Logan Colbert took their slaves, goods, supplies, and arms for the tribe and his personal use. Through his piracy, Colbert acquired many black slaves and much valuable property.

It is also important to note that James Logan Colbert had 150 slaves by 1782 which means he had the capacity to farm large tracts of land. These black slaves were probably taken from the French and Spanish who Colbert considered his enemy; therefore, just based on his slave holdings, Colbert was a very wealthy man. He definitely got some of his fortune through his piracy activities. His friend Colonel John Montgomery was officially charged with helping James Logan Colbert in pirate raids on Spanish shipping on the Mississippi River. In addition, one of the men who was a pack horseman and trading for Colbert was Richard Hyde whose father by the same name worked

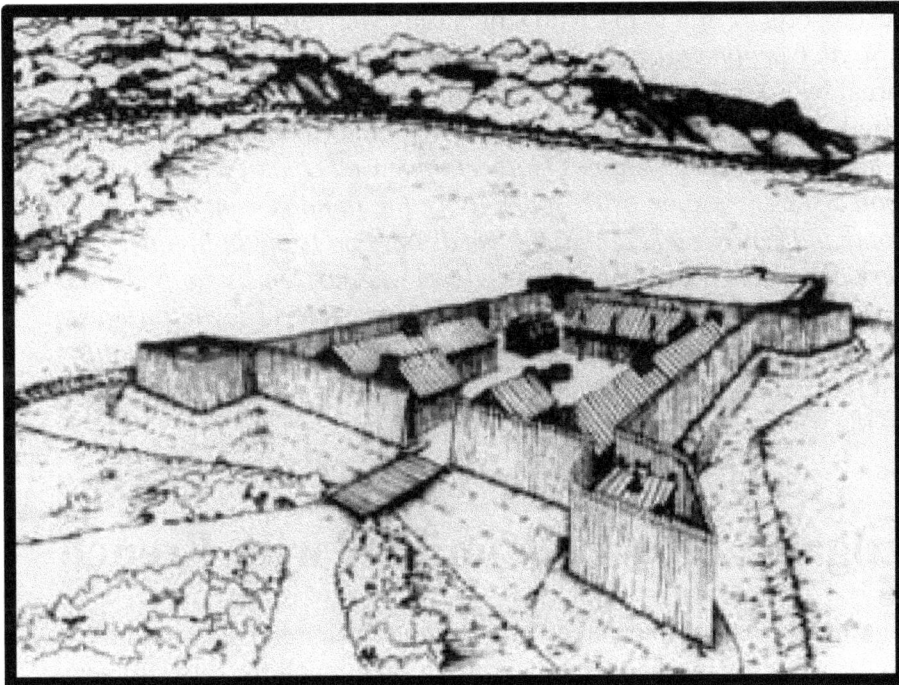

**Illustration of Fort Prince George on Cherokee Path
Built in 1753 on Keowee River in Pickens County, SC**

with the famous Pirate Black Beard, who was killed in 1718; therefore, through his acquaintances Colbert had knowledge of piracy. It is documented by the Spanish merchant Silbestre Labadie that James Logan Colbert participated in raiding his boats on the Mississippi River as a pirate.

Trader—James Logan Colbert's primary occupation was that of a trader to the Chickasaw Nation in northwest Alabama and northeast Mississippi. On January 22, 1766, James Logan Colbert was found on a list titled *Traders and Pack-horsemen* which was found in the records of England. During an interview in 1767, Malcolm McGee was asked to describe the Indian traders who lived with the Chickasaws. McGee described the traders by their place of birth: Adair, Irish; Bubby, English; Buckles, English; Hightower, Dutchman; Colbert, Carolinian. All the traders, according to McGee, had a Chickasaw wife except Colbert who had three. McGee deduced that the above traders had lived with the Chickasaw for over twenty years because by 1767 all of them had full-grown "half-breed" children.

The following is probably a trading expedition led by James Logan Colbert and is one of the earliest reports of him being with Chickasaw warriors. The information was found in *The South Carolina Gazette*, Number 1368, October 11-18, 1760, and was published in a journal by a Mr. Langley. His September 26, 1760, entry made at Fort Prince George, stated, *"Soon three or four other fellows (Indians) came, and were at our bake house when to our surprise, James Colbert appeared coming up, with signal and two letters upon a stick. As soon as he spoke to us, the Indians went off. He then returned to the mouth of Crow Creek, about 400 yards off, and brought in four Chicasahs that were concealed there. The poor fellows were extremely fatigued and their leader Jockey's son was sick, having a fever every other day. They left Augusta about the 18th of August, and on their way staid some time at a fort the inhabitants were building twist this and Savannah River, and were obliged to leave five others of their party sick, in the woods a days-journey from the said fort."*

James Logan Colbert's Conflicts with French

James Logan Colbert—When James Logan Colbert first moved into the Chickasaw Nation, the Chickasaws had been in conflict the French for some 40 years; however, prior to the end of the French and Chickasaw wars James Logan Colbert had become a highly regarded leader among Chickasaw people. The French perceived

Colbert as a great annoyance and danger to their shipping interests on the Mississippi River.

According to Cushman (1899), the French applied James Logan Colbert's name to the Mississippi River and referred to it as the Rivere de Colbert as follows: *James Logan Colbert came with some of the early traders and adventurers who assisted the Chickasaws in their wars against the French. At an early day he was a renowned - leader among them, and to that degree of celebrity, that one of the names given to the Mississippi River by the early French writers, during the days of their wars with that people with whom he had identified himself, was Rivere de Colbert sustaining the conjecture, that Logan Colbert was the name of the most famous chief among the Chickasaws; who at that time swayed the scepter of absolute authority over the country along the east banks of the Mississippi River to the great annoyance and danger of the French in ascending and descending that mighty stream. Though little else of the life of Logan has escaped oblivion, except he lived, he died; yet his name has been handed down to posterity in that of his noble line of descendants, who figure upon the pages of history as being among the influential families of that Nation* (Cushman 1899).

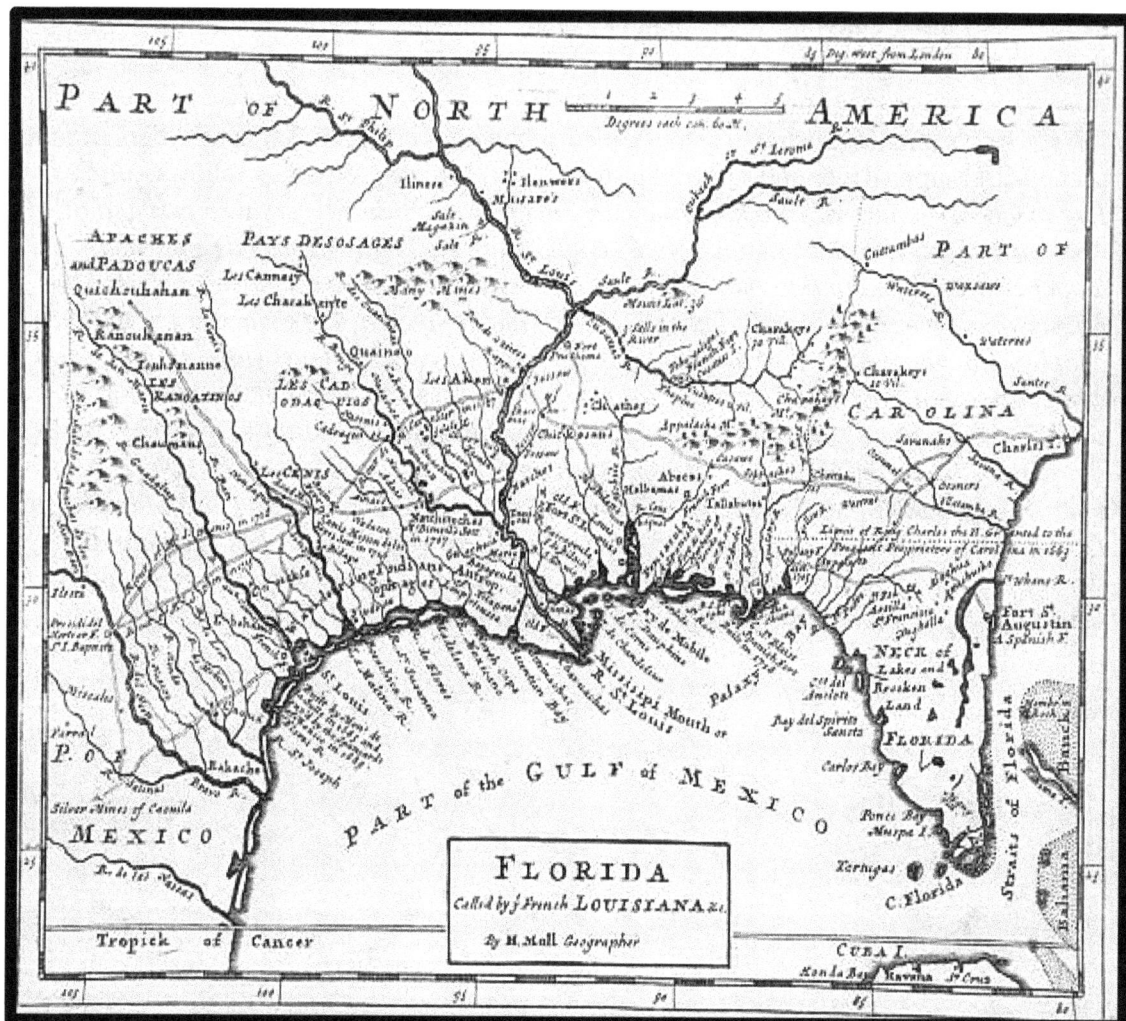

French Louisiana Land Claims

French Land Claims—The French published a southeastern United States map in 1733 and referred to a trail which follows portions of the High Town Path as the Chemin de la Caroline. The Chemin de la Caroline is interpreted as a route to and from the Carolinas. The Chemin de la Caroline map shows a trail passing through Oakfuskee then proceeding northwest through the center of Alabama to the Chickasaw towns on the upper Tombigbee River System. The western portion of the Chemin de la Caroline appears to travel westerly along the High Town Path route from Flat Rock Camp to the French Landing on the Chattawatchee River which is now Cotton Gin Port of the Tombigbee River.

16

According to the 1663 map, the French land claim southern boundary was south of the Tennessee River in Alabama and followed along the Tennessee Divide which was the same line as the Spanish northern boundary. The French Territory lay to the north of the divide with the Spanish claims to the south of the Tennessee Divide (Buggey, 1980). The French tried to control most of the Indian trade in the Mississippi River Valley which included the Tennessee Valley. They had an established trading post located at the Muscle Shoals by 1715. In addition, French officials regarded it as essential to establish French presence and power in that region to thwart the English thrust which had nearly reached the Mississippi.

Reports from French traders in the Northwest warned that "the English are coming," confirming the English traders' relentless march from their base at Charleston, South Carolina to the West. French and English traders inevitably were the vanguard of troops, fortifications, and settlements. Their daring and intensively competitive attempts to establish commercial relations with tribes in the lower Mississippi Valley prompted the early incidents in the long and bloody contest for control of this region which lasted from the 1680s to 1763. At times, Spain was a reluctant participant in this power struggle which centered on the Chickasaws (Gibson, 1971). However, the British maintained greater influence with the Chickasaws and Cherokees than did the French. The British goods were half the price of French goods and usually much better. The French had a much greater alliance with the Choctaw than either the Chickasaws or Cherokees.

First French-Chickasaw War—French troubles with the Chickasaws began in 1698 because of the undermining influence of the English from Carolina. The French tried to block the Carolina trader paths using Choctaw Indians, with whom they had a strong alliance. The French were unable or unwilling to supply the amount of trade goods desired by the Chickasaws; therefore, they turned to the English who delivered large pack trains and caravans loaded with quality goods to the Chickasaw Nation. By 1720, the first French-Chickasaw War broke out with the killing of a French trader. The first Chickasaw-French War ended early in 1725 when French officers led their Choctaw companies from ambush positions on the Carolina trader paths back to the Choctaw Nation (Gibson, 1971).

Second French-Chickasaw War—The second French-Chickasaw War started in 1731 because of the burning of three captured Chickasaws and refusal by Chickasaws to release Natchez refugees to the French. Bienville, French Governor of Mobile, methodically plotted his major offensive against the Chickasaw Towns in the upper

Tombigbee. In 1736, Bienville was determined to defeat the English supported Chickasaws.

Allied with Choctaws, Bienville's army camped six miles from the upper Tombigbee Chickasaw Towns ready for an assault. The following account from Albert James Pickett's *History of Alabama*, 1851, pages 156-160 gives the situation, *"May 24, 1736: His intention, at first, was*

BIENVILLE'S FORT

On May 22, 1736, a military force commanded by Jean Baptiste Le Moyne de Bienville, Governor of French Louisiana, landed nearby to attack the Chickasaw. A palisade of 600 log posts was built near here as a base of operations. Defeated in the Battle of Ackia at Tupelo, Bienville retreated to the fort and to Mobile on May 29.

to march to a circuitous direction, around the Chickasaw villages...The Chickasaws had fortified themselves with much skill, and were assisted by Englishmen, who caused them to hoist a flag of their country over one of their defenses. The French troops, as they advanced, were not a little surprised to see the British Lion, against which many of them had often fought in Europe, now floating over the rude huts of American Indians, and bidding them defiance...The brave Chickasaws maintained their positions in the fortified houses, and, from loop holes, riddled the French with their unerring rifles... When the French had retreated some distance towards Bienville's headquarters, the Choctaws, by way of bravado, rushed up to the Chickasaw fortifications, as if they intended to carry them by storm, but receiving a general volley from the enemy, they fled in great terror over the prairie...Night now shrouded the scene with its sable mantle, and the French troops reposed behind some trees which had been felled for their protection.

French Map showing the location of Fort Tombeche
Fort Tombeche at top of map under Les Chicachas

 The Chickasaws remained quiet within their entrenchments. At length day dawned, and exhibited to Bienville a painful sight. On the ramparts of the Chickasaws were suspended the French soldiers and officers, whom Beauchamp was forced to leave upon the field. Their limbs had been separated from their bodies, and thus were they made to dangle in the air, for the purpose of insulting the defeated invaders. Many of the officers wished to rush again upon the villages, but Bienville was determined to retreat, as the Choctaws were of no assistance to him, and he was without cannon to batter down the fortifications...If the Chickasaws had followed up the French, they

19

could easily have destroyed Bienville's army at this time. At length the army reached Fort "Tombechbe," now Jones Bluff. Bienville, sending on a portion of the troops, and the sick and wounded to Mobile, disembarked at the fort. He remained there, however, but one day...the governor entered his boats, and continued the voyage until they were moored at the town of Mobile" (Pickett, 1851).

Fort Tombechbe—Fort Tombechbe was a stockade fort built to support Bienville's war against the Chickasaws. The fort was located on the Chattawatchee River, present-day Tombigbee River in what is now Sumter County, Alabama. It was constructed under the leadership of Bienville in 1736-37 as trading post for the Choctaws and to provide supplies in the war the French were waging against the Chickasaws. Tombechbe was a major French outpost built on Choctaw lands about 270 miles up the Tombigbee River from Mobile, Alabama on an 80-foot limestone bluff and would play a major role in the French efforts to stop English intrusions into the area. Bienville claimed that the new fort was to protect the Choctaw from the Chickasaws.

**Jean Baptiste LeMoyne,
Sieur de Bienville**
2/23/1680-3/7/1767

Control of the fort passed to the British in 1763, who renamed it Fort York, where present-day York, Alabama gets its name. In 1793 the Spanish got control of the area and built a new fort named Fort Confederation. In 1802 the United States got possession of the fort and General George S. Gaines used it as a trading post for the Choctaws beginning in 1816. The United States stopped using the post in 1823 and it was basically abandoned until 1980 when it was eventually turned over to the University of West Alabama.

James Logan Colbert came to the Chickasaw Nation shortly after they had won the second war with the French. The French under command of Bienville suffered a bitter defeat at the hands of the Chickasaws. The second French-Chickasaw War ended in February 1740 with both sides agreeing to end hostilities and exchange prisoners. After serving as Governor of Mobile for forty years, Bienville was returned to France because of being unable to defeat the Chickasaws.

Third French-Chickasaw War—Trouble between the French and Chickasaw continued with raids occurring at frequent intervals. James Logan Colbert was living with the Chickasaws and had several half-blood Chickasaw children by the time of the third French-Chickasaw War began in 1752. During this war, the French were determined to annihilate the Chickasaw Nation. Marquis de Vaudreuil, the new French Governor of Mobile, organized seven hundred French regulars and a large number of Choctaws to invade the Chickasaw Nation. The invasion force followed the route of Bienville up to the Tombigbee and met with the same fate as his predecessor. Therefore, after three bloody wars the French were unable to defeat the English supported Chickasaws. France finally relinquished the area to the English on January 1, 1763.

According to *Two Hundred Years at Muscle Shoals*, "*Oka Kapassa was established as a Cherokee village about 1770 on the west bank of Coldwater, or Spring Creek, at its confluence with the Tennessee, about one mile west of the present Tuscumbia. This site was resorted to by neighboring Indians for the purpose of trading with the French who still persisted on the Wabash, and became the source of great vexation and numerous outrages to the Cumberland settlements about our present Nashville*" (Leftwich, 1935). Eventually, the French were defeated in several battles by the British Alliance with the Chickasaws and Cherokees; however, toward the end of the 1770s, French influence greatly diminished. Cumberland settlers organized a campaign against the French Trading Post at Coldwater in present-day Tuscumbia and wiped them out.

James Logan Colbert's American Conflicts

Captain James Logan Colbert worked with the British and eventually led Chickasaw warriors against the Americans at Fort Jefferson that had been built on hunting grounds of the Chickasaws and Cherokees by the State of Virginia on orders of Virginia Governor Patrick Henry and Governor Thomas Jefferson.

According to the 1918 Tennessee Historical Magazine, *"The Chickasaws, as has been stated, resented the appropriation of their hunting grounds without their consent. Upon the erection of Fort Jefferson they at once put themselves in communication with the British at Pensacola. November 23, 1780, Major General John Campbell, commanding his Majesty's forces in the province of West Florida, appointed James Colbert, leader and conductor of such volunteer inhabitants, and Chickasaws, Choctaws, Creeks, and other Indians as should join him, for the purpose of annoying, distressing, attacking, and repelling the King's enemies.*

Colbert conducted the siege of Fort Jefferson. At the end of five or six days the garrison was reduced to the utmost extremity, when they were fortunately relieved by Colonel (George Rogers) Clark; the post, however, which had been inconsiderately established, was evacuated and about the last of August, 1782. Simon Burney and two Chickasaw warriors, under a flag of truce,

FORT JEFFERSON SITE

Built in 1780 by George Rogers Clark as part of impressive plan of settlement. conceived by Gov. Patrick Henry of Virginia, later pursued by and named for Gov. Thomas Jefferson. The fort was to protect US claim to its western border and to be a key trading post. It was abandoned, 1781. Over. Resettled after Jackson Purchase. Important Union post in Civil War.

delivered to Colonel Logan, of Lincoln County, Kentucky, a talk signed by Poymace Tankaw, Mingo Homaw, Tuskon Patapo, and Piomingo, in which they expressed their desire for peace. They admitted they had done mischief in Kentucky, as well as on the Cumberland, but alleged that the building of Fort Jefferson on their hunting ground, without their consent, made it necessary to take up arms to defend what they deemed their natural right; but that the cause being then in some measure removed, they desired to be again at peace with the American States" (Goodpasture, 1918).

Another version of the siege at Fort Jefferson was given in Z. F. Smith's History of Kentucky as follows: *"In the summer of 1780, Governor Thomas Jefferson of Virginia, having sent instructions to place a post on the Mississippi River, with cannon to fortify it, Colonel George Rogers Clark with some soldiers, left Louisville and proceeded to the Iron Banks, at the mouth of the Mayfield Creek, five miles below the mouth of the Ohio. He there erected Fort Jefferson. The Chickasaws at this time were the owners of the country west of the Tennessee River, including the ground where Fort Jefferson was erected. The Governor's instructions to buy the site or get the Indians' consent were not complied with, and their resentment was aroused. They commenced to maraud and to kill members of the families that had settled around the fort. Mr. Music's entire family, except himself, was killed.*

A white man was taken prisoner and forced to reveal the condition of the fort, etc. There were about thirty men in the garrison, under Captain George. Many of these were sick. They were reduced in supplies of food on account of those who had taken refuge there, and the destruction of their crops near-by, by the Indians.

"In this condition, and under the lead of a Scotchman named Colbert, who had lived with and acquired a great influence over these Indians, they appeared in force, several hundred strong, and began a siege and attack upon the fort in the summer of 1781. After resistance of five days the respective leaders, Colbert and George, met under a flag of truce to try to agree on terms of capitulation, a summons to surrender within an hour having been refused. Terms could not be arranged, and the fighting was resumed. The issue was near at hand, as a messenger had been dispatched to Kaskaskia for aid. A desperate night assault was made by the Indians in force.

When they had advanced in short range and in close order, Captain George Owens, who commanded one of the block-houses, had the swivels loaded with rifle and musket balls, and fired them into the crowded ranks. The fire was very destructive and the slaughter excessive. The enemy, repulsed and disheartened, fell back to their camps.

Soon after, Colonel Clark arrived with a relief force and the Chickasaw army gave up the siege. This fort was some time after abandoned, from its isolated position, and the difficulty of supplying so remote a garrison. The evacuation was the signal for peace, which was tacitly accepted by the Indians and faithfully

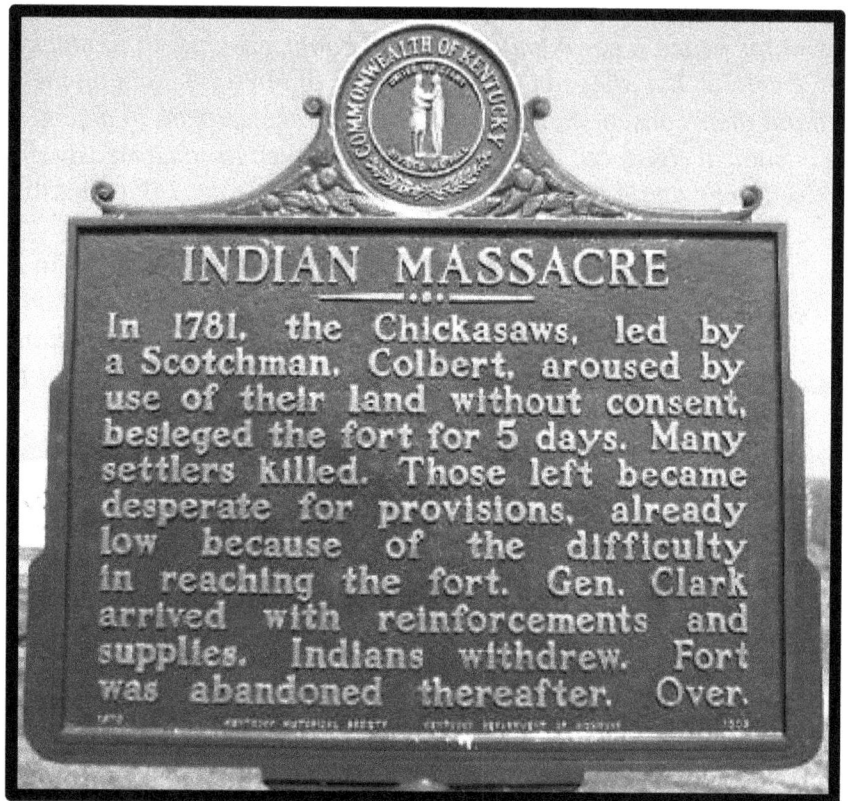

COMMONWEALTH OF KENTUCKY

INDIAN MASSACRE

In 1781, the Chickasaws, led by a Scotchman, Colbert, aroused by use of their land without consent, besieged the fort for 5 days. Many settlers killed. Those left became desperate for provisions, already low because of the difficulty in reaching the fort. Gen. Clark arrived with reinforcements and supplies. Indians withdrew. Fort was abandoned thereafter. Over.

observed by both parties after" (Smith, 1891).

After the siege of Fort Jefferson, James Logan Colbert led the Chickasaw delegation in negotiations with the State of Virginia. Later one of the negotiators gave this description of James Colbert: *"From his education and mode of life, being bred among the Indians from his infancy, it will naturally be supposed he is illiterate, which is the case, but possessed of strong natural parts"* (McDonald, 2007).

Initially, James Logan Colbert had sided with the British because he had a great dislike for both the Spanish and French. Since the British had assisted Colbert and the Chickasaws during their conflicts with the French and Spanish, he remained loyal to the British during most of the American Revolution. After his siege at Fort Jefferson, and toward the end of the Revolutionary War, James Logan Colbert agreed to terms of peace with Americans in Virginia.

James Logan Colbert's Conflicts with Spanish

James Logan Colbert did not like the Spanish and led several attacks against them in support of the English. According to Robert Haynes' (1976) book _The Natchez District and the American Revolution_, James Logan Colbert had remained steadfast in his attachment to England and like his close friends, had cultivated a bitter distaste for Spaniards.

Infuriated by the treatment given Blommart, Alston, and other Natchez insurgents, Colbert—together with the insurgent Turner—began harassing Spanish shipping on the Mississippi between Natchez and St. Louis. On April 25, 1782, Turner and fourteen of his compatriots captured a vessel commanded by Captain Eugenio Pouree and disarmed the crew. While being escorted in a canoe to the Chickasaw country, the Spanish prisoners surprised and overpowered their captors. The Spaniards toppled over the canoe and managed to kill six Englishmen and two blacks by beating them over the head with oars as they came up for air. Although Turner was among these thrown into the water, he and one of his slaves recovered the canoe and escaped without injury...The Spanish policy of instant retaliation failed to have the desired effect of apprehending the culprits responsible for the Pouree incident or deterring Colbert and his band of marauders from further aggressive activity. Instead, it stiffened Colbert's determination to undertake additional reprisals against Spanish commerce. Through the assistance of several sympathetic British settlers in Natchez, he learned the contents of almost every Spanish vessel going upstream, as well as the approximate time they were scheduled to pass by Chickasaw Bluffs. Early on the morning of May 2, 1782, Colbert and his raiders captured a particularly valuable prize when they seized a boat owned by Silbestre Labadie, a St. Louis merchant, and containing not only a cargo of provisions and 4,500 pesos, but also the wife of commandant of St. Louis, Francisco Cruzat, and her four sons. As his vessel approached Chickasaw Bluffs, Labadie spotted a boat tied to the bank and, thinking it belonged to a friend, approached it. One of Colbert's men inquired if Madame Cruzat were aboard, leap ashore when some forty men rushed out of a concealed trench near the bank and, with raised muskets, ordered the Spaniards to surrender. "In clear and intelligible French" one of the men cried out, "you are prisoners, and if you move or shake your head we will fire upon all of you and kill you". The raiders refused to identify themselves other than to say they were Englishmen and to insist that their possessions were all the orders they needed.

Colbert's men escorted the prisoners, partly by small boat and partly on foot, through the thick underbrush laced with thorns, over rugged hills, across almost impassable streams to a clearing in the interior where they locked the Spaniards in "an uncomfortable, make-shift jail". Although Colbert was openly contemptuous of all Spaniards, he treated Madame Cruzat and her sons with unexpected kindness, although she and the other prisoners watched in dismay as their captors divided the spoils. Colbert and his men began auctioning off the tableware, then the slaves, and ended up by distributing the guns, clothing, and money among themselves. The next day, some 200 Chickasaw warriors arrived for a major celebration at which they received powder and brandy from the appreciative Englishmen. To the Spanish captives, it appeared as if the Indians were tolerating without approving the escapades of their British allies, although they obviously enjoyed the festivities immensely.

Alexander McGillivray
12/15/1750-2/17/1793

Although Colbert and a few of his Lieutenants talked rather freely of their plans with Madame Cruzat and Labadie, they candidly displayed a good deal of uncertainty about how to dispose of their prisoners. The primary purpose in taking Madame Cruzat was to exchange her and her children for the English settlers still under guard in New Orleans. On May 15, 1782, Alexander McGillivray, a young half-breed who would one day become the principal chief of the Creek Nation, arrived in camp and quickly devised the plan which Colbert eventually used in trying to gain the release of his English friends. McGillivray drew up a "Parole of Honor" in which Labadie and nine other prisoners consented to go to New Orleans and arrange for the exchange after they had pledged to consider themselves prisoners of war and to "return to any of the British Dominions if called upon" before the release took place. Before Labadie left, his captors also forced him to repurchase his own boat "for four hundred pesos" and to ransom "one of his own Negroes" for an additional 250 pesos.

On May 22, 1782, Labadie and eleven sailors, accompanied by Madame Cruzat, her four sons, and a black female servant, departed for New Orleans. They carried a letter written by McGillivray, but bearing the name of Colbert, for the governor of Louisiana explaining the terms of their agreement with the prisoners and requesting his immediate compliance. The letter also contained a protest against the practice prevalent in West Florida (especially at Mobile) of "offering great rewards to Indians for the heads of particular men in the Indian country" (Haynes, 1976).

James Logan Colbert and Alexander McGillivray

The Creeks, Chickasaws, and Cherokees were initially friendly with each other and were members of the Chickamauga Confederacy warring against the Americans who were taking their lands. Three important leaders emerged as friends and cooperated with the British during the Chickamauga War. Their fight against the United States during the American Revolution brought these men together: Doublehead with the Lower Cherokees; James Logan Colbert with the Chickasaws; and, Alexander McGillivray with the Upper Creeks.

James Logan Colbert and Alexander McGillivray developed a close friendship and he knew McGillivray was smart and educated; therefore, Colbert depended on McGillivray for advice when dealing with government officials. McGillivray actually wrote the letter telling of the death of James Logan Colbert. James Logan Colbert's oldest son William Colbert and Alexander McGillivray married sisters and were brother-in-laws.

Alexander McGillivray was born *Hoboi-Hili-Miko* (Good Child King) in the Coushatta village of Little Tallassee on the Coosa River, near present-day Montgomery, Alabama. His father, Lachlan McGillivray, was a Scots-Irish trader who built trading-posts among the Upper Towns of the Muscogee Confederacy, who had traded with French Louisiana. Alexander's mother, Sehoy Marchand, was the daughter of Sehoy, a mixed-race Creek woman of the prestigious Wind Clan, and of Jean Baptiste Louis DeCourtel Marchand, a French officer at Fort Toulouse near Montgomery, Alabama. Alexander and his siblings were born into the Wind Clan, as the Muscogee had a matrilineal system, based on the mother's family lineage.

Sehoy Marchand—Sehoy was portrayed as a beautiful black-eyed Indian princess, with whom McGillivray was instantly love struck. Sehoy Marchand and Lachlan McGillivray's marriage was recognized by the Creek Nation. Sehoy Marchand was a high-status woman of the Koasati (Coushatta) and her mother was also named Sehoy, of the Wind Clan. Hers was a politically powerful family of the Upper Creek Nation, which had matrilineal system of descent and property. Sehoy's immediate family included several important chiefs within the tribe.

Historical and circumstantial evidence suggest the marriage may have been strategic for both sides, as he gained by

Sehoy Marchand
1702-1772

being allied with a high-status family of Creek, and Sehoy and her family had benefits from a connected European-American trader. They had three children: Alexander, Sophia, and Jeanne. Jeanne McGillivray married French officer Le Clerc Milfort. Sophia McGillivray married Benjamin Durant and named her oldest son Lachlan McGillivray Durant. Sophia was mother to a large family and may have died at the Fort Mims massacre in which her nephew Red Eagle was involved. The children lived most of the time with their mother in the Creek tribe and learned its language and ways, although the father sent Alexander to a European-American school in Charleston and Augusta.

After her marriage Lachlan ended, Sehoy II Marchand married Malcolm McPherson and Chief Tuckabatche. She had a daughter Sehoy (Sehoy III). Sehoy III married Charles Weatherford, and one of their sons was William Weatherford, better known to history by his Creek name, translated as Red Eagle.

28

Lachlan McGillivray—Lachlan McGillivray was one of several Scottish Highlanders recruited by James Oglethorpe to act as settler-soldiers protecting the frontiers of Georgia from the Spanish in Florida, the French in the Alabama basin, and their Indian allies. On January 10, 1736, Lachlan and 176 emigrants, including women and children, arrived on board the Prince of Wales to establish the town of Darien, Georgia, originally known as New Inverness. He was a prosperous fur trader and planter in colonial Georgia with interests that extended from Savannah to what is now central Alabama. He established a fur trading post and plantation at Little Tallassee near today's Wetumpka, Alabama, possibly on the site of the former Fort Toulouse. He prospered and invested his trading and plantation profits in businesses on the Atlantic coasts of Georgia, eventually settling in Savannah, Georgia as a man of considerable wealth. He was the father of Alexander McGillivray and the great-uncle of William McIntosh and William Weatherford, three of the most powerful and historically important American Indian chiefs among the Creek Indians of the Southeast.

Lachlan McGillivray
1718-1799

Alexander was born on December 15, 1750 (or 1740) and as a child, he briefly lived in Augusta with his father, who owned several large plantations and was a delegate in the colonial assembly. In 1773, he was sent to school in Charleston, South Carolina, where he learned Latin and Greek, and was apprenticed at a counting house in Savannah,

Georgia. He returned to Little Tallassee in 1777 where the revolutionary governments of Georgia and South Carolina confiscated the property of his Loyalist father, Lachlan McGillivray, who returned to Scotland. He continued correspondence with his son Alexander and other friends and relatives in the United States. After his son's death in 1793, Lachlan McGillivray paid for Alexander's orphaned children, Alleck and Mary, to be brought to Scotland. Lachlan McGillivray died in his native Scotland in 1799 at around 80 years of age. His estate and place of interment are not known. Alleck and Mary McGillivray were still living with him in Scotland at that time. Alleck died as a young adult shortly after his grandfather; Mary McGillivray remained a resident of Scotland but no records of her life have been found.

Alexander McGillivray—According to Carolyn Thomas Foreman (1929), Alexander McGillivray's description is as follows: "*He was of slender build, tall, with a commanding figure, and the immobile face which showed his Indian blood. Possessed of inordinate ambition and ability and a keen intellect, he was soon surrounded by warriors and adventurers...He was a very striking looking man, six feet tall, and erect in carriage. He had remarkably fine, piercing eyes and his forehead must have been very noticeable as all writers in describing him speak of the extraordinary expansion which commenced at his eyes and widened to the top of his head. He is said to have been handsome and to have had long tapering fingers with which he wielded a pen with remarkable rapidity. He was dignified and his manners were polished. He ordinarily dressed in a combination of Indian and American garments but he was provided with uniforms of Great Britain, Spain, and the United States which he wore on proper occasions, being careful not to appear in his American uniform when he was to meet Spaniards. In his homes he entertained distinguished visitors with lavish hospitality and while he was ambitious and unscrupulous he had many fine traits, the best of which was his kind heart; he was celebrated for his kindness to captives and his last work in behalf of his nation was an effort to secure teachers for them*" (Foreman, 1929).

During the American Revolution, Alexander McGillivray was commissioned as a colonel in the British army. He brokered a British Indian alliance with Doublehead of the Lower Cherokees, James Logan Colbert of the Chickasaws, and other Chickamauga leaders. Colonel Alexander McGillivray was a skillful diplomat and a great military strategist, but he rarely participated in battle. At one time, McGillivray wielded great power commanding from 5,000 to 10,000 Creek warriors that became a major faction in the Chickamauga Confederacy.

In 1783, Colonel Alexander McGillivray became the principal chief of the Upper Creek towns. His predecessor, Chief Emistigo, died while leading a war-party to

30

relieve the British garrison at Savannah, which was besieged by the American Continental Army under General Mad Anthony Wayne. Chief Alexander McGillivray died on February 17, 1793, and was buried in Pensacola, Florida at his friend William Panton's home, trading posts, and warehouses. Panton, a powerful Scots Irish trader of both British and Spanish goods, was a loving and dear friend of McGillivray; and he provided a place in his beautiful garden for McGillivray's last resting place. After his death, Alexander's nephew William (Red Eagle) Weatherford would emerge as an important leader among the Creeks, and he would eventually surrender to Andrew Jackson after the Battle of Horseshoe Bend.

William (Red Eagle) Weatherford surrenders to Andrew Jackson in 1814
Red Eagle 1765-3/24/1824

After the death of James Logan Colbert on January 7, 1784, the Scots Irish father of some important Chickasaw chiefs, the Chickasaws agreed to terms of peace with the United States Government. As the Chickasaw people allied themselves with the United States and began helping the Americans who were pressuring the Creeks from the east and taking their lands, conflicts arose between the tribes. Beginning in 1786, McGillivray commanded the Creeks to start making raids into the Chickasaw Nation, because the Chickasaw supported the United States Government efforts to force the Creeks from their homelands.

Even though the High Town Path was considered the Creek's northern boundary in Lawrence County, Alabama, they used trails crossing the Moulton and Tennessee Valleys in route to their buffalo hunting grounds near the French Lick (Nashville, Tennessee). Probably the only historic battle between the Creeks and Chickasaws to take place in Lawrence County was the Battle of Indian Tomb Hollow. The story about the Creek-Chickasaw battle which occurred in the 1780's, some 7 miles south of Moulton, was published in the Moulton Democrat newspaper on November 7, 14, and 21, 1856.

After the death of Alexander McGillivray, a temporary peace was established between the Creeks and Chickasaws in 1798; however, in 1814, peace between the Creeks, Chickasaws, and Cherokees was soon forgotten when the United States Government demanded the Chickasaws and Cherokees take up arms against the hostile red stick Creeks. Upon the death of Doublehead on August 9, 1807, the Creek Nation lost a friend and the support of the Lower Cherokees. Eventually, the Chickasaws and Cherokees would help Andrew Jackson defeat the Creeks at Horseshoe Bend on March 27, 1814. As a result of Indian assistance, the once powerful Creek Nation fell to Andrew Jackson's forces. The Treaty of Fort Jackson in 1814 relinquished thousands of acres of Creek Indian claims south of the High Town Path. After Jackson's defeat of the Creeks, the land of the Black Warrior (Bankhead Forest) was opened for settlement. In 1815, Richard McMahan became the first documented white settler in the area near the present day Town of Haleyville.

James Logan Colbert and Doublehead

According to Chickasaw interpreter Malcolm McGee in 1841, *"William Colbert had the old man's property. William's first war exploits was in the Red Nation; had joined the Cherokees and aided in their warfare against the whites, under Dragging Canoe in 1776 at the Tatum Flats; then about 16 and his father was along"*. Based on McGee's statement it appears that James Logan Colbert carried his sons into battle with him as he rode with the Cherokees during the Chickamauga War. Not only did James Logan Colbert become friends and fight conflicts against the American settlers with Creek Chief Alexander McGillivray, but he was also friends and fought with Dragging

32

Canoe and Doublehead in the Chickamauga War. Initially, James Logan Colbert, William Colbert, George Colbert, and other Chickasaws became allied with Doublehead and his Chickamauga Confederacy during the Chickamauga War that lasted from 1775 through June 1795.

George Colbert was the double son-in-law of the last Chickamauga Cherokee Chief Doublehead who arrived in the Muscle Shoals area by 1770. Doublehead used marriage to strengthen his position and his iron clad grip on the Muscle Shoals area of north Alabama and having two of his daughters to marry George Colbert was a brilliant move that secured his position among the Chickasaws. When Doublehead's occupation of Muscle Shoals came into question, Chief George Colbert of the Chickasaws confirmed that Doublehead had his permission. The agreement of George Colbert was probably greatly influenced by the fact that he had married two of Doublehead's daughters.

James Logan Colbert became acquainted with Chickamauga Cherokee Chief Doublehead during the 1770's because of their mutual support by Celtic traders of the English. In addition, at least two of James Logan Colbert's daughters-in-law were the children of Doublehead. Also both James Logan Colbert and Doublehead were supported by Creek Chief Alexander McGillivray who not only advised both leaders, but also provided

Dragging Canoe
1738-3/1/1792

33

Creek warriors to help them in their campaign against the Americans. Also Doublehead worked at building alliances with other tribes associated with the Great Bend of the Tennessee River during the Chickamauga War that started as a result of the Treaty of Sycamore Shoals in 1775. The British supported both the Chickasaws and Cherokees in their efforts to prevent their lands from being taken by the American settlers.

The Cherokees occupied the Great Bend of north Alabama under the leadership of Doublehead and established several villages along the Muscle Shoals which represented the southwestern portion of their nation that overlapped with Chickasaw claims; however, George Colbert told General James Robertson that Doublehead was at the shoals by his permission. The villages in the shoals area were occupied by members of the tribes of the Chickamauga Confederacy which included the Chickasaw, Lower Cherokee, Upper Creek, Shawnee, Delaware, and Yuchi. Doublehead ruled over the Chickamauga villages along the shoals while Dragging Canoe controlled the territory in northeast Alabama, southeastern Tennessee, and northwest Georgia.

Chickamauga Chief Doublehead or Talo Tiske, meaning two heads, established Doublehead's Town in the 1770's on the south bank of Tennessee River at the head of Elk River Shoals at Brown's Ferry in present-day Lawrence County, Alabama. In early 1802, Doublehead moved to Shoal Town to be near his trading post at the mouth of Blue Water Creek in Lauderdale County, Alabama. The area from Chickasaw Island near Huntsville, Alabama and west along the Muscle Shoals had always been an area of dispute between Chickasaws and Cherokees, though it was known as Chickasaw

General James Robertson
6/28/1742-9/1/1814

34

Hunting Grounds and legally became Chickasaw land by the treaty with the United States on January 10, 1786.

Doublehead and Dragging Canoe disapproved of the Treaty of Sycamore Shoals in 1775 with the Henderson Company which gave up large tracts of Cherokee hunting grounds. Dragging Canoe vowed that settling the beloved buffalo grounds in middle Tennessee and Kentucky would be dark and bloody. Within a short period of time after the 1775 land sale to the Henderson Company, the start of the Chickamauga War began in east Tennessee. Doublehead's German father-in-law Christian Priber had advocated a large Indian confederacy in order to form a Red Empire, and both Dragging Canoe and Doublehead pursued the dream of a united Indian force during the Chickamauga War in order to prevent the loss of their sacred hunting grounds. James Logan Colbert and his sons assisted Dragging Canoe and Doublehead with the Chickamauga War, but shortly after Colbert's death in 1784 most of the Chickasaws left the confederacy and agreed to peace with the Americans.

Even though Doublehead was leading war parties on killing and stealing raids, he became more vicious after the murder of his brother Chief Old Tassel, one of the Cherokees most well-known and beloved chiefs. When Old Tassel was murdered in 1788 with the help of the white soldier James Hubbert, Doublehead went on a violent killing rampage, attacking white settlers throughout the Cumberland Mountains of Tennessee and into Kentucky. During several raids on the Cumberland settlements, Doublehead led his warriors against General James Robertson forces at Fort Nashborough and surrounding stations. On at least two occasions, General James Robertson's forces tried to kill Doublehead.

The 20 year warpath of Doublehead lasted from 1775 to 1795 and is well documented, even to the point of cannibalism. Doublehead's last major raid was against Valentine Sevier, the brother of Colonel John Sevier. In June 1795, Doublehead and some 40 fellow Creeks were said to be somewhat intoxicated when they viciously attacked the settlement of Valentine Sevier. Even though Doublehead had signed a peace treaty with President George Washington in June 1794, he ended his bloody war about one year later and was not known to participate in another raid or battle. Doublehead's terrible atrocities certainly add up to a significant sum and Haywood said he had more blood on his hands than anyone at that time in history.

After the end of his warpath, Doublehead became a changed man and sought peace with the settlers. Though he began to mimic the ways of the whites and built a large house in Lauderdale County, Alabama, Doublehead continued to defend the

Cherokees land rights; however, in various treaties he accepted bribes which eventually led to his death. Doublehead with the help of John D. Chisholm formed the Doublehead Company that leased 1,000 acres to more than 50 white settlers between the Elk River and Cypress Creek. Doublehead's change of heart was characteristic of other Cherokees during this time, many of whom adopted the manners and customs of the whites.

After Doublehead's death on August 9, 1807, George Colbert and the Chickasaws demanded the white settlers living on Chickasaw land be removed; therefore, the government established Fort Hampton in Limestone County, Alabama to remove white squatters on Chickasaw lands. Later, George and William Colbert along with other Chickasaw and Cherokee warriors joined with General Andrew Jackson's Army to defeat the Creeks on March 27, 1814.

James Logan Colbert and John Montgomery

James Logan Colbert became a very wealthy man during the time he and fellow Chickasaws were acting as pirates of the Mississippi River. He along with his sons and other Chickasaws gained great wealth by stealing from both French and Spanish vessels that traveled up and down the river. For many years the family of James Logan Colbert was one of the most powerful families in the Chickasaw Nation that had a great dislike for both the French and Spanish. The Spanish implied that Colonel John Montgomery of the Cumberland was assisting Colbert and the Chickasaws in their pirating raids. *When Colonel (James) Robertson, having located two negroes, one taken at Mattattock and the other on the Arkansas, offered to assist in their recovery if the owners could be found, Monsieur Cruzat replied that Colbert and his people, scattered in several bands, were carrying on war by robbery and pillage everywhere, and consisted of so large a number of persons that it was impossible to procure the necessary proofs* (Goodpasture, 1918).

Colonel John Montgomery's association with James Logan Colbert was not compelling enough for him to be found guilty of providing assistance to Colbert in his pirate activities against the Spanish; however, Montgomery not only had to defend himself before the Virginia Commissioners, but he also had to defend himself locally before the Committee of Cumberland who investigated him for assisting Colbert. Even though James Logan Colbert with the assistance of the Chickasaws had for some years been conducting extensive piratical activities against the Spanish on the Mississippi River, the Cumberland settlements feared that Colbert's activities would cause additional hostilities against their people; therefore on March 15, 1783, the Committee of Cumberland charged Colonel John Montgomery with being an accessory to Colbert's pirate operations against the Spanish and also annulled his appointment as Sheriff.

According to Bill Thayer (2009) in the Tennessee Historical Magazine, *on June 3, 1783, the Committee of Cumberland sent two men with letters to the Spanish governor in Illinois denying any connection or sympathy with Colbert's proceedings. Moreover, this charge was carried to the Governor of North Carolina, who issued a proclamation for Montgomery's arrest. Accordingly, the County Court of Davidson County, at its first term in 1784, placed Colonel Montgomery under bond to appear at the next term of the Court, and answer the charge of aiding and abetting Colbert. But before the next term of the Court, the Governor, being better informed, withdrew his proclamation, and the proceedings in the County Court were dismissed as a matter of course* (Thayer, 2009).

Colonel John Montgomery worked with James Logan Colbert in order to maintain peace with the Chickasaws and the Cumberland River settlements. After being charged and investigated for assisting Colbert in his pirating activities, Montgomery was cleared and court proceedings were dropped; since, the Spanish were not considered friends of the newly established American government, Colbert's pirate operations against the Spanish was not as important as maintaining peace with the Chickasaws. Montgomery's military career and accomplishes were recognized by the Governor, and he realized the charges were politically motivated; therefore, all charges were dropped.

Colonel John Montgomery—Initially, James Logan Colbert and the Chickasaws were a faction of the Chickamauga until approximately 1782 when Piomingo and other leaders of their tribe agreed to peace with General James Robertson, Colonel John Montgomery, and members of the Cumberland settlements. Later Colonel Montgomery was the leader of a major campaign against the Chickamauga Indians that destroyed Nickajack and Running Water Towns which were west of present-day Chattanooga, Tennessee. Montgomery's troops delivered a severe blow that broke the power of the Chickamauga and eventually led to peace with the Cherokee faction around 1794 some ten years after the death of James Logan Colbert; however, Montgomery would shortly be killed by the Creek faction of those same Chickamauga people while on a hunting trip. He made a valiant stand to assist a wounded friend, but he paid with his life which was taken by the Indian people that he had fought for years during the Chickamauga War.

The following is the details of the deaths of Major Evan Shelby, Jr. and also of Colonel John Montgomery who were killed by factions of the Chickamauga Indians as given by the Tennessee Historical Magazine: *In the meantime the discerning eye of Colonel Montgomery had discovered in the rugged hills that crown the forks of Cumberland and Red Rivers a superior site for the location of a town; and at the very time the county court was ruling him to bond, to-wit, January, 1784, he and Martin Armstrong were entering the land on which the City of Clarksville is now located. In the fall of the same year they had it surveyed, and Armstrong, who was a practical surveyor, laid off the plan of a town on it. The town was named Clarksville, in honor of General George Rogers Clark, the commander and friend of Colonel Montgomery in the Northwestern campaign, and was established by legislative authority in 1785. Colonel Montgomery, who made his home there, was the first named among its Commissioners. It was the second town established in Middle Tennessee, Nashville, chartered in 1784, being the first. Martin Armstrong never lived in Clarksville.*

Colonel Montgomery was one of the justices of Tennessee County from its establishment in 1788 until his death. In 1794 he commanded the territorial troops in the Nickajack campaign, the last, and one of the most important and successful enterprises undertaken against the

General George Rogers Clark
11/19/1752-2/13/1818

38

Indians, in which the towns of Nickajack and Running Water were destroyed, and the power of the Chickamauga completely broken. This was Colonel Montgomery's last public service.

A party of Creek Indians from Tuskegee was doing much mischief on the Cumberland in 1794. It was the same party who had killed Major Evan Shelby in 1793. They began their operations this year on upper Red River, where they killed Miss Betsy Roberts on the twelfth, and Thomas Reasons and wife on the fourteenth of November. Soon afterwards they moved down to the mouth of Red River. Colonel Valentine Sevier, after the fall of the Franklin Government in 1788, had emigrated to Tennessee County and erected a station on the north side of Red River, near its mouth, and about a mile from Clarksville. The Indians surprised his station on the eleventh of November, and massacred many of its inhabitants. They then returned to the country around Eddyville, Kentucky (Thayer, 2009).

It should be noted that in April 1779, Major Evan Shelby, Jr. led the first American attack that destroyed Chickamauga Town and other Indian villages. The raid led by Shelby also destroyed the British stores of John McDonald that were supplying arms and ammunition to the Cherokees, Creeks, Shawnees, and other Chickamauga tribes taking up arms against the Americans; therefore, Shelby was on the hit list of the Chickamauga. In addition, Chickamauga Cherokee Chief Doublehead was with a hunting party of Creeks who became somewhat intoxicated and attacked the station of Colonel Valentine Sevier in 1795. Doublehead's brother Old Tassel had been killed in 1788 under a flag of truce by soldiers under the command John Sevier, Valentine's brother. Prior to his death, Old Tassel wrote to John Sevier and told Sevier that he had tried to kill him for many years. Doublehead was often assisted by the Creeks and was the leader of many raids during the Chickamauga War which originated at Doublehead's Town at the Muscle Shoals. Doublehead's Town was the home of Lower Cherokees, Upper Creeks, Shawnees, Chickasaws, and mixed-blood warriors that fought together during the Chickamauga War.

After his return from Nickajack, Colonel Montgomery led a hunting excursion to the neighborhood of Eddyville, where the party of Creeks was lurking. November 27, 1794, they surprised him in his camp. His party, taken at a disadvantage, retreated, when Colonel Hugh Tinnon, one of the party, who was impeded by a wound, asked Colonel Montgomery not to leave him. With the courage and devotion so often found among the pioneers, he threw himself between Colonel Tinnon and the Indians, until a bullet from one of their guns took effect in his knee, when, finding him disabled, the Indians rushed upon him and killed him with their knives. John Rains, on his way from

Fort Massac, reached Eddyville on the day of the tragedy, and met Julius Sanders, one of the hunting party, who had escaped, though shot in four places. Sanders told him the last he saw of Colonel Montgomery an Indian was stabbing him repeatedly with a large knife. The next day Rains went with a party, including a son of Colonel Montgomery, and found his body, which they buried where a tree had been uprooted by the storms (Goodpasture, 1918).

In 1772 Isaac Bledsoe married Katherine Montgomery, a sister of the veteran frontiersman Colonel John Montgomery. The Bledsoe family lived at Mansker's Fort in 1782-83, but moved into Bledsoe's Fort about 1784. They had eight children. Indians shot and killed Isaac Bledsoe while he was working in a field near his fort on April 9, 1793. Eleven months later, his son Anthony fell mortally wounded in an Indian attack near Daniel Smith's Rock Castle home (Durham, 2009).

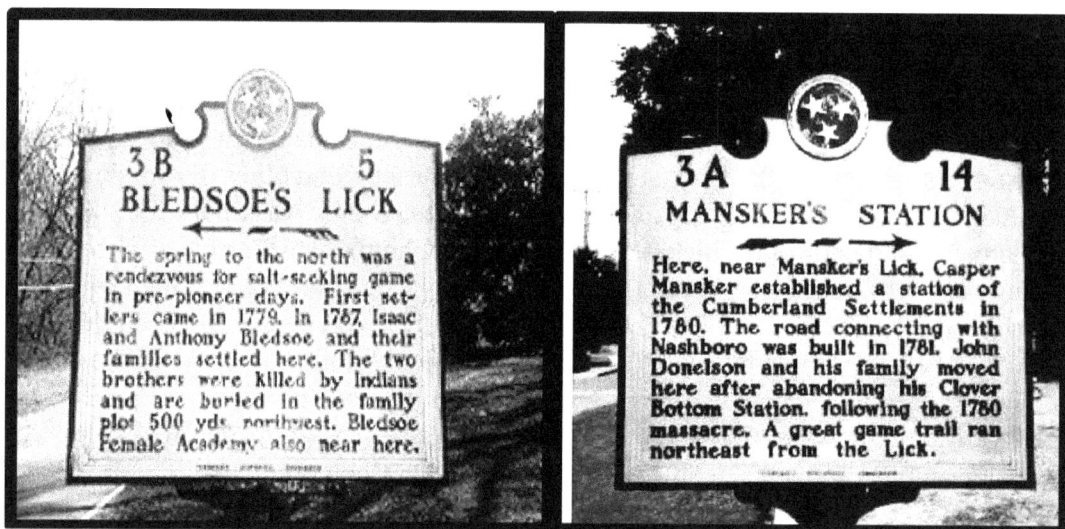

Both Colonel John Montgomery and his brother-in-law Colonel Isaac Bledsoe had fought in the war against the Chickamauga Indians. As seen in the paragraphs above, the men were eventually killed by Chickamauga warriors. They paid with their lives after trying to help secure the safety of settlements along the Cumberland River.

Two years later, when Tennessee County gave up its beautiful name to the State, it took the name of Montgomery, in honor of the brave Colonel John Montgomery, who had been her leading citizen, and was second in command of the national heroes, who, under General George Rogers Clark, had conquered and saved to the United States the great West, from the Alleghany Mountains to the Mississippi River (Goodpasture, 1918).

Tecumseh—General Clark defeated the British to take the Northwest Territory that the British ceded to the United States by the Treaty of Paris in 1783. Later, the remaining Indian forces were defeated by the American forces clearing all resistance to the Northwest Territory. On October 5, 1813, Tecumseh, leader of the Shawnee Indian confederacy, was killed at the Battle of Thames near Moravian Town and his confederacy surrendered to William Henry Harrison at Detroit.

Tecumseh was a Shawnee chief that tried to develop an Indian confederacy as did Dragging Canoe and Doublehead. Tecumseh had been with Dragging Canoe and fought with him and Doublehead during the Chickamauga War. On August 27, 1811, Tecumseh and his party of 20 delegates from the northwestern tribes passed the home of Levi Colbert in the Chickasaw Nation. His Indian group consisted of 20 people that included six Shawnees, six Kickapoos, six other northwestern Indians, and two Creek guides. George Colbert was curious as to Tecumseh's activities in his country; therefore, George met with him to inquire about his intentions and to find out what he was doing in the Chickasaw Nation. Tecumseh told Colbert that he would make his intentions and mission

Tecumseh-Shawnee
3/1768-10/5/1813

41

known at Tuckabatchie where he was to speak to the Creek Nation.

Prior to the Red Stick Creeks fighting the Americans, legend has it that Tecumseh came to Cotton Gin Port, Mississippi near the home of Levi Colbert to speak to the Chickasaws and enlist their support in August 1811, beneath a large tree referred to as the Council Tree on the bluff near Colbert's home. There is a concrete marker beside the road at Cotton Gin Port marking the site. The council tree was also destroyed by fire; some say it was struck by lightning in the late 1800s. Other historians say careless boys camping under the long dead tree burned it accidentally in the early 1900s.

Death of James Logan Colbert

According to a Chickasaw interpreter Malcolm McGee in 1841 James Logan Colbert was killed by his slave, Cesar as given in the following: *In 1784, or near that time, old James Colbert was killed while on his way from the nation to Georgia, as was supposed, by one of his own Negros, who was along and returned to the Nation with the story that the old man's horse had thrown and killed him. The Negro was of bad character and William Colbert took him to Natchez, sold the Negro, Cesar and he was among the number who went from that place perhaps to Texas at that early day and was killed.*

James Logan Colbert died January 7, 1784, in Alabama at 62 years of age. After conducting some business in St. Augustine in 1783, he began his journey home. James Logan Colbert had stopped by his friend and advisor Creek Chief Alexander McGillivray's house for a short stay. He then left there about January 4, 1784. Three days later his horse threw and killed him or his black slave Cesar killed him.

Governor Esteban Rodriguez Miro
1744-6/4/1795

42

Another version of Colbert's death is given by Robert Haynes (1976), *Spanish Governor Miro sent a strong note of protest to Captain James Logan Colbert upbraiding him for undertaking military action after the treaty of peace was signed and demanding that he release all Spanish prisoners still in his custody. In his reply of August 3, 1783, Colbert stated that upon learning of the termination of hostilities between the English and Spanish, he had released all prisoners and had urged the Chickasaws to do the same. He accused Cruzat of failing to live up to his end of the bargain with the Chickasaws by refusing to release the prisoners seized by the Kickapoos during their southern raid. Colbert momentarily broke off further negotiations with the Spanish officials to travel to St. Augustine, where he consulted with Alexander McGillivray on how to treat the recent demands of the governor of Louisiana that he and his men compensate Spain for the damages they had inflicted on Spanish property on the Mississippi. Three days out of St. Augustine, while on his return home, Colbert was thrown from his horse and died before his servant could come to his aid* (Haynes, 1976).

Malcolm McGee—Malcolm McGee was born in 1757 and his father was killed that year in the struggle for Fort Ticonderoga. His mother then removed to Illinois country, where in 1767 they came in contact with Chickasaw agent John McIntosh. McIntosh took McGee back to Chickasaw country and sent him to school at Mobile. Upon his return to the Indian country, McGee married a Choctaw named Kanahhoya, settled near present Old Houlka, Mississippi, and fathered a son named Samuel. Later, after his first wife's death, he married Elizabeth Oxberry, a Chickasaw, and fathered a daughter named Jane. They separated in 1821. McGee was the Chickasaw tribe's principal interpreter from 1786 to 1818; however, in 1794, he was replaced temporarily by William McLish for dealing with the Spanish. In 1804, he refused to interpret any longer without a raise, and his salary was raised to $500 a year.

Malcolm McGee not only provided valuable historical information on James Logan Colbert, he was a member of the extended Colbert family by marriage. Since Malcolm McGee gave tremendous insight on historical elements of the Colbert's, a short description of him is given by Horatio Cushman (1899). *Malcolm McGee, of Scotch parentage who had recently emigrated from Scotland, was born in New York City about 1757, his father having been killed shortly before, at the battle of Ticonderoga, in the French and Indian War where he fought with the Colonial troops. While he was quite young, his mother removed to and settled on the north bank of the Ohio River, in southern Illinois, at Fort Massac, and immediately across the river from the Chickasaw country. McGee had no schooling, but served as an interpreter among* the Chickasaws, for forty years. It is said, "He assumed the Indian costume and conformed to all their customs except their polygamy."

He married Elizabeth, a daughter of Christopher and Mollie (Colbert) *Oxbury* as his second wife, about 1819, and had one daughter, Jane. Shortly thereafter Elizabeth left him, taking the child with her. The mother later returned the child and she was placed by McGee in the home of Dr. T. C. Stuart, to be educated at Monroe Mission. In 1849, Malcolm McGee removed from Mississippi to the old Indian Territory, where he lived at the home of his daughter, Jane (Mrs. William R. Guy), at Boggy Depot, and where he died on November 5, 1849. Cyrus Harris became the guardian of their minor children whom he reared and educated (Cushman, 1899).

On May 7, 1826, Mollie Colbert joined the Monroe Mission Church according to the following church record; "*Mollie Colbert, a native, came forward and offered herself as a candidate for admission into the church. Her examination being sustained, she was accordingly received*". Mollie's daughter Elizabeth married Malcolm McGee and had a daughter Jane who she left with McGee shortly after having the child. Malcolm McGee carried his daughter Jane to Reverend Thomas C. Stuart, Superintendent of Monroe Mission and left her with Stuart to be educated at the mission.

Monroe Church, Pontotoc County, Mississippi

In a letter from Mill Creek in the Chickasaw Nation, Governor Cyrus Harris on August 10, 1881, wrote to Mr. Harry Warren of the Mississippi Historical Society. In the letter, Harris tells about his step-father Malcolm McGee as follows: *Malcolm McGee was my step-father. He had one daughter by my mother and named her Jane. My sister Jane married Robert Aldridge, a white man who lived at Tuscumbia, but after they came to this country (Indian Territory) he got so trifling she drove him off. He then went to Texas and died. They had one daughter who is yet living. Jane afterwards married a nice gentleman by the name of William R. Guy and soon after she and Mr. Guy were married they went after sister Jane's father, old man McGee, and had him with them at Boggy Depot, Chickasaw Nation, but he, being very old, lived but a few months after getting there. I saw the old man die and was at his funeral. Old man McGee was a little over one hundred years old when he died. He was a long time United States Interpreter for the Chickasaws and it was said he could beat the Chickasaws talking their own tongue. Mr. and Mrs. Guy had nine children when Mrs. Guy died at Boggy Depot. About a year after her demise, William Guy died at Paris, Texas being there on a visit"* (Warren, 1908 and 1927).

45

George Colbert's Family Genealogy

Genealogy is not an exact science and neither is the family lineage given in the following breakdown of all of George Colbert's siblings and descendants. The information was derived from the best available sources and by no means definitive or without mistakes. References used for identifying the Colbert family tree include Rootsweb.com, FamilyTreeMaker.com, Chickasawhistory.com, Natchezbelle.org, archival microfilm, and historical books. Since the genealogical material has been mixed and combined from various sources, information on individual family members will not be cited separately, unless it is direct quotes from historical literature.

George Colbert's Siblings and Family

George Colbert's father James Logan Colbert married three times. His first marriage was to a full-blood Chickasaw woman in the Chickasaw Nation around 1740. His second wife was also a full-blood Chickasaw woman that he married before 1742. His third marriage was to a half-blood Chickasaw woman that he married before 1768. His half-blood wife died in 1822 at Tockshish in the Chickasaw Nation in Mississippi Territory.

Another source states that, *"Among the most influential mixed-bloods of the Chickasaws, were the five sons of James Logan Colbert, a Scotsman who came to live among the tribe in 1729 and married three Chickasaw women. Four of his sons became chiefs of the tribe. One Colbert had three wives, one Indian and the other two were white women. Both were sisters with the last name Allen"* (Warren, 1904). Notice, Warren's book, _Some Chickasaw Chiefs and Prominent Men_ (1904), states that two wives were white sisters named Allen while the other wife was a half-blood, but the statement does not particularly identify which son of James Logan Colbert married the two white women named Allen.

James Logan Colbert became an important leader of the Chickasaws and a legend among his people. Even though he was a Scotsman who lived among the Chickasaws, James Logan Colbert adopted their ways, married three Chickasaw women, and even led them into battle. Two of his wives were full-blood Chickasaw and one was a half-blood Chickasaw. From his three wives, James Logan Colbert fathered nine children. His first wife gave him a son and two daughters: William, Sally, and Celia. He fathered four sons by his second wife: George, Levi, Samuel, and Joseph.

James Colbert's third wife bore him another son, James, and another daughter, Susan. Seven of those children were half-blood Scots and half-blood Chickasaw with the last two children being three fourths Scots Irish and one fourth Chickasaw. He had six sons: William, George, Levi, Samuel, Joseph, and James, and of these six sons, of mixed Chickasaw and Scots Irish blood, four became chiefs of the Chickasaws. Notice that James Logan Colbert's last two sons were named after his father, Joseph Calvert, and maternal grandfather, James Logan.

Children—First Marriage of James Logan Colbert

I. General William (Billy) "Chooshemataha" Colbert

President Andrew Jackson
3/15/1767-6/8/1845

William was the eldest son of James Logan Colbert. He was also called "Chooshemataha", "Pyaheggo" and "Billy Colbert". He was a celebrated fighter and was an ally of the Americans not only against hostile Indians, but also when a struggle against Spain for the possession of the Mississippi seemed imminent.

According to Goodpasture (1918), *General William Colbert, or Chooshemataha, was a military character of consequence. He fought for his own people against the Creeks, and, it has been stated, assisted Andrew*

47

Jackson against the same tribe. "Old Hickory" presented him with a military coat, which the chief wore on important occasions until the end of his days. He lived a few miles south of Tocshish which was south of Pontotoc, and was put on old maps as "McIntoshville." Under the Treaty of Chickasaw Council House in 1816, General William Colbert was allowed an annuity of $100.00 for life.

Piomingo—*William Colbert was the friend and follower, as well as the successor, of Piomingo. The following incident will illustrate their relations. In the fall of 1792 Piomingo, with a company of Chickasaws, went to Philadelphia after goods for their tribe, who were to meet him at Mussel Shoals on his return. Being delayed beyond the appointed time, the Chickasaws feared that some accident had happened to him. Their foreboding was strengthened by a report circulated by the Creeks, that the Cherokees had killed him and all his party. This report so exasperated them that William and George Colbert collected a party of Chickasaws on either side of the Tennessee, for the purpose of cutting off six canoes of Cherokees, who were moving down the river, but Levi Colbert and some others prevailed on them to desist until their information could be confirmed. Shortly after these canoes went by another appeared, loaded with corn, and having on board one man, two women, and two children. William Colbert hailed them, and ordered them to come ashore. They disregarded his order and kept on their way, which he construed into a confession of guilt, and gave chase. The canoe paddled to the shore, the man landed and hid himself in the bushes, and the others continued down the river, but were soon overhauled and brought back. William Colbert found the man, tomahawked and scalped him.*

Piomingo was the great war chief of the Chickasaws before William Colbert had won his spurs. He proposed peace to Kentucky and Cumberland in 1782; he fought with the Americans under St. Clair; Dragging Canoe spent the last effort of his life vainly trying to induce Piomingo to join the confederacy of southern Indians against the United States, while they were engaged in a momentous struggle with the Indians of the Northwest; when the Spaniards of Louisiana made large offers to the Chickasaws if they would forsake the Americans in 1793, Piomingo treated the offer with contempt. He was a true and good man, had great natural ability, and possessed in a high degree the fundamental elements of statesmanship. He merits a high place among the great chiefs of his Nation, and deserves to be remembered by the Americans for his unfaltering devotion to their cause, after the treaty of French Lick on the Cumberland, November 12, 1783 (Goodpasture, 1918).

William's war with the Creeks—*William was visiting his wife's relatives in the Creek Nation when war broke out, and was forced to flee to the Choctaw Nation. In*

June of 1794, George and William Colbert accompanied Piomingo to Philadelphia, where the chiefs received a certificate from Washington on July 21 guaranteeing to the tribe all lands claimed by Piomingo at the Nashville Indian Conference, encompassing all of western Kentucky, central and western Tennessee, northern Mississippi, and northwestern Alabama. They also received a $3000 annuity in consequence of their aid to St. Clair in 1791. Piomingo and William Colbert then journeyed to the Ohio country, where they joined the army of General Anthony Wayne against the same Northwestern Indians.

A general disintegration of relations between the Chickasaws and Creeks led to renewed hostilities in the winter of 1794-1795. In January, William Colbert and a band of Chickasaw warriors took five Creek Scalps on the Duck River in the Chickasaw country, perhaps in retaliation for raids by the Creeks against the Cumberland settlers and Chickasaw hunters during the previous four months. On January 13, Colbert and a party of 100 Chickasaws that included his Creek wife and several of his children carried the scalps to agent Robertson at Nashville. The white citizens there, frustrated by twelve years of Creek depredations, treated the Chickasaw entourage with affection. Robertson organized a lavish "Entertainment" for Colbert. A company of cavalry was assigned to escort them while in the city.

William Colbert visited Nashville again on July 22, 1795, to ask Governor Blount for more guns. He got no satisfaction from the Governor, who he believed had been duped by the Creek peace talks. Leaving Jessie Moniac Colbert in Knoxville, he rounded up Chiefs William McGillivray, John Brown, Piomingo, and interpreter Malcolm McGee and set out for Philadelphia. The delegation received an audience with President Washington on August 22 but again received no encouragement in the prosecution of a new war with the Creeks. The Americans felt that Colbert's Duck River raid had initiated the new round of hostilities. Colbert also met with Secretary of War Timothy Pickering who stated: "I found Major Colbert singularly difficult to please, perhaps because the President would not satisfy his wishes in making war against the Creeks. I have given Major Colbert four hundred dollars to buy an elegant stallion, but he seemed to consider this sum as hardly sufficient. As I said before, it was not easy to please him."

The returning Indians received shocking news. Two days earlier, a thousand Upper Creeks had invaded Oldtown at the instruction of Mad Dog. Most Chickasaw warriors had been away on the fall hunt at the time. According to the story, Levi Colbert had then mustered some 200 old men and boys to repel the attack. Levi's fierce *resistance and an unaccountable panic had forced the Creeks to flee in terror; the bodies of twenty-six Creeks and seventeen Chickasaws now strew the village.*

Late in 1798, Piomingo died and the control of the tribe then fell to Wolf's Friend and George and William Colbert. Wolf's Friend actually assumed the informal title of principle chief of the tribe, but delegated much of his authority to the Colberts, who without hesitation accepted. William Colbert assumed the role of statesman emeritus, and it was George Colbert who began proving his mettle as a tribal leader of the first note.

In October of 1891, the U.S. sent commissioners to the Chickasaw Nation with orders to secure right of way for a road and to obtain permission from the Chiefs for white settlers to operated lodges along the road. The road would follow the Natchez Trace which was already a series of crude paths; the United States had no more to do than to improve it to a width of twelve feet (Martini, 1986).

Creek Indian War—*General William Colbert, who succeeded Piomingo as the principal chief of the Nation, distinguished himself as the friend of the United States. He served under General Wayne against the Indians of the Northwest, and in 1794 made war on the Creeks to avenge their depredations in the Cumberland settlements. When the Creek war broke out in 1813, he hastened to join the third regiment of United States infantry for service against the old enemies of the Chickasaws. He served five months in the regular infantry, when he returned to his Nation and raised an independent force which he led against the hostile Creeks, whom he pursued from Pensacola almost to Apalachicola, killing many, and bringing eighty-five prisoners back to Montgomery. In June 1816, he headed a Chickasaw delegation to Washington, and in the treaty that followed, he is styled Major General, and is granted an annuity of $100 during life* (Goodpasture, 1918).

General William Colbert was a man of a military turn of character, and in that capacity rose to considerable distinction in the Creek War of 1814. He won the confidence of General Andrew Jackson in that war, by his manly bearing and noble conduct, and was presented by Jackson, as a testimonial of his esteem, with a fine military coat made after the American style, which Colbert carefully kept to the close of his life as one among the most highly treasured relics of the past, and only wore it on important national occasions (Cushman, 1899).

President George Washington—*Major William Colbert, a son of James Logan Colbert, became a famous war chief among the Chickasaws and early in life took an*

50

active part in the political affairs of the tribe. He represented his people at Washington, upon numerous occasions, and in the very early days, was received by President Washington, in Philadelphia. At the solicitation of Washington, he led a contingent of Chickasaw warriors in support of General Anthony Wayne at the battle of Fallen Timbers, Ohio, on August 20, 1794, against Little Turtle and the Northwestern Confederation of Indians. Major William Colbert served nine months in the 3rd Regiment of United States Infantry in the War of 1812, concluding his military career by an effective participation in the war against the recalcitrant Creeks. As a commissioner from the Chickasaws, he was a signer of the treaty of October 4, 1801, and the treaty at Washington, of September 20, 1816. By the terms of the latter treaty, he was granted an annuity of $100 for the remainder of his life and was also styled a major-general. He also signed the Chickasaw Treaty of October 19, 1818. The major signed these treaties by mark, which would indicate his lack of any scholastic training, although he is recognized as a character of pronounced native courage, ability and fine judgment. Major Colbert married a Chickasaw Indian woman by the name of Mimey and lived at Tokshish, Mississippi, some four miles southeast of Monroe, and doubtless was largely instrumental in securing the establishment of the celebrated mission at that place. He was a contemporary of the famous Chief Piomingo of the Chickasaws, and passed away at an advanced age, sometime shortly before the Chickasaw removal of 1837-8 (Meserve, 1937).

William also made a trip with his half-brother George Colbert and Wolf's Friend to meet with President John Adams in Philadelphia in 1798.

William Colbert's Whiskey—In his journal, half-blood William Mizle, a Chickasaw interpreter who married a daughter of Piomingo, mentions that, to accommodate his trade, he stored whiskey at the great Holly Springs some miles south of Chickasaw Bluffs in Spring Hollow. A traveler stated that he spent several days at the home of General William Colbert who lived near the Federal Agency located about two miles south of the present village of Old Houlka in Chickasaw County. He stated that, *"William Colbert was a great drinker and, having run out of whiskey, walked to Mizle's post at the holly springs and bought seven kegs of whiskey; Colbert then started home and, just after arriving there, drank the last of the seventh keg, having consumed three days upon the trip."*

Death of William Colbert—William was born in Chickasaw Nation about 1742 and died May 30, 1824, in Tockshish, Pontotoc County, Mississippi at 81 years of age. The best evidence of General William Colbert's death is found in some old Chickasaw Agency records. One is a receipt from Ishtanaha to Benjamin F. Smith, Chickasaw Agent, for the pension of General Colbert. The receipt is dated July 15, 1824, for $40 in full for, *"... the amount settled on my husband General William Colbert by the Government of the United States up to May 30, 1824, at which time he deceased."* Additionally, in Smith's Chickasaw Agency expenditure accounting on September 27, 1824, he list a payment to, *"... Ishtanaha Colbert for the Pension of General William Colbert...."* And again in his accounts accepted by United States auditor William Stuart on December 4, 1824, Smith states that $40 was paid, *"to the wife of General William Colbert in full to May 30, 1824."* His body was interred in Pontotoc City Cemetery, Pontotoc County, Mississippi.

He lived a few miles south of a little place then known as Tokshish a corruption of the word Takshi, (bashful). He died in 1826, honored by his people while living, and mourned by them when dead as an irreparable national loss (Cushman, 1899).

William Colbert's Marriages—William married twice with his first marriage to a Creek woman known as Jessie "Wayther" Moniac in Chickasaw Nation, before 1780. Jessie was the daughter of a Creek, William Dixon "Dick" Jacob Moniac, and Sehoy III, daughter of Creek Chief Tuckabatche. Jessie was not listed on the 1818 Chickasaw Roll, so she was either dead by then or no longer Colbert's wife. Jesse was a sister to Elise Moniac who was the wife of Creek Chief Alexander McGillivray; therefore, William Colbert and Alexander McGillivray were brother-in-laws.

William's second marriage was to Ishtanaha "Mimey" in Chickasaw Nation, before 1824. Ishtanaha died after 1839 in Indian Territory. She was baptized at the Monroe Mission in Pontotoc County, Mississippi on June 5, 1830. She sold land on March 31, 1836 in Pontotoc County, Mississippi; and she purchased land May 3, 1837, and September 12, 1837, in Pontotoc County, Mississippi. She migrated from Mississippi to Indian Territory on board the steamboat Fox and arrived on November 21, 1837.

Children of William Colbert and Jessie "Wayther" Moniac

A. Mary "Mollie" Colbert—Molly first married James Gunn, a white Loyalists who settled among the Chickasaws. James and Molly had a beautiful daughter named Rhoda Gunn. Rhoda Gunn became *"the belle of the Chickasaws, and the fairest rose that bloomed in the wilderness, whose glossy locks to shame might bring the plumage of the raven's wing."* She was the mixed-blood daughter of the loyal Gunn, and passed her childhood years in Lee County, Mississippi. Rhoda was mostly Scots-Irish, but part French, Creek, and Chickasaw. She married Samuel Colbert, but they separated after having one child, a girl, who grew up, married and left the county. Rhoda, after her separation from Colbert, married Joseph Potts, a white man, by whom she had two sons: Taylor and Joseph.

According to Meserve (1937), *Molly Colbert Gunn also married to Christopher Oxberry, a Cherokee. An interesting character among the Chickasaws in Mississippi was Mollie, daughter of Major William Colbert. As a young woman she married*

Governor Cyrus Harris
8/22/1817-1/6/1888

Christopher Oxberry, a mixed-blood Cherokee, a proficient interpreter and a person of high standing among the Chickasaws. They lived upon her comfortable estate three miles south of Pontotoc, Mississippi, where her daughter Elizabeth or Betty was born. Her interesting home stood upon an ancient mound, the highest point in that part of the State, and surrounded by 1,000 acres of beautiful table-land. All of her children were born there as well as her famous grandson, Cyrus Harris, who was born there on August 22, 1817.

Cyrus Harris—The identity of the father of Cyrus Harris is somewhat confused. He is reputed to have been a white man by the name of Harrison, the name being subsequently shortened to Harris. Elizabeth's marriage to him was of brief duration, as she soon left him and returned to the home of her mother, where her son, Cyrus Harris, was born. The father declined to remove with the Chickasaws, at first, although he later attempted to join his son in the old Indian Territory. Cyrus Harris declined to have anything to do with him. Elizabeth married Malcolm McGee, very shortly but again returned to her mother at Pontotoc. Mollie sold her famous home about 1830, to Robert Gordon, who thereafter erected the spacious plantation home "Lochinvar" upon the site and where his son, Colonel James Gordon, afterwards a United States Senator from Mississippi, was born. After the sale, Mollie removed with her children, including Elizabeth, to Horn Lake, in what is today DeSoto County, Mississippi, where she passed away shortly before the removal of the Chickasaws, in 1837-8. Elizabeth removed in the party with her son, Cyrus Harris, to the old Indian Territory, late in 1837, where she died some years later, at Mill Creek, at the home of her famous son.

Mill Creek Residence of Chickasaw Governor Cyrus Harris

Cyrus Harris with his mother, Elizabeth, left Horn Lake, on November 1, 1837, for Memphis, to join a party of the emigrants led by A. M. M. Upshaw, the emigrant agent. Within the next few days they crossed the Mississippi and proceeded overland to Ft. Coffee. He tarried for a brief two weeks in camp at Skullyville and in the following year settled on the Blue River, in what is today Johnston County, Oklahoma. He removed again in November, 1855, to Mill Creek, northwest of Tishomingo, where he continued to reside until his death.

Cyrus Harris again was sent as a delegate to Washington, in 1854, and upon the adoption of the new constitution, in August, 1856, was chosen as the first governor of the Chickasaw Nation. In this memorable first election there were several candidates, but when the results were totaled, it appeared that no one of the aspirants had secured a majority of the votes cast, and as a consequence, the choice was delegated to the legislature, with the result that Cyrus Harris was chosen by that body by a majority of one vote. The young governor organized the new government, served through the two year term and was succeeded by Dougherty (Winchester) Colbert (Meserve, 1937).

B. Elijah Colbert

C. Jamison Colbert was born before 1804 and was listed as a resident in the 1818 census report in Chickasaw Nation. He resided in Skullyville, Skullyville County, Choctaw Nation, Indian Territory in 1855.

D. Ishtonnarhay Colbert was listed as a resident in the 1818 census report in Chickasaw Nation. This person may in fact be a female and the same as Ishtahana, a wife of General William Colbert.

E. Tooklaishtubby Colbert was born before 1818. He was listed as a resident in the 1818 census report in Chickasaw Nation.

F. Balbarhubby Colbert was born before 1818. He was listed as a resident in the 1818 census report in Chickasaw Nation.

G. Meharchubby Colbert was born before 1818. He was listed as a resident in the 1818 census report in Chickasaw Nation.

H. Immarhollochetubby Colbert was born before 1818. He was listed as a resident in the 1818 census report in Chickasaw Nation.

I. Logan Colbert was born before 1818 and died about 1870 in Indian Territory. He was listed as a resident in the 1818 census report in Chickasaw Nation and in the 1847 census report in Chickasaw Nation.

J. Shemarhoye Colbert was born before 1818. He was listed as a resident in the 1818 census report in the Chickasaw Nation in Mississippi.

K. Wileky Colbert was born before 1818. He was listed as a resident in the 1818 census report in Chickasaw Nation.

L. Schtimmarhoye Colbert was born before 1818. He was listed as a resident in the 1818 census report in Chickasaw Nation.

M. Onnarhoketay Colbert was born before 1818. He was listed as a resident in the 1818 census report in Chickasaw Nation.

N. Apalartubby Colbert was born before 1818. He was listed as a resident in the 1818 census report in Chickasaw Nation.

O. Nancknitubby Colbert was born before 1818. He was listed as a resident in the 1818 census report in Chickasaw Nation.

P. Nuzeka "Nossaecachubby" Colbert was born before 1818.

Q. Margaret Colbert was born after 1818 and died 1850 in Lowndes County, Mississippi at 31 years of age. She married Major John L.

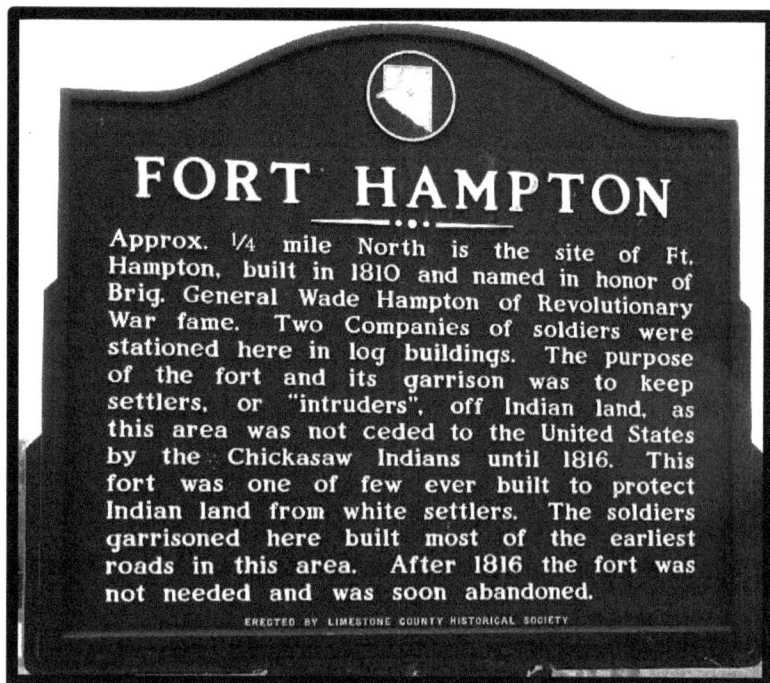

FORT HAMPTON

Approx. ¼ mile North is the site of Ft. Hampton, built in 1810 and named in honor of Brig. General Wade Hampton of Revolutionary War fame. Two Companies of soldiers were stationed here in log buildings. The purpose of the fort and its garrison was to keep settlers, or "intruders", off Indian land, as this area was not ceded to the United States by the Chickasaw Indians until 1816. This fort was one of few ever built to protect Indian land from white settlers. The soldiers garrisoned here built most of the earliest roads in this area. After 1816 the fort was not needed and was soon abandoned.

ERECTED BY LIMESTONE COUNTY HISTORICAL SOCIETY

Allen in Mississippi before 1842. John was born about 1789 and was the son of David Allen and Nancy McConnell. John was baptized at Monroe Mission in Pontotoc County, Mississippi on April 5, 1834. He was listed as a resident in the census reports in Lowndes County, Mississippi in 1836, 1840, and 1850. He settled among the Chickasaws in 1796, but later served as postmaster at Paris, Tennessee, and as commander of Fort Hampton in Limestone County, Alabama. He was sub-agent for the Chickasaws from 1829 to 1837, was deputy postmaster in the Chickasaw Country in 1832, and ran a tavern near Pontotoc, Mississippi in 1837. In 1842 in Lowndes County, Mississippi, Margaret Colbert was involved in a lawsuit against her husband, John L. Allen over some Chickasaw Indian Nation land. After removal, he relocated to Columbus, Mississippi where he died after 1850.

II. Sally (Incunnomar) Colbert

Sally Colbert was born about 1743 and married Thomas Love in Chickasaw Nation around 1782. Thomas, the son of William 'English Bill' Love, was born in Virginia and died 1832 in Holly Springs, Marshall County, Mississippi. He was listed as a resident in the Chickasaw Census report in 1818, and was a trader by occupation before 1832. "Thomas Love was probably a white man and a refugee Tory or Loyalist. The Indian nations were often asylums for refugee Loyalist or Tories, in the early days."

One source says that Thomas Love fathered 13 children by two wives. One supposedly a daughter of trader James Logan Colbert and the other a full blood Chickasaw named Emahota. Other sources indicate that he had only one wife Sally Emahota Colbert, the oldest child of James Logan Colbert (Martini, 1986).

Emahota was born in 1791 and some consider the second wife of Thomas Love. She sold land in Marshall County, Mississippi on April 8, 1836. She was listed on the 1840 LaFayette County census. She removed to Indian Territory in November, 1844. The1847 census lists her as half white, head of household, consisting of one male over 18 and 2 females over 16. She died at Burneyville on September 25, 1873.

The Thomas Love family was one of the larger mixed-blood families in the Chickasaw Nation. After Thomas Love's father had been killed, he took off through a briar patch and made his lifesaving escape. He assisted in marking the Creek-Chickasaw boundary in 1796. Another countryman, John McIntosh, appointed him administrator of his estate in 1803. He was still living in 1818 and apparently died about 1830.

By the 1820's, most of the Love family was living in a prosperous farming community located about six miles southwest of the present Town of Holly Springs, Mississippi. In 1826, a Presbyterian missionary located a station they called Martyn Station near Henry Love's home which stood at the crossing of two Indian trails near Pigeon Roost Creek. Many of the family's children attended school there. Seven of his sons became Chickasaw leaders, particularly during and after the removal to Indian Territory.

Children of Sally Colbert and Thomas Love

A. Delilah "Liley" Love was born in Chickasaw Nation in Mississippi and died before 1847 at Fort Washita in the Chickasaw Nation of Indian Territory in the west. Delilah was listed as a resident in the 1818 census report of the eastern Chickasaw Nation and immigrated west in December 1842 to the Chickasaw District of the Choctaw Nation.

Delilah's First Marriage—Delilah first married Samuel Mitchell in Chickasaw Nation, Mississippi about 1807. Samuel, the son of Joab Mitchell and Mary Henderson, was born in Tennessee on April 13, 1765 or September 30, 1766, and died about 1811. Samuel was a lawyer and early settler of Tennessee. He was appointed by President Thomas Jefferson as agent of the Chickasaw and Choctaw Nation of Indians, which post he held from 1797 to 1806 up to the time of his death.

Samuel proposed to Margaret 'Peggy' Allen in Chickasaw Nation, Mississippi about 1804 and was promptly turned down. He carried his suit to her grandmother, a dominating Colbert. The old lady considered it an excellent match and sent Peggy off to the agency where Mitchell presided with a string of well-loaded packhorses and ten Negro slaves as her dowry. The lovely Peggy, whose mother had been only one-eight Indian, was as determined as her grandmother. She made the trip to Mitchell's house, but that was as far as she would go. She stubbornly refused him, saying that she would never marry a drinking man white or Indian; therefore, she refused to marry him; and instead, she married Simon Burney.

Delilah Love and Samuel Mitchell had the following children:
(1) Joseph Greer Mitchell was born on February 28, 1808.
(2) Catherine "Kitty" Mitchell was born 1812.

Delilah's Second Marriage—Delilah second marriage was to John B. Moore in Mississippi after 1812. John, the son of John Moore and his white wife, was born in Louisiana in 1782. John died in the spring of 1840 in Holly Springs, Marshall County,

Mississippi at 57 years of age. John made his will on September 26, 1839, which was probated in Holly Springs, Marshall County, Mississippi on June 24, 1840.

Delilah 'Liley' Love and John B. Moore had the following children:
(3) Catherine Caroline Moore was born 1816.
(4) Harriet Moore was born on February 17, 1818.
(5) Mary Moore was born in 1819.
(6) Eliza B. Moore was born about 1822.
(7) Martha Jane Moore was born about 1822.
(8) John D. Moore, Jr. was born in Mississippi Territory on September 4, 1831.
(9) George Clendenen Moore was born in 1832.

B. Thomas Love, Jr. was listed in the 1818 census report in the Chickasaw Nation.

C. Colonel Henry W. Love was born bout 1785 and married Sarah Ann Moore and Elizabeth Meezell. Henry Love had the following children: John Benjamin Love married Narcisso Love; Amanda M. Love married James Hamilton Willis; Elvira Love married Aldredge W. Jones, James Hamilton Willis, and Dr. William P. Worthington; Overton Love married Elizabeth Guess; Frances Love; Charlotte Love married James Tyson and Nathan Coffee; Littleton H. Love married Elizabeth Humphreys; Catherine Love married Ben G. Mitchell, David Love, and Elizabeth Love married James Holmes Colbert.

D. Elizabeth "Betsy" Love was born about 1790 and married James B. Allen. They had the following children: George G. Allen married Charity Colbert; Tennessee Allen married Richard Overton; Sarah Sally Allen married Martin Colbert; Mississippi Allen married Charles Colbert; Alexander Allen married Elizabeth Allen; Louisiana Allen married Martin Colbert; Susannah Allen married David Wall and John Guest; Elizabeth Allen married Calvin Love; Mourning Tree Allen married Maxwell T. Frazier and Charles Edward Gooding; Mary Polly Allen; and Samuel Allen.

E. Colonel Benjamin Love was born about 1795 and married Charlotte "Lotty" Burney. They had the following children: Narcisso Love married George D. James and John Benjamin Love; Emily Love married John Taylor Potts; Agnes Love married George D. James; Matilda Alma Love married George A. Criner; Mary Jane Love married Thomas J. Grant; and Melvina Love married William Gaddis.

F. Isaac Love was born about 1797 and married Eliza McKinney. They had the following children: Elzira Elisa Love married William "Well" L. Lewis; Delilah Love; Sarah Love married James Preston Roark; Benjamin Stephen "B.S." Love married Eveline Colbert; Mary Ann Love married Charles Banhier; Wyatt Call Mitchell Love married Sarah Sparlin; Leander R. Guy Love; Henry Love married Martha Ellen Lane and Jennie Goldsby; and Emily Love married John Preston Roark and David Calhoun Burney.

G. Slone Love was born about 1807 and married Lottie Gaines and Sarah M. Allen. They had the following children: Calvin S. Love married Elizabeth Allen; Wilson Love married Elizabeth Allen; Nancy Love married Richard McLish and Jourdan Anderson Smith; Nathaniel B. Love married Sophia Humphreys; Daniel Love; Gabriel Love; and Mary Frances Love married Benjamin Ben M., Jr. Stewart.

III. Celia Colbert

Before 1824, Celia married John McLish, who was a half-blood raised and educated in Tennessee. John was the son of a Chickasaw mother and Chickasaw interpreter William McLish, who is last mentioned in 1805. He was first mentioned in May, 1815, when Andrew Jackson wrote that he was staying at "McLish'es" on the Buffalo River. By the Chickasaw Treaty of September 20, 1816, John was the recipient of a tract of land on the north bank of the Buffalo River and lived there until 1822. He sold part of his reservation and moved to a site six miles northeast of the Chickasaw agency. John was listed as a resident in the 1818 Chickasaw Census, Mississippi Territory. John McLish resided for some time in Lewis County, Tennessee; before 1826 he moved to Pontotoc County, Mississippi. In the fall of 1837, he moved to Indian Territory and died there in January or February, 1838.

Children of Celia Colbert and John McLish

A. William McLish (II)

B. David McLish

C. Sampson McLish

D. Martin Colbert McLish

E. George Frazier McLish was born in 1824 and married Ginny "Jincy" Colbert, Sarah "Sally" McIntosh, and Julie Tontubby. They had the following children: Edward Colbert McLish, Julia Ann McLish, Louisa McLish, Ellen McLish, Wyley McLish, Henry L. McLish, and Alexander "Muggs" McLish.

Children—Second Marriage of James Logan Colbert

IV. Colonel George "Tootemastubbe" Colbert

George Colbertwas born about 1744 and will be discussed in detail later in this book.

V. Major Levi "Itawamba Minco" Colbert

Major Levi "Itawamba Mingo" Colbert was born in 1759 and died June 2, 1834, at Buzzard Roost, Colbert County, Alabama at 74 years of age. He lived near Cotton Gin Port, Mississippi and was buried at Buzzard Roost in Colbert County, Alabama. Levi Colbert was possibly the wealthiest and most powerful of the Colbert family. He lived just west of Cotton Gin Port located in Monroe County, Mississippi. He owned four thousand cattle, five hundred horses, a large herd of sheep, and several head of swine. At one time, Levi had a part interest in Colbert's Ferry on the Natchez Trace which was said to have been worth $20,000 annually; Levi's brother George Colbert was the principle owner and operator of the ferry.

In the 1818 census report, Levi was listed as a resident of the Chickasaw Nation in Mississippi; he was Chief of the Chickasaw Nation, Mississippi, before 1834. Levi's will was probated in Monroe County, Mississippi on November 24, 1835. Levi Colbert died soon after the Chickasaw Treaty of 1834 was signed. He had served with the United States troops under General Andrew Jackson in the Battle of New Orleans; he was recognized as an important counselor to his Chickasaw people. Levi Colbert had 25 children with 14 sons and 11 daughters; however, he may have had more children and probably there were more than three wives.

Levi married at least three times. 1) His **first marriage** was to Ishtimmarharlechar, who was listed as a resident of the Chickasaw Nation in

Mississippi on the 1818 census report . 2) His **second marriage** was to Temusharhoctay 'Dollie' (Schtimmarshashoctay) who was born before 1780 and was listed as a resident of the Chickasaw Nation in Mississippi in the 1818 census report. 3) His **third marriage** was to Mintahoyo House of Imatapo who was born before 1799 and died after 1839. She was listed as a resident in the 1818 census report in Chickasaw Roll; and on May 24, 1834, but she was a resident of the Chickasaw Nation in Indian Territory in the 1839 census report.

Cotton Gin Port—Cotton Gin Port was located at major Chickasaw trail crossings of the Tombigbee River close to the home of Levi Colbert, Itawamba Mingo. The large Chickasaw town located at the site sat on the bluff west of the river. One trail which crossed the Tombigbee River at Cotton Gin Port was known as Gaines Trace and was surveyed from Melton's Bluff on the Tennessee River in present-day Lawrence County, Alabama by the Captain Edmund Pendelton Gaines of the United States Army beginning in December 1807. Another fork of Gaines Trace ran to Colbert's Ferry on the Tennessee River in present-day Colbert, County, Alabama. In addition, the High Town Path and Old Chickasaw trail crossed the Tombigbee River at Cotton Gin Port.

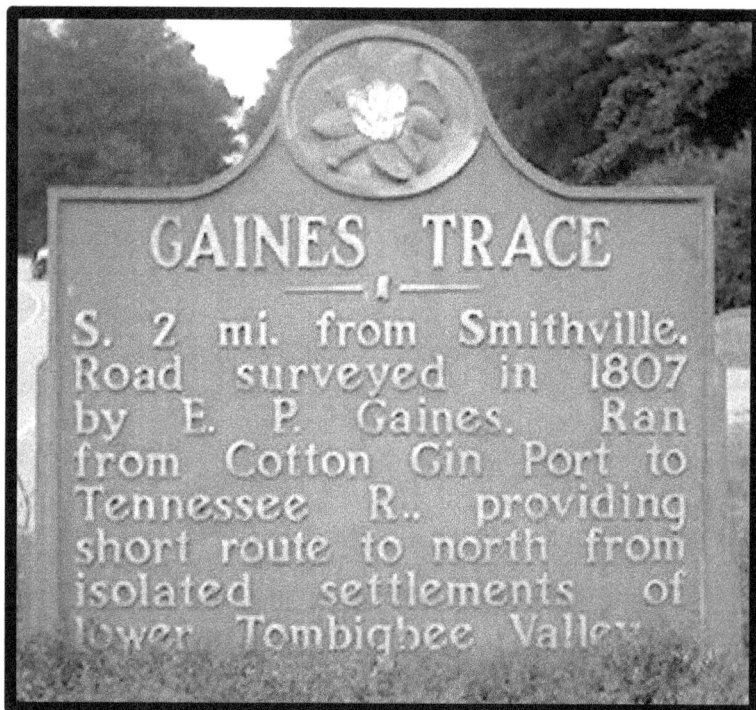

GAINES TRACE

S. 2 mi. from Smithville. Road surveyed in 1807 by E. P. Gaines. Ran from Cotton Gin Port to Tennessee R.. providing short route to north from isolated settlements of lower Tombigbee Valley

Gaines Trace was laid out as an early road along the Chickasaw trail that crossed the Tombigbee at the Cotton Gin Port. In 1816, the Chickasaws ceded their territory east of the Tombigbee and southeast of Gaines Trace to the United States.

In about 1801, the United States government agreed to build cotton gin on the west side of the river for the Chickasaw who lived on the bluff above the crossing. The

Americans hoped to improve relations with the Chickasaw who had been allies of the English, and to encourage the growing of cotton. According to one legend, the cotton gin was a gift from George Washington to one of the Colbert Chickasaw chiefs.

After the passage of the Indian Civilization Act in 1801, the United States government established a cotton gin on the west side of the river in an attempt to convert the Chickasaws into peaceful farmers and to win the support of the tribe that had long been allied with the English. The United States built the cotton gin on the site of the Old French Fort starting about around 1802 because the bluff was a good boat landing place. Although documents do not indicate clearly that a cotton gin was constructed by the United States Government for the Chickasaws at Cotton Gin Port, many think that the gin was part of the treaty of December 1801 authorizing Natchez Trace.

The exact location of the cotton gin is suspect, but it was probably built on the high bluffs southwest of the Old French Fort where a number of Indian trails converged. Some people claim that the cotton gin was constructed within the old fort site.

An explanation on the destruction of the cotton gin is given by Jack Elliott (2004) in *The Buried City*: *The gin was constructed in 1801 under the supervision of Indian agent John McKee as a part of the federal government's policy of encouraging the Indians to adopt commercial agriculture as an alternative to their traditional combination of horticulture, hunting, and gathering. Gin components were purchased in Natchez and hauled for hundreds of miles to the river crossing, which was accessible to the Chickasaw settlements and provided a means of shipping the ginned fiber downstream to Mobile. A gin house was built, and the gin began its operation. The Chickasaws were not able to use it for long, however. Possibly angered at not receiving a gin themselves, a group of Choctaws set fire to the gin house, reducing it to ashes within minutes and retarding plans for encouraging cotton culture among the Chickasaws* (Elliott, 2004).

The cotton gin saw little use since it was burned in a few months of being constructed; it is believed that a raiding band of Choctaw Indians burned the gin because they did not get one. Other historians say the Chickasaw burned it themselves; other sources say that a jealous husband burned it because his wife liked the operator. Finally, some historians speculate the cotton gin burned because of an accident.

Across the Tombigbee River and half a mile north of the ruins of the Cotton Gin Port ferry, a flat mound stands in the middle of a soybean field. Artifacts found here prove that the surrounding area was inhabited as early as 600 B.C., possibly earlier. This region was one of a number of large centers of Mississippian culture in the Tombigbee Basin. The mound itself was built during this period, dating from 1000 to 1700 A.D., by the ancestors of the Chickasaw Tribe. In area the mound measures about fifty yards square and is elevated over eight feet, clearly above high water level (Bryan, 1971).

Bell Mission—Bell Mission School, an agricultural and industrial mission school for the Chickasaws, was located just south of Cotton Gin Port in 1820. The Cumberland Presbyterian Church in Tennessee sent Reverend Robert Bell to Cotton Gin Port to start a mission for the Chickasaw Indians. Also known as Charity Hall, the school was located on the west side of the Tombigbee River about three miles south of Cotton Gin Port.

Reverend Robert Bell resided in Monroe County, Mississippi, not far from the Indian border. He was induced to assume charge of the Cumberland mission. Bell made a visit to James Colbert soon after the South Carolina and Georgia Messengers Humphreys and Stuart had left to go back home. Colbert showed Bell the written agreement between the Chickasaws and the South Carolina and Georgia missionaries. Bell got a copy of the agreement, and with alterations, a similar agreement was adopted by the Chickasaw council with reference to the Cumberland missionaries.

BELL
INDIAN MISSION

Six miles south is site of
first industrial school in
Mississippi. Presbyterian
Indian mission founded in
June, 1870, by the Rev. and
Mrs. Robert Bell.

Therefore in the year 1820, the Chickasaws granted two charters in nearly the same wording for two different missions. Bell, having gotten his agreement approved by the Chickasaw council, went home and at once moved to Cotton Gin Port to begin his missionary work. When Mr. Stuart got to Monroe Station in January 1821, he received word that the Cumberland Presbyterians were already at work. The South Carolina brethren were the first to get permission to come, but the Tennessee brethren were nearer the Chickasaws and were the first to establish a mission. Reverend Robert Bell established a school and preached to the Indians two and a half miles northeast of Cotton Gin Port.

The Cotton Gin and Monroe Station missions continued till the Chickasaws were removed to the West in 1837. In 1834, Reverend Bell settled near Pontotoc, Mississippi, where he lived the remainder of his days.

Itawamba Mingo—*Levi Colbert, or Itawamba mingo, was the best known and the most influential of the brothers. While he used broken English and was devoid of education himself, he seems to have believed in schools and gave all of his numerous sons an education. His title Itawamba, means "Bench Chief" and was given him as a reward for distinguished services rendered the tribe against their enemies the Creeks. Levi was a merchant. His sons were named Martin, Charles, Alex, Adam, Lemuel, Daugherty, Elijah, Commodore, and Lewis. His four daughters were called Charity, Mariah, Phalishta and Asa. We find his name mentioned in the treaty of 1816 with the Chickasaws as the recipient of $150 cash, and two forty acre tracts of land, two and one-half miles below Cotton Gin Port, on the Tombigbee River* (Warren, 1904).

In Horatio Bardman Cushman (1899) was born in the Choctaw Nation about 1824, and lived among the Choctaws and Chickasaws for some 75years. With first-hand knowledge, Cushman gave a detailed report on Levi Colbert as follows: *Major Levi Colbert resided near a place then known as Cotton Gin Port. He was truly a man wise in the councils of his Nation and valiant in defense of his Nation's rights. In early manhood, or rather in boyhood, he was elevated by an act of gallantry to the high position of "Ittawamba micco," as has been so oft published by different writers, and meaning, as given in the wisdom of their interpretation, "Bench Chief, or King of the Wooden Bench." There is no such; word in the Chickasaw language as "Itta wamba micco," and it can be but the fabrication of imaginative ignorance. The Chickasaw words for Bench Chief (if there ever was such a personage among them) would be, "Aiobinili (a seat) falaia (long) Miko chief.pro. Ai-ome-bih-ne-lih-far-li-yah Meenkoh, The chief on the long seat -or bench—in our phraseology, The chief in the Chair of State.*

Major Levi Colbert's act of gallantry, by which he was at once elevated to the high position of chief, consisted in having defeated, when but a youth a war party of Muscogees who had invaded the Chickasaw Nation, at a time when all the warriors of the invaded district were away from home on a hunting excursion. Young Levi at once collected the old men and boys and formed them into a war company and started for the depredating Creeks, whom he successfully drew into an artfully planned ambuscade, by which all the Muscogees were slain, not one being left to return to his own country and tell of their complete destruction. The little stream upon whose banks the battle took place was afterwards called (so says a writer in one of his published articles) "Yahnubly," and gives its signification as "All killed"; bill unfortunately for his erudition, no such word is known in the Chickasaw language. There is, however, the word yanubih (pro. yarn-ub-ih) in their language but its signification is iron-wood. While the Chickasaw words for "All killed" (same as the Choctaw) are momaubih; the land or place where all were killed.

When the warriors returned from their hunt and learned of the battle and to whom the safety of their families was due, and also the honor of the victory, a council was immediately called and the young hero summoned to attend; when he appeared and the statement of facts had been laid before them, they, without a dissenting voice, and as men who quickly discerned true merit and knew how to appreciate it, elevated him to the responsible position of a chief in their Nation.

The following publication appeared a few years ago as a valuable piece of Chickasaw history: "Ittawamba was the name of an office. The word signifies King of the Wooden Bench. The individual who held the high title was elected by the national council. A part of the imposing ceremony by which the officer elected was initiated was as follows: At a given signal he jumped from a wooden bench to the floor in the hall of state where the magnates of the Nation sat in conclave. At the moment his feet touched the earth the whole of tire assembly exclaimed Ittawamba! The honored individual who heard this voice became the second magistrate of the Nation. Thus he received the orders of Chickasaw Knighthood, Ittawamba micco, or Bench Chief.

No doubt of it. But the greater mystery is, how anyone could jump "from a wooden bench to the floor in the hall of state," and "the moment his feet touched the earth," not to become instantly a notorious "Bench Chief." Verily, a problem that must be left for solution to the unprecedented wisdom of the author of the above historical piece of information. But the whole article is such an exhibition of pitiable nonsense, that in reading it to some Chickasaw friends, they ill exclaimed': "What a fool"; The most ridiculous, absurd and utterly false articles ire continually appearing in print, in regard to the Indians, from the pens of those whose knowledge of that unfortunate people, against whom lies enough have been fabricated and published to satisfy the devil, is about as much as might be expected to be found in an African Bushman.

But be what "Ittawamba" may, nevertheless the young initiate, Levi Colbert, after his initiation into its wonderful mysteries, proved himself worthy to be not only a "king of the wooden bench," but also, by his talents, purity of principles, energy and force of character, a king upon a regal throne to bear rule over a nation. For several years he shaped the policy, and presided over the destinies of the Chickasaw people with wisdom and discretion.

John Coffee—*On the 27th and, 28th of September, 1830, the Choctaws, by a treaty with John Coffee and John Eaton, United States commissioners, ceded their lands, east of the Mississippi River to the United States. Major Levi Colbert, having heard what they had done, immediately called upon his friend, Mr. Stephen Daggette, and asked him to calculate the interest for him of four hundred thousand dollars at five, six, seven and eight per cent. The Choctaws had taken government bonds at five per cent; Major Colbert at once seeing that they had been badly and most outrageously swindled, exclaimed in a loud and highly excited tone of voice, "God I thought so." He then informed Mr. Daggette that he was anxious to obtain the calculation, that he might be enabled to explain it to his people in their own language. He also stated to Mr. Daggette that "the United States would soon make an effort to buy the lands of the Chickasaws also, and I want to be ready for them."*

This conversation between Lev Colbert and Mr. Daggette took place two years before the treaty with the Chickasaws, which was made on the 20th of October, 1832, at

67

the house of a Chickasaw called Topulka—a corruption of Tahpulah; (to halloo or make a noise), but was known, says a writer of the yahnubbih and Ittawamba order of expounders, in his publication, as "Pontaontac," which he also interprets as signifying "Cat Tail Prairie"; but unfortunately for him also, the Chickasaw words for his classic name "Cat Tail Prairie" are Kutus Hasimbish Oktak (pro. Kut-oos (cat) Harsim-bish (tail) Oke-tark prairie; therefore he also must seek elsewhere than in the Chickasaw language for his "Pontaontac" and its signification "Cat Tail Prairie," as there is no such word in the Chickasaw language, nor in any other North American Indian language, it is reasonable to suppose. Pontotoc, the name of a town in north Mississippi, is a corruption, as has been before stated, of the words Paki Tukohli—grapes hung up; hanging grapes.

But such are the gross and ridiculous errors made by those of the present age who not only prove their terrible ignorance by their unmerciful butchery of the Indian languages, but equally so in the exhibition of their shameful prejudice unreasonably cherished against that unjustly persecuted people, concerning whom, in every particular, they assume to be infinitely wise; and though totally ignorant of the subject, presume to talk and write about them with arrogant duplicity to the infinite injury of the Indians and disgrace of their languages.

When the United States had resolved to gobble up the Chickasaw country also, as they had the Choctaws' two years before, John Coffee was sent to the Chickasaw Nation to order Ben

General John Coffee
6/2/1772-7/7/1833

Reynolds (the Chickasaw Agent) to immediately assemble the chiefs and warriors in council to effect a treaty with them.

Three treaties (or rather articles) were drawn up, but were promptly rejected by the watchful and discerning Chickasaws. Then the fourth was written by the persistent Coffee; but with the following clause inserted to catch the noble and influential chief, Yakni Moma Ubih, the incorruptible Levi Colbert, which read as follows; "We hereby agree to give our beloved chief, Levi Colbert, in consideration of his services and expense of entertaining the guests of the Nation, fifteen sections of land in any part of the country he may select. Stop! Stop! John Coffee shouted the justly indignant chief in a voice of thunder, "I am no more entitled to those fifteen sections of land than the poorest Chickasaw in the Nation. I scorn your infamous offer, clothed under the falsehood of our beloved chief, and will not accept it, sir. A frown of disappointment momentarily rested, no doubt, upon the face of Coffee.

Then a fifth treaty was written out by Coffee, and the council again called together to consider upon its merits; and which, after due deliberation, was finally accepted. The Chickasaws agreed, to take United States bonds, but were unable to satisfactorily comprehend the six per cent promised them, until their interpreter, Ben Love, illustrated it as a hen laying eggs. Those one hundred dollars would lay six dollars in twelve months, which they at once fully understood...

Ishtehotopa, the king, first walked up with a countenance that betokened the emotions of one about to sign his jury's death warrant, and with a sad heart and trembling hand made his mark. Then Tishu Miko advanced with solemn mien and did likewise; then the other chiefs with countenance sad and forlorn; and last of all, the pure, the noble Levi Colbert, whom gold could not buy, or cause to ever from the path of honor.

Levi's Death—*Soon after the treaty had been signed, Major Levi Colbert stated to Mr. Daggette he was not satisfied with some clauses in the treaty which he did not at first correctly understand. Mr. Daggette advised him to go immediately to Washington and get it changed to his satisfaction before it is confirmed by the Senate. Colbert, with other delegates, started immediately to Washington City, but only got as far as his son-in-law, Kilpatrick Carter's, in Alabama (Buzzard Roost Spring in Colbert County), where he was taken sick and died, to the great sorrow and loss of the Chickasaw Nation. The other delegates continued their journey to Washington, and secured the desired alteration in the treaty...*

But, in justice, it must and shall be said of the Chickasaw Agent of 1832, Benjamin Reynolds, that he was an honest man. As agent to the Chickasaw people for the United States Mr. Reynolds annually paid them twenty thousand dollars for several consecutive years as annuity. Previous to the treaty Mr. Daggette affirms he assisted Mr. Reynolds in paying to the Chickasaws their annuities, and that Mr. Reynolds distributed the last cent among them, giving to each his or her dues honestly and justly, though every opportunity was offered to defraud them, and lived and died an honest and pure man; and then, no doubt, went above to receive the glorious welcome (Cushman, 1899).

1) Levi's Children by Ishtimmarharlechar

A. Charlotte "Lotty" Colbert was born prior to 1818 and married Davis James, who was born in1811 and died on 2/9/1856. They had at least three children: Roberson James who married Mary James; Walton James; and, Lucy James.

B. Chersey "Kersey" Colbert was listed as a resident in the 1818 census report in Chickasaw Nation. Chersey was listed as head of a family in the 1839 Chickasaw Nation Indian census in Choctaw Nation, Indian Territory, living alone over age 50 and owning 14 slaves.

C. Lesila Colbert was listed as a resident in the 1818 census report in Chickasaw Nation.

D. Dorothy Colbert was listed as a resident in the 1818 census report in Chickasaw Nation.

2) Levi's Children by Temusharhoctay 'Dollie'

E. Alexander "Alex" Colbert was born before 1818 and died after 1837. He married Diana Colbert and they had at least two children: Eveline Colbert married Benjamin Stephen Love who was born 2/18/1825 and died 12/26/ 1856; and, Stephen Colbert.

F. Leila (Alizra or Elzira) Colbert married John Junior Pitchlynn and they had the following children: Levi Pitchlynn; John Jack Pitchlynn; and, Hiram Pitchlynn who married Desire A. Morrow.

G. Ailcy Colbert

H. Martin Colbert was born circa 1795 and married Sarah Allen, Louisana Allen, and Sally Oxberry. Martin and his wives had the following children: Benjamin Franklin Colbert married Martha Jane Moore, Martha McKinney, Melinda Factor, George Ann McCarthy, and Anna "Amanda" Louise Goldsby; James Allen Colbert married Athenius Folsom; Margaret Colbert married Henry McKinney; Rebecca Colbert married Ed Nail; Adolphus Colbert married Orilla Folsom; Buck Colbert married Louisa Kemp; Minerva Colbert married Bill Finch; John Calvin Colbert married Emma Frances Nail and Rosabell Davis; and, Henry Clay Colbert married Ellen Nora Willis and Louisa Kemp.

Benjamin Franklin Colbert
12/18/1826-3/11/1893

Benjamin Franklin Colbert operated a ferry in Indian territory that crossed the Red River from Oklahoma to Texas. He bought the ferry that had been built by Joseph G. Mitchell in 1842 and Mitchell operated the ferry until he died five years later.

When Benjamin Franklin Colbert, a Chickasaw Indian, purchased the property in 1849, he hired Pennsylvania-native Joseph Bonaparte Earhart to make improvements on Mitchell's previous ferry operations. Earhart later became personally involved in the Butterfield line, managing a stage station to the west at Hog-Eye Prairie, on the Jack-Wise county line.

In 1858, Colbert obtained a license for a toll ferry from the Chickasaw Legislature. Two years later, in 1860, he encountered problems with the owner of the ferry landing across the river in Texas, M.A. McBride. McBride wanted a piece of the ferry business, and in resolving the dispute, forced the Native American to purchase his property. Colbert's Ferry was a stage stand on the Butterfield Overland Mail from 1858-1861, and carriages, wagons, and livestock crossed here until 1893. Travelers passing through here included Frederick Grant, son of Ulysses S. Grant, as well as Frank and Jessie James and the Younger Brothers (Britton, 1978).

I. Adam Colbert was born in 1805 in the Chickasaw Nation. Adam died after 1847 in Indian Territory. On April 11, 1836, he bought property in Monroe County, Mississippi.

J. David "Dave" Colbert was born circa 1811 and married Amy Mamie. They had the following children: Frances Colbert married Charles Adams, Samuel Hunter Cochran, Theophilus H. East, and Daniel David Green.

K. Abijah Jackson Colbert was born 1813 and married Rhoda Hillhouse. They had the following children: Amos Henry Colbert married Icy Hamilton.

L. Commodore Colbert was born in Chickasaw Nation and died about 1844 in Indian Territory. He was listed as a resident in the 1818 census report in Chickasaw Nation. The 1839 census in Choctaw Nation, Indian Territory shows him the head of his family living alone at age 25-50. He bought property in DeSoto County, Mississippi on March 3, 1837.

M. Dolly (Dicey) Colbert married Noah Doran Colbert and they had the following children: Susan Watkins married James McCauley; and, Mary Watkins married Charlie Juzan and James T. Leedy.

N. Martha "Patsey" Colbert was born 1820 and married Jackson Kemp. They had the following children: Jackson Kilpatrick Kemp; and, Alexander Commodore Kemp married Emma Jane Gordon and Alice Love.

3) Levi's Children by Mintahoyo

O. Lemuel Colbert married Parthena and Carter Elzira Hoyt and they had the following children: Mary Eliza Colbert married Edard G. Yerion and Simon Burney Kemp; Elvira Kemp married Simon Burney Kemp; Elvrin Colbert; and, Elzira Colbert.

P. Phalishta "Pat" (Malacha) Colbert married Kilpatrick Carter and lived at Buzzard Roost Spring in Colbert County, Alabama. They had the following children: Pamela Carter married Frances Montgomery Reynolds; Colbert Kilpatrick Carter married

Elizabeth Humphreys; Melena Carter married a McDonna and a Colbert; Susan Carter married William M. Walner; and, Eliza Carter married Jackson Kemp.

Levi Colbert Historic Marker

Levi Colbert died at the home of his daughter, Phalishta "Pat" Malacha Colbert Carter, at Buzzard Roost Spring in Colbert County, Alabama. Levi originally lived at the Buzzard Roost site and had Kilpatrick Carter to build a new home on the site; however, supposedly during the construction of the home Carter fell in love with Levi's daughter and married her. Levi told Carter if he would build him another house at Cotton Gin Port that he would give his daughter and Kilpatrick Carter the home at Buzzard Roost Spring which was done. Then in 1834 after Levi and the Chickasaws negotiated a treaty with John Coffee, they realized that changes should be made before the treaty was ratified; and therefore, a delegation of Chickasaws including Levi Colbert started from Cotton Gin Port to Washington, D.C. Levi got sick and stopped at his daughter's house at Buzzard Roost Spring where he died. He is supposedly buried at the old home site in Colbert County, Alabama.

Q. Lewis Colbert

R. Monroe Colbert was listed as Munro, a resident in the 1818 Chickasaw Census report in Chickasaw Nation.

S. Robert Colbert married Elsey Mollie (Mah La To Ka) Toka and had the following children: Frances Colbert; Cub Colbert; Emily Colbert; Elzira Colbert married Levi Kemp; Levina Piney C. Colbert married Alfred Wright Folsom; and, Catherine Kitty Colbert married Thomas Suggs Barker.

T. Charity Colbert was born 1805 and married George C. Allen. They had the following children: Martin Allen; Elsie Allen married Zachariah Colbert; and, Emily Allen married Robert Lewis Boyd.

U. Charles C. Colbert was born circa 1812 and married Mississippi Allen. They had the following children: Rebecca Colbert married John Brooks and Steve Bussell.

V. Asa Colbert was listed as a resident in the census report in Chickasaw Nation, 1818.

W. Daugherty Colbert was born circa 1819. The capable Cyrus Harris inaugurated the new government as its first governor to be succeeded in the fall of 1858 by Daugherty (Winchester) Colbert.

Daugherty Colbert
1810-1880

Winchester Colbert— *Daugherty (Winchester) Colbert although listed as a son in the large family of Levi Colbert which consisted of twelve sons and eight daughters and although he was reared as a member of that family, a verification impels the conclusion that he was not, in fact, a son of Levi Colbert. He is reputed to have been the natural son of an itinerant, adventurous white man by the name of Darrity. His* *mother was a Chickasaw Indian woman and he was born in the Tombigbee River country near Cotton Gin Port, Monroe County, Mississippi in 1810. In his early years, this child of romance was received by adoption into the family of Levi Colbert and was reared and educated by that distinguished Chickasaw leader. Chickasaw law offered no defined procedure relating to such adoptions but the practice was not unusual among the Indians. The communistic impulses of these simple folk inclined their hearts to extend shelter, care and protection to the homeless of their race irrespective of circumstances. He was invested with the family name of Colbert his own father's name being employed as his first name, but Darrity Colbert soon became Daugherty Colbert occasioned not only by a similarity in the names but also probably influenced by the fact that a near relative of Levi Colbert bore the name of Daugherty Colbert. The name Winchester Colbert was adopted by the young man some years later and so through life he sometimes was recognized as Daugherty Colbert and at other times as Winchester Colber*t (Meserve, 1940).

X. Mariah Colbert was born circa 1822 and married Joel I. Kemp. They had the following children: Simon Burney Kemp married Eliza Colbert and Elvira Colbert; Frances Elizabeth Kemp married Benjamin Franklin Roark, Sanford Minor Mead, and Albert Henderson Moberly; Joel Carr Kemp married LaNora McSwain and Elizabeth Minerva Tunna Perry; Lillie Kemp; Mary Jane Kemp married William R. George; Charity Kemp; Daisy Kemp; Laura A. Kemp married John Horton Mashburn and James Easky; and, Isabella Abigail Kemp married John M. Webb.

Y. Andrew Morgan Colbert was born 1825 and had a daughter, Mary Ann Colbert.

VI. Samuel Colbert

Samuel was born about 1761 and was killed by northern Indians about 1782. He married Nancy Frazier who was the daughter of Alexander Frazier and Mollie (Mary) Perry. Nancy died before 1889. She was listed as a resident in the census report in Batapanbogue, Choctaw Nation on November 28, 1834. She was listed as a resident in the census report on 1855 Choctaw Roll, Chickasaw District, Indian Territory on December 1856.

Children of Samuel Colbert and Nancy Frazier

A. William James Colbert, Jr. died about 1837 and married Kunnoyie who died about 1838. They had the following children: Joseph Colbert; Tennessee Colbert; and, James Samuel Colbert who married Sarah Blazier.

B. Martin Vann (Van) Colbert

C. Winchester (Daugherty) Colbert was born in 1810 and died in 1880. He married Annica Kemp, Easter Ibbahfoquatubby, Silsey Ibbahfoquatubby, and Rhoda Ibbahfoquatubby. They had the following children: Harley Humphrey Colbert married Elmira Parker and Selina Hamilton; Margaret Peggy Colbert married Fred O. Lee and Benjamin Franklin Perry; Viney Colbert; Noah Colbert; George Washington Colbert; Isabelle Bebe Colbert; Elizabeth Colbert; Lucy Bransford Colbert; James Logan Colbert; Jackson Colbert; Isaac Colbert; Wilson Colbert; Mary Colbert; David Dave Colbert; and, Julia Colbert.

D. Robert Colbert was born before 1818 and his wife was not known. He had the following children: Emily Colbert married Allen Latta; Lindsay Colbert; and, Vina Colbert.

E. Hettie Colbert was born before 1820 and died before 1889. She married an unknown Colbert and they had the following children: Ben Colbert; and, Selina Colbert.

VII. Joseph Colbert

Joseph was born about 1767 and died at Colbert's Ferry on the Tennessee River in Alabama. He served as an interpreter for the Chickasaw Nation in 1799 and also for missionary Joseph Bullen.

Children—Third Marriage of James Logan Colbert

VIII. Major James Colbert

James was a quarter blood Chickasaw born about 1768 and died May 1842 in Doaksville, Towson County, Choctaw Nation, Indian Territory, at 73 years of age. He was listed as a resident in the 1818 census report in Chickasaw Nation, Mississippi. James was Chickasaw Chief in Chickasaw Nation before 1842. In the early 1780's, James was placed under the tutelage of the firm of Panton, Leslie, and Company of Pensacola by his father, James Logan Colbert, there to obtain an education and employment. This is the same company that had very close ties to Creek Chief Alexander McGillivray. McGillivray was actually buried on his Panton friend's property at Pensacola. James returned to the Chickasaw Country by 1789 and within six years became a tribal interpreter. From 1814 to 1818, he was employed as United States interpreter to the tribe at a salary of $400 a year.

James Colbert, the youngest of Logan Colbert's sons, was also, as his renowned brothers, a man of great integrity and firmness of character. He acted, for many years, in the capacity of the national secretary. The archives of the Chickasaw Nation were placed in his hands for safe keeping, the majority of which being in his own hand writing; and truly it may be said, antiquaries, in coming years of the far future, may decipher with much interest and profit, the documents written by James Colbert (Cushman, 1899).

The youngest of the four brothers was Major James Colbert, at one time interpreter for the nation, who also lived in Alabama, some forty miles south of Levi and George. They were all constant and active friends of the United States (Goodpasture, 1918).

James Colbert married three times. 1) His **first wife** was Susan (Susannah) James before 1799. Susan was born March 27, 1783, and was the daughter of Benjamin James. Susan died on December 3, 1863, at 80 years of age, and she was interred in Soper, Choctaw County, Oklahoma. She married Major James Colbert in Mississippi on June 24, 1799. James was divorced from Susan (Susannah) James in Mississippi before 1830. Susan was listed as a resident in the census report in Chickasaw Nation, Mississippi in 1818. Susan was a Presbyterian and was baptized at in Monroe Mission,

Pontotoc County, Mississippi on January 6, 1828. She resided in Marshall County, Mississippi on March 22, 1841, when she filed the following: *"Susan Colbert of Marshall County, Mississippi for love of my daughter Susan M. James and her daughters Amelia James and Margaret James, who are also my granddaughters,"* a Deed of Gift of Negro slaves.... *"all of which Negros are in the possession of my son Joseph Colbert in Chickasaw Nation West of Mississippi River; also to Margaret James in her own right Negro girl Mary, 8 years and now in possession of her father Samuel M. James and to remain so until Margaret reaches 18 years or shall marry."* The deed was witnessed by William B. Spinks and Green Davis. The deed was acknowledged in Marshall County, Mississippi by Gordentia Waite, Clerk Probate Court on March 24, 1841. The deed was filed in Red River County, Texas, Deed Record Book G on page 172. She was listed as a resident in the census report on 1855 Choctaw Roll, Kiamitia County, Choctaw Nation, Indian Territory on November/December 1856.

The Natchez Road
Later called the Natchez Trace

Showing some of the stands and towns that developed along the Road before the 1830s.

© Frederick Smoot 2002

Tennessee R.   Cumberland R.

Nashville ☆

Tennessee

JOSLIN'S STAND
GORDON'S STAND
Duck R.
KEG SPRINGS STAND
SHEBOSS STAND
DOBBIN'S STAND
McLISH'S STAND
Columbia
YOUNG FACTOR'S STAND
GRINER'S STAND
JACKSON'S STAND
TOSCOMBY'S STAND
SESSUM'S STAND

CHICKASAW BLUFFS

Memphis

Mississippi River

GEORGE COLBERT'S STAND
BUZZARD ROOST STAND
LEVI COLBERT'S STAND
BROWN'S STAND
OLD FACTOR'S STAND
LEVI KEMP'S STAND
JAMES COLBERT'S STAND
JAMES ALLEN'S STAND

Florence

Alabama

TOCKSHISH'S STAND
WALL'S STAND
PIGEON ROOST STAND

Mississippi

MITCHELL'S STAND
FRENCH CAMP STAND
HAWKIN'S STAND
SHOAT'S STAND
ANDERSON'S STAND
CROWDER'S STAND
DOAK'S STAND
WARD'S STAND
BRADSHERS'S STAND
OGBURN'S STAND
DEAN'S STAND
RED BLUFF STAND
HAYES'S STAND
ROCKY SPRINGS
WOOLRIDGE'S STAND
GRINDSTONE FORD
COON BOX STAND
GREENVILLE
UNIONTOWN
SELSERTOWN
WASHINGTON

Jackson

Port Gibson

Natchez

Pearl R.

Notice on the map, James Colbert ran a stand along the Natchez Trace along with his half-brothers, George and Levi Colbert. James Colbert's Stand was in the southern portion of the Chickasaw Nation some forty miles south of George Colbert's Stand at the Tennessee River crossing of the Natchez Trace. Susan Colbert's husband James Allen ran a stand to the south of her brother James Colbert.

1) Children of James Isaac Colbert and Susan James

A. Molcy (Molsey) Colbert was a physician in Chickasaw Nation in Indian Territory and died after 1856. She was listed as a resident in the 1818 census report in Chickasaw Nation and in Indian Territory in 1847. Molcy was baptized at Monroe Mission in Pontotoc County, Mississippi on May 7, 1826. She resided in Kiamitia County, Choctaw Nation in Indian Territory during 1855.

B. Charles Colbert died July 23, 1800 in Mississippi and he was buried on July 24, 1800. On July 24, 1799, Charles was baptized in the Chickasaw Nation in Mississippi.

C. Thomas Colbert died in the winter of 1841 or 1842 before January 24, 1842 in Arkansas. Probate records state that he was "late of Arkansas". He was listed as a resident in the 1818 census report in Chickasaw Nation. On January 24, 1842, Thomas' will was probated in Marshall County, Mississippi.

D. Sukey Colbert was listed as a resident in the 1818 census report in Chickasaw Nation and a resident in the census report on 1855 Choctaw Roll in Kiamitia County of the Choctaw Nation, Indian Territory on November/December 1856.

E. Joseph Edwin Colbert was born January 5, 1801, and died before 1898. He married Elmira Elzira Oxberry and they had the following children: Frank Colbert; William Colbert; Joseph Colbert; Henry Colbert married Louisa Lou Humphreys; Emily Colbert married Charles Sealy and John Houston Fleetwood; Lavinia Vine Colbert married John Thomas Pitchlynn; Jane A. Zile Colbert married John Thomas Howell; Albert D. Colbert married Mary McCassland; Edmund Colbert; Elizabeth Colbert married an unknown Fletcher; and, Elvina Colbert married an unknown Fleetwood.

F. James Isaac Colbert, Jr. was born September 10, 1802, and died about 1860. He married Sarah "Sally" McLish and Catherine Caroline Moore and they had the following children: Nathaniel A. Colbert married Melinda McCurtain; James "Bushy Jim" Colbert married Katrinka Countess De Rudczinsky, Sylvia Blackburn, and Mary Polly Nelson; Sophia Colbert married Charles Messick; Christopher Columbus "Tum" Colbert married Nancy M. Bourland; Rebecca Colbert married William Venson Alexander; Mary Colbert; Frances Colbert; Jenny Lind Colbert married William Venson Alexander and Joseph B. Moore; James "Old" Holmes Colbert married Elizabeth Love; and, Harriet Colbert married Albert Perry Eastman.

G. Tennessee Robinson Colbert was born May 6, 1805.

H. Susan Miller Colbert was born 1814 and married Lovard M. James.

I. Samuel A. Colbert was born November 14, 1816, and died August 27, 1880. He married Rhoda Gunn, Mary unknown, and Lucinda "Lina" or "Ciney" Love. Samuel and his wives had the following children: Mary Susan Colbert married Doctor P. Loman; Atwood Colbert; George Washington Colbert married Elizabeth "Lizzie" Sorrells and Dora McCarty; Virginia Colbert; Sarah Love Colbert married Hilburn Harrison; Caroline Colbert; Isabella Colbert; Samuel Colbert; Ellen Colbert; Wilson McAlester Colbert; Delilah Colbert married L. P. Parshall; and, Edward Colbert married Lena Hereford.

J. Elizabeth "Betsy" Colbert was born 1819 and died January 5, 1872. She married Charles Frances Eastman who was born in 1800 and died on October 16, 1874. They had a son Charles Frances Jr. Eastman.

K. Matilda Colbert was born June 10, 1820.

2) Children of James Colbert and Half-breed Chickasaw Frazier

2) James' **second wife** was Mrs. Half-breed Chickasaw Frazier after 1799.

L. Daughter Colbert died at age 18.

3) Children of James Colbert and Nellie

3) James' **third wife** was Nellie about 1841. She was listed as a resident in the 1855 census report on Choctaw Roll, Chickasaw District, Indian Territory, December 1856.

M. George Colbert was born 1842 only 12 days after his father died. He was listed as a resident in the 1855 census report in Choctaw Roll in the Chickasaw District of Indian Territory in December 1856.

IX. Susan "Susy" Colbert

Susan was born about 1770 and died after 1848 in Indian Territory. She filed a claim as a self-emigrating Chickasaw on November 15, 1848. She first married James

B. Allen in Chickasaw Nation, Mississippi about 1790. James B. Allen and James Logan Colbert's daughter Susan Colbert had a daughter, Peggy. She was very beautiful and married a handsome young man from the neighborhood of Natchez.

James B. Allen was born in North Carolina and died 1835 and buried in Toccopola, Mississippi. He was listed as a resident in the census report in Chickasaw Nation, Mississippi in 1818 and 1830. James was baptized at in Monroe Mission, Pontotoc County, Mississippi on July 6, 1828. James Allen, a North Carolinian, was well-educated and of a family in easy circumstances. He came to Nashville, intending to settle there as a lawyer, but from some disgust, entered the Chickasaw Nation, where he soon found the favor of a wealthy half-breed, General William Colbert. According to Martini (1986), *"James Allen, a native of North Carolina and reputedly at one time a lawyer in Nashville, Tennessee, arrived in the Chickasaw Nation sometime before 1793. By 1797, he was married to Susan Colbert, the youngest daughter of trader James Logan Colbert, and two years later their daughter, Peggy, was baptized by missionary Joseph Bullen. Allen was also married in 1797 or 1798 to Betsy Love, daughter of trader Thomas Love."*

In the Chickasaw Nation during 1818, Susan Colbert was listed as a resident in the census report and on the Chickasaw Roll in Mississippi. Susan registered to pay taxes in Yalobusha County, Mississippi in 1834-1835. She sold property in Yalobusha County, Mississippi on February 9, 1835. She bought property in Yalobusha County, Mississippi on February 9, 1836. In 1835 and 1840, she was listed as a resident in the census report and tax list in Yalobusha County, Mississippi. She bought property in Mississippi on May 22, 1843; her reserve was suspended in the later months of 1843.

Susan Colbert was listed as a resident in the 1847 census report in Indian Territory; she was listed as a full blood over the age of 50. She was residing in Indian Territory on November 15, 1848. The missionaries in 1799 indicate that Susan Colbert was the youngest daughter of James Logan Colbert; therefore, she was only one quarter like her brother James Colbert.

Jonathan Daniels in his book, *"The Devil's Backbone - The Story of the Natchez Trace,"* refers to Peggy Allen, who married Simon Burney, as the great-granddaughter of James Logan Colbert; stating that she was the daughter of Susan Colbert and James Allen. However, Peggy was actually a granddaughter of James Logan Colbert.

There does exist in the Monroe County, Mississippi records the following; *"Susan Perry, Yalobusha County, Mississippi, to daughter Margaret Burney of the*

Chickasaw Nation, slaves. February 9, 1825." Margaret (Allen) Burney was most often referred to as Peggy, (Peggy is a well-known nickname for Margaret), and was the daughter of Susan Colbert and James Allen.

Margaret married Simon Burney; plural marriages were certainly consistent with Chickasaw Tribal Law at that time and many white traders took advantage of that fact. Susan Colbert married the Perry before 1818. Susan (Colbert) Allen must have been alive in 1825, and living in Yalobusha County, Mississippi. Three things affirm this: Yalobusha County, while on the border line of the Chickasaws and Choctaws in Mississippi, was considered Choctaw land; Susan Colbert's last name was later given as "Perry" and not "Allen"; and, James Allen had by 1798 married to Betsy Love, daughter of trader Thomas Love; therefore, something happened to the marriage of James Allen and Susan Colbert.

Susan (Colbert) Allen married a man named Perry and moved to the edge of the Choctaw Nation. There were a number of prominent Perrys in the Choctaw Nation and it is probable that Susan (Colbert) Allen married one of them. Susan was alive in 1825, and there is a Susan Perry listed with the Colbert family on the 1818 Census and she may be the same person as a Perry widow by 1818.

Susan's brother James Colbert was destitute in 1830, and was trying to get back the slaves that he had inherited from his father James Logan Colbert, but had given or sold to a number of his friends or relatives. Listed among those friends or relatives was Benjamin Love, who had married Charlotte Burney (a granddaughter of young James Colbert's sister Susan), David Burney (a brother of Charlotte's), Simon Burney (the father of Charlotte and David, as well as the husband of Margaret "Peggy" Allen), Susan (Colbert) Perry, John Perry, and Joseph Perry.

It is quite possible that the slaves held by the Burneys and Benjamin Love, were among the slaves given to Margaret (Allen) Burney by her mother Susan (Colbert) Perry. The 1818 Chickasaw Census does list an individual named Susy Perry Colbert apparent member of the house hold of James Colbert, Susan's brother.

Children of Susan 'Susy' Colbert and James B. Allen

A. Margaret "Peggy" Allen was born about 1790 and married Simon Burney. They had the following children: Charlotte "Lottie" Burney married Benjamin Love and Calvin S. Choate; Levi Burney; David Calhoun Burney married Lucy James and Emily Love; Mary Burney; and, Annie Burney married Benjamin Franklin Smallwood.

George Colbert: Wives and Children

George Colbert was the half Chickasaw and half Scots son of a Chickasaw woman named Sofa or Minta Hoye and James Logan Colbert, who was a Carolinian of Scots descent and lived with the Chickasaws at a young age. Some historians believe that George married at least three daughters of Doublehead, but there appears to be clear historical evidence that George married the two oldest daughters of Doublehead and Creat Priber: Saleechie Doublehead and Tuskiahooto Doublehead. There is no record of George and Tuskiahooto having any children.

George Colbert, or Tootemastubbe, was perhaps the most well-known and pleasing in appearance and manners of James Logan Colbert's sons. He was illiterate but had much influence, stood acceptably fair, and talked very common English. He was opposed to innovation, education, missions, and whiskey; however, it is documented that he sold whiskey to travelers, had a very successful farming operation, and tolerated missionaries. He lived for a while at Colbert's Ferry in present-day Colbert County, Alabama and later on Wolf Creek some four miles west of Tupelo, Mississippi. George Colbert and Saleechie moved to the West where he died two years later on November 7, 1839.

Description of George Colbert—According to McDonald (2007), *various accounts describing George Colbert's appearance and character present an interesting study of this leader among the Chickasaws. Cyrus Harris, Governor of the Chickasaw Nation after their removal, described him as "illiterate but had some influence and stood tolerably fair; talk common English". A Methodist preacher called him a "very shrewd, talented man and, withal, very wicked." Dr. Rush Nutt, a Natchez Planter, said that he was the "greatest of the Chickasaws, displays genius and talent...but is an artful designing man." Colonel Return J. Meigs, Cherokee Indian Agent, described him as: "extremely mercenary miscalculates his importance, and when not awed by the presence of the officers of the government takes upon himself great airs"...*

James Simpson grew up across the river at Florence. As a boy of ten years, he was fascinated when George Colbert and other Indians came to town and bought supplies at his father's store. As an old man, Simpson wrote about these scenes of the past and gave an interesting description of George Colbert: He was tall and slender and handsome with straight black hair that he wore long, which came well down to his shoulders. His features were that of an Indian but his skin was lighter than that of his tribe. He wore the dress of a white man of his day and always appeared neat and clean. He frequently ate dinner at my father's house in Florence, Alabama. The building now known as the Commercial Hotel was my father's store and he had reputation among the Indians as being an honest and just man and as a consequence of the Indian trade. George Colbert often crossed the river in canoes with thirty or fifty of his tribe to purchase goods in Florence. The Indians seemed to enjoy roaming over the store looking at everything. They wore buckskin clothes of their own making. Some of them wore feather head dress (McDonald, 2007).

Chickasaw Chief George Colbert
1744-11/7/1839

George Colbert was unwilling to allow individual traders to sell merchandise to the Chickasaws because it would diminish his profits. George Colbert organized trading activities to Florence, Alabama and was able to oversee trade in the Chickasaw Nation. George Colbert did not allow outside traders unless he approved of the transactions. He would accompany large numbers of his people to stores in town to make sure that the Chickasaws were treated fairly by the white merchants.

George Colbert's Home at his ferry—The date of the construction of George Colbert's home was after the treaty of 1801, with some claiming it was completed by 1808 and possibly much earlier. Most historians agree that the house was part of the agreement of General James Wilkinson and George Colbert that provided for a new ferryboat and lodging at the Natchez Trace crossing of the Tennessee River. The two storied house was originally located in present-day Colbert County, Alabama within a few hundred yards of George Colbert's Ferry.

According to McDonald (2007), *one historian, Frank King, of Leighton, Alabama, recorded the date as 1790. He inspected the old house in 1923 and wrote: "The house is built of the best heart material and fastened together with wooden pins. The two front rooms, one above the other, are twenty four feet by eighteen with a nine foot ceiling. The back room is the same size. The foundation is stone and the front porch is held up by well-dressed black walnut columns, seven or eight inches square with the corners nicely beveled. The stone chimney, since removal of the mantle, is the most attractive feature of the place. It is ten feet broad at the base, maintaining a width of eight for more than twenty feet from the ground where it tapers to about six. It was plastered with cement of a good quality. The mantle was sold to a Cincinnati party about 30 or 40 years ago for $100.00 and was stored in a Government building at Riverton (old Chickasaw), which unfortunately was burned and the mantle lost.*

In a private letter to Dr. James M. Glenn, Atmore, Alabama, dated April 26, 1928; King sent a photograph of the house along with the following note: "You will notice the double stone chimney in this building is down but quite a lot of the old stones are yet to be seen. I remember years ago to have seen the chimney in good shape. I also remember a dozen or more Negro cabins which Colbert had for his Negro slaves. They consisted of four poplar logs about 30 inches wide to the walls of the cabins. They have long since fallen into decay."

One traveler, probably not having seen a decent dwelling during his long journey through the wilderness, was so captivated by (George) Colbert's house that he described it as: "...a country palace with its abundance of glass in the doors and windows" (McDonald, 2007).

1924 picture of George Colbert's Home at Colbert's Ferry

McDonald continues, *according to one legend, Colbert and* (Andrew) *Jackson had an altercation during this 1816 Council when the General swung at Chief* (George) *Colbert with his sword. A notch in one of the porch columns was pointed out as where Jackson's sword hit when it missed Colbert.*

As with most old houses, Chief's Colbert's home did not escape the inevitable ghost stories. As late as 1969 a former resident reminisced about her childhood days when her family lived in the house. She told about the eerie sounds that could be heard in the night, as if feet were ascending and descending the stairs. She reasoned, though, that it had something to do with the beams or rafters that were cut at angles which allowed the timbers to move back and forth as the temperature changed.

Frank R. King reported in the September 10, 1929, issue of Arrow Points the destruction of Chief Colbert's home by fire. According to him, this happened, during the week of July 12, 1929 (McDonald, 2009).

In the 1834 treaty, George Colbert was granted a portion of a reservation consisting of four sections to be divided between Levi, Levi's oldest son Martin, Isaac Albertson, Henry Love, and Benjamin Love. George made sure that his portion included some sixty yards south of his Colbert's Ferry home so as to include the burial site of his wife Tuskiahooto. After the Civil War the area of the ferry and home became known as George Town, in honor of Chickasaw Chief George Colbert. In 1870, Leander Hyatt operated the ferry for two years which he closed because of poor business.

George Colbert's Service—Colonel George Colbert was listed as a resident of the Chickasaw Nation, Mississippi in the1818 census report and on the Chickasaw Roll. On the death of his brother Levi Colbert on June 2, 1834, leadership of the Chickasaw Nation passed into the hands of George Colbert. According to McDonald (2007), *George Colbert was a spokesman for his people a number of years before he began operating the ferry on the Tennessee River. He continued in this role although his home was some distance from the center of the Nation located near what would become Tupelo, Mississippi. His first attendance at a conference with the white man was at Nashville in 1792. In 1794 he was among the Chickasaw delegates at Philadelphia, Pennsylvania. In 1801 he was involved in rather lengthy negotiations, and in 1802 visited Washington. His other services as Chickasaw spokesman were in 1805, 1816, 1818, 1826, 1827, 1830, 1832, 1833, and 1834.*

George Colbert's home at the ferry was the site of a significant conference between the Cherokees, Creeks, Choctaws, Chickasaws, and the U. S. Government in September 1816. His home was designated for this meeting as the "Chickasaw Council House". Representing the government were Andrew Jackson, David Meriwether, and Jesse Franklin. At this conference the Chickasaws ceded their land north of the Tennessee River, as well as some territory south of the river. However, certain tracts were reserved. George Colbert was given sixteen square miles on the north bank of the river, including his ferry landing, in what eventually became Lauderdale County, Alabama.

George Colbert deeded this land back to the United States on May 15, 1819. However, prior to this time he had sold certain parcels of land to white settlers; including a rather large farm to the Walston family that was located south of what was to become the Oakland Community. Colbert's Lauderdale County land became known as "The Reserve". At one time a U.S. Post Office was located there with the designation as Reserve, Alabama (McDonald, 2007).

George Colbert was the recognized chief of the Chickasaw Nation at the time of removal and until his death on November 7, 1839. He was buried with honors at Fort Towson, for he was a veteran of the American Revolution, having served under General Washington and having been commissioned a major in the army and awarded a sword. He also served under General Jackson by whom he had been commissioned a colonel in the Seminole Wars. George died at 95 years old on November 7, 1839, in Fort Towson, Towson County, Choctaw Nation, Indian Territory and his body was interred at Fort Towson.

Doublehead—Chickasaw Chief George Colbert was the double son-in-law of Doublehead. He took two of the daughters of Chickamauga Cherokee Chief Doublehead and Creat Priber as his wives-Tuskiahooto and Saleechie. By the Chickasaw Boundary Treaty of January 10, 1786, most of area north of the High Town Path and west of the Flint River in Madison County, Alabama became Chickasaw land; however, Doublehead was permitted to stay in this area of north Alabama because his daughters'- Tuskiahooto and Saleechie - marriages to Chickasaw Chief George Colbert.

George Colbert's two Cherokee wives were said to be among the most beautiful women in the region. George's wife Saleechie lived at Tupelo, Mississippi. He had one adopted son Pitman and he fathered seven children: Jane, Susan, George, Jr., Vicy, Vina, and John. Some say that George also had a daughter named Nancy Colbert. His adopted son, Pitman, had a very fair education.

Saleechie (Standing Fern) Doublehead

George first married Saleechie (Shullachie or Salechie) Doublehead before 1797 and was one-fourth German and three-fourths Cherokee. She was the daughter of Chickamauga Cherokee Chief Doublehead. She was listed as a resident in the census report in Chickasaw Roll, Chickasaw Nation in Mississippi in 1818. Saleechie (Salitsi) Doublehead was born about 1762 in Monroe County, Tennessee, and she died February 1, 1846, in Oklahoma, Indian Territory. George and Saleechie (Standing Fern) had seven children who were one eighth German, three eighths Cherokee, one quarter Scots-Irish, and one quarter Chickasaw. Pitman Colbert was adopted by George and Saleechie. Through Chief George Colbert's children, his siblings, and many relatives, a

89

large number of people in northeast Mississippi and northwest Alabama are related to the historic Colbert family.

1. **Samuel "Pitman" Colbert** was born about 1797, and he married Sarah McGillivray. Pitman died February 26, 1853, in the Choctaw Nation in Indian Territory (Pitman was said to have been adopted by George and Saleechie).Major Pitman (Samuel B.) Colbert and Sarah 'Sallie' McGillivray had the following children: 1) Harriet Colbert, 2) Susan Catherine "Kitty" Colbert was born February 10, 1825. 3) Henry Colbert was born before 1842. His body was interred in Doaksville, Towson County, Choctaw Nation, Indian Territory. 4) Zachariah Colbert was born before 1848. His body was interred in Doaksville, Towson County, Choctaw Nation, Indian Territory. He married Elsie Allen who was the daughter of George G. Allen and Charity Colbert.

2. **Jane Colbert** was born prior to 1800 and married Charles Frazier and had five children-Jane Frazier was born 1811, Andrew Jackson Frazier was born 1815, Mary Frazier, Maxwell T. Frazier, and Emily Frazier. She died about 1827 in the Chickasaw Nation, Mississippi.

3. **Susan "Sukey" Colbert** was born about 1810 at Colbert's Ferry, and first married John Mclish, and then the second marriage was to Robert McDonald Jones. She had one son by Mclish whose name was Benjamin Franklin McLish, born in 1830. She had three children by Jones: 1) George Washington Jones was born 1840, 2) Frances Jones was born 1842, and 3) Joseph Jones was born before 1856. Sukey died January 13, 1860, in Hugo, Choctaw Nation of Indian territory.

4. **George Colbert, Jr.** was born in Chickasaw Nation before 1818. George died before 1836 in Chickasaw Nation. Prior to removal, George Colbert, Jr. was thrown from a horse and killed. He was listed as a resident in the census report in Chickasaw Roll, Chickasaw Nation, Mississippi in 1818. Some historians say George Colbert, Jr. died in 1879.

5. **Levica "Vicy" Colbert** was born before 1818 and died in January 1846, in Indian Territory. Vicy first married William Duncan and had one son named John Duncan. John Duncan married Mary Hargett and they had 1) Mary Elizabeth Duncan who was born in 1845, 2) unknown daughter, 3) Jonathan Duncan was born in 1824, 4) William Duncan was born in 1838, 5) Morketts Annie Duncan was born in 1840, 6) Lucinda Duncan was born in 1841, and 7) Sara Emmiline Duncan was born in 1844. Vicy's second marriage was to Doctor James McDonna and they had one daughter.

Vicy Colbert was an educated woman, and wealthy, as wealth was counted in those days. She owned three sections of land, all of which Colonel Doxey sold to William Duncan for $13,000.00. She lived south of the old Chickasaw King, though she lived for a while in the Cherry Creek neighborhood. She went west with the Chickasaws during removal.

6. Vina Colbert was born before 1818. She was listed as a resident in the census report in Chickasaw Nation, 1818.

7. John Colbert was born before 1818 and married Rachel Perry and they had three children-1) Aley Colbert, 2) Kittie Colbert, and 3) Alfred Colbert. John Colbert died before 1834.

8. *Nancy Colbert was about 1805 and died in 1875 or 1878 in Colbert, Alabama. Nancy Catherine Colbert married Hezekiah Tharp in 1830 in Franklin County, Alabama. Hezekiah Tharp lived from 1795 to 1873. Hezekiah and Nancy Colbert Tharp had a large family of children: Hulda Caroline Tharp, 1828-1914; Robert F Tharp, 1830-1878; Thomas F Tharp, 1836; Martin Tharp, 1837-1864; Elizabeth Tharp, 1838-1860; Permelia A Tharp, 1841; Nancy Catherine Tharp, 1842-1939; Hezekiah Tharp, 1842-1864; Presley Tharp, 1844-1892; Rufus Tharp, 1847; Lancey Tharp, 1850; James Tharp, 1850; and Reece Tharp, 1855-1921 (Remembering the Shoals, 2011).*

One descendant, Robert F. Tharp was born May 11, 1830, in Franklin, Alabama and died October 12, 1878, in Colbert, Alabama. He married Sarah Ann Prentice who was born January 5, 1839, in Marshall, Alabama and died May 15, 1904, in Colbert Heights, Colbert County, Alabama. The text of their marriage certificate is given as:

The State of Alabama, Lauderdale County
To any Judge, Minister of the gospel or Justice of the Peace legally authorized

You are hereby authorized and required to solemnize the rights of Matrimony between Robert Tharp and Sarah Ann Prentice agreeable to the state in such case made and provided and a due return make to the Office of Probate for the County aforesaid.

Given under my hand this 1st day of May 1858 W. T. Hawkins P. Judge. The rites of matrimony solemnized by me this 16th day of May 1858. B. F. Kursman, J. Peace

To this marriage were born the following children: James Orman Tharp, 1853-1940; Martha E. Tharp, 1856; Mary Jane Tharp, 1861-1946; Safronia McClellan Tharp, 1865-1919; Robert Tharp, 1868-1914; Caldona Tharp, 1870-1900; Mary Jane Tharp, 1873-1880; Susan Evaline Tharp, 1873-1961; William Coleman Tharp, 1847; and James Tharp, 1877.

Martha F. Tharp born 1856 in Franklin County, Alabama married James R. Yocum who was born May 11, 1830, in Franklin County and died October 12, 1878, in Colbert County, Alabama. They married November 10, 1871, in Colbert County, Alabama. Their children were: Laura E. Yocum, 1873-1890; Sarah A Yocum, 1875; James R. Yocum, 1877; and Mary Julia Julie Yocum, 1879.

Martha Tharp Yocum and James R. Yocum's daughter Laura Yocum died sometime after 1890 probably in Franklin County, Alabama. Laura married November 13, 1871, to William Houston "Bud" Fisher who was born in 1868 and died in 1909 in Franklin County, Alabama. Together they had Mary Florence Fisher who was born September 15, 1890, and died in June 1982 in Russellville, Franklin County, Alabama (Remembering the Shoals, 2011).

Tuskiahooto Doublehead

Based on tradition, Tuskiahooto was considered one of the most beautiful women in the country and was the favorite wife of George Colbert. She was George's principal wife and lived at the Colbert's Ferry home until she died around 1817. In the treaty of 1834, George made sure to include his wife's burial site in the reserve that was set aside for his personal use.

According to McDonald, "*Tuskiahooto, Colbert's principal wife, reputed to be the, fairest of all the Indian princesses, presided over George Colbert's household at the ferry. Old families of Colbert County recall with some amusement this rich Indian lady's refusal to ride in the elegant carriage provided according to her means. She followed this vehicle, which was driven by a slave, astride her favorite pony seated on a colorful blanket, and quite often she was barefoot.*

Washington socialites were likewise amused when she accompanied her husband (George Colbert) to a dinner at the White House dressed in the latest fashion and barefoot. It was a dark day for the Chief when Tuskiahooto died. He was never the same afterward."

Tuskiahooto Doublehead's grandfather Christian G. Priber was a German genius; therefore, she was one-fourth German and three-fourths Cherokee. George's second marriage was to Tuskiahooto Doublehead before 1807. She was born about 1760 in Tellico Plains and was also the daughter of Chickamauga Cherokee Chief Doublehead. She died at her and George's home at Colbert's Ferry which was adjacent to the Natchez Trace in Colbert County, Alabama.

According to the description in the 1834 treaty with the Chickasaws and the United States, George buried his beautiful wife within 60 yards south of their dwelling house at Colbert's Ferry. Tuskiahooto, reputed to be one of the most beautiful Indian princesses in all the land, rests in an unmarked grave on a beautiful and serene hillside overlooking the south bank of the Tennessee River. George seemed to never get over her loss and shortly after her burial, he moved to Tupelo, Mississippi with Saleechie. Today, the Tuskiahooto's burial site is protected as part of the Natchez Trace Parkway at Colbert's Ferry in present-day Colbert County, Alabama. George and Tuskiahooto did not have any known children.

Family of Saleechie and Tuskiahooto

Doublehead was the father of Saleechie and Tuskiahooto; he was believed to be married at least five times and possibly more. His first wife was Creat (Drags Blanket) Priber, half German and half Cherokee, who was born between 1735 and 1740 in a Cherokee town at Tellico Plains in Monroe County, Tennessee. Creat Priber was the daughter of Christian Gottlieb Priber (Anglo-German) who was born on March 21, 1697, and Clogittah (Cherokee) who was the daughter of the great Cherokee Chief Moytoy. Clogittah was born between 1705 and 1720 and died about 1790. Clogittah was the aunt of Doublehead; therefore, Creat Priber was Doublehead's first cousin.

Christian Gottlieb Priber—Christian Gottlieb Priber, the German father-in-law to Doublehead, was the grandfather to George Colbert's wives Tuskiahooto Doublehead and Saleechie Doublehead; and therefore, Priber was the great grandfather to George's children by Saleechie. George and Tuskiahooto did not have any children that were recorded.

Christian Gottleib Priber, a Utopian Socialist (Black Robe or Jesuit), was born in Saxony, Germany on March 21, 1697. On June 13, 1735, he petitions London to be allowed to leave the country on the next ship to Georgia in America. He left a wife and four children in Saxony when he was forced to leave the country, they would not go with him. Priber said, *"I was married to Christiane Dorothea Hoffman in Zittau, Germany and we had four girls together. She was a portrait painter and very educated woman. Her father was the rector of the Classical College, a senator and noted printer. I had wanted to bring my wife and children with me when I left Germany, but her father wouldn't allow it."*

Priber arrived in Charles Town and he soon after was preparing to go to the Cherokee Nation which he did in 1736 where he took up residence in Great Tellico. Through his good works and marriage to Cloggitah, Moytoy's daughter, Priber established himself firmly in the confidence of the Cherokees. Priber founded an empire, crowned Moytoy Emperor, and declared himself the prime minister. He declared Moytoy the Emperor and gave high sounding titles to all the chief warriors. He called them the His Majesty's Red Court. He made himself the Imperial Majesty's Principle Secretary of State.

Over the next several months, trader James Adair grew to like the man. Adair was then sent south to trade with the Creeks, but asked Priber to continue correspondence with him. Priber agreed, but after the attempts to capture him by the English, he lost trust in Adair and told the Cherokee that Adair was the devil's clerk. Priber claimed to be Jesuit acting under orders of his superior in Germany to bring steady industry, an organized government, and civilized living to the Cherokees. He has a strong memory, stronger than anyone Adair has ever met and would be considered genius. He learns their language in about a month.

The English were soon out to get Priber. They were convinced that he was an agent to turn the Cherokee's against them and favor the French. Priber actually did not attempt to turn the Cherokee against the English, he only taught them the use of weights and measures and how they were getting short changed in trading. He also taught them to play the French against the English to obtain better prices for the goods they traded.

The South Carolina governor said, *"The French envy our American colonies. Their choice of the man Priber as their emissary was genius, although the man was a stranger to the mountains and wilds, as well as to their language, his sagacity has won through and given him the proper place among them. He is slowly forming a red empire and that to the great danger of our southern colonies."*

After seven years of living with the Cherokees and convincing them to set up an alliance with the Creeks, Priber was making his way to Mobile to unite the Creeks with the Cherokees in his Republic. The empire was about to expand into a powerful force with this unification. He wanted to unite all the southern tribes of Indians including the Chickasaw, Creek, Yuchi, Shawnee, Choctaw, and western Mississippi Indians into a Republic as a model to be set up in Europe at a later date.

Fort Frederica on Saint Simons Island, Georgia

He landed one evening at Tallapoose Town at nightfall. His black slave jumped from the canoe into the river to make his escape and the English traders shot him dead. Priber was seized by English traders among the Creeks, convinced the Creeks of his dangerousness, and took him to Georgia, where he was imprisoned for the remainder of his life. The traders bound him and carried him to Fort Augusta where Captain Kent was in command. Kent apologized to Priber for the traders' rough treatment and then sent him on to Fort Frederica.

General James Edward Oglethorpe knows that the English all refuse to believe Priber is a Jesuit, but he also knows their reputation for scholarship, devotion and courage. Oglethorpe's first impression of Priber was that of an Indian. Priber tells Oglethorpe, *"All I am is a poor Jesuit Priest acting under orders from my superior. He asked me to introduce habits of industry, art and a regular form of government to these poor people. Before leaving Germany, I served as a government counselor of the Supreme Court in Zittau, Germany in 1732. I traveled over 500 miles by mountain trails to reach the Cherokees. I taught the Indians the use of weights and measures. I tried to help them not be taken advantage of in trade by the Europeans and that is what I am guilty of. I also helped them learn the use of gunpowder and iron works. The Europeans want to exploit the Indians for their own greed."* Oglethorpe knew that

Priber would still be a free man if what he taught the Indians had not interfered with the greed of the English.

Oglethorpe still suspects that Priber was consorting with the French and the Spanish. Oglethorpe was impressed that Priber spoke Cherokee, Creek and some other Indian languages. He allowed Priber to collect quite a library in his cell, but his papers are confiscated and destroyed. Priber does not know of this destruction. Oglethorpe later allows Priber's wives and children to come to Fort Frederica and live with him until his death. He came down with a fever in 1744 and died. Christian Gottleib Priber rests in an unmarked grave in Frederica, Georgia today. Some historians indicate he was buried on Saint Simon's Island off the coast of Georgia.

General James Edward Oglethorpe
12/22/1696-6/30/1785

Doublehead and Creat—Doublehead's oldest brother Red Bird was married to Susan Priber who was thought to be a sister to Creat. Creat was said to have died from severe abuse and beatings by Doublehead. Doublehead was known as a wife abuser and was known to kill another wife to whom he had a violent relationship. She was a sister to James Vann's wife and was one of the reasons that Vann agreed to be the leader of the assassination group that would kill Doublehead.

Doublehead and Creat were thought to have five children who were one quarter German and three fourths Cherokee. They were Tuckaho, Tuskiahooto, Saleechie, Nigodigeyu, and Gulustiyu.

With one double son-in-law (George Colbert) and two daughters in the western portion of the Tennessee River territory and another double son-in-law (Samuel Riley) and two daughters in the eastern portion of the Tennessee River territory, Doublehead was able to know what was happening in a vast section of the river valley. Through these marriages of four of his daughters, Doublehead basically controlled an area of the Tennessee River from Mississippi through north Alabama and into the middle of east Tennessee. After his assassination in 1807, some 1,131 of his family and loyal supporters moved west of the Mississippi River to Arkansas.

George Colbert's Ferry

George was born on the west side of Bear Creek where it empties into the Tennessee River in the present-day northeastern most corner of Mississippi. In December 1801, the United States Government agreed to build cabins for travelers, a store, stables, a large dwelling house, a new ferry boat, and other facilities for George to operate a ferry where the Natchez Trace crosses the Tennessee River in present-day Colbert County, Alabama.

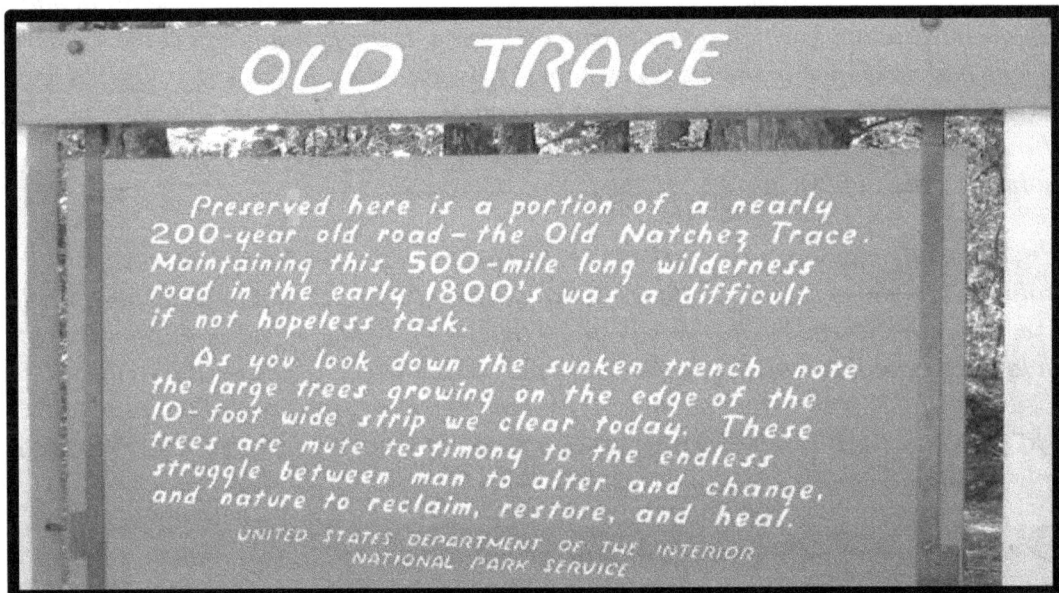

> ## OLD TRACE
>
> Preserved here is a portion of a nearly 200-year old road – the Old Natchez Trace. Maintaining this 500-mile long wilderness road in the early 1800's was a difficult if not hopeless task.
>
> As you look down the sunken trench note the large trees growing on the edge of the 10-foot wide strip we clear today. These trees are mute testimony to the endless struggle between man to alter and change, and nature to reclaim, restore, and heal.
>
> UNITED STATES DEPARTMENT OF THE INTERIOR
> NATIONAL PARK SERVICE

Andrew Jackson—One of the largest paydays for George Colbert for providing supplies to the Tennessee Volunteer troops across the Tennessee River was $22,816.00; however, Jackson himself secured Colbert's payment for the assistance provided to the Tennessee Volunteers as seen in the following: *On the day following* (December 30, 1796), *Mr. Andrew Jackson presented a petition from George Colbert, a Chickasaw Chief, who asked compensation for supplies furnished by his tribe to a detachment of*

Tennessee volunteers. The petition was referred to the Committee on Claims. After which, the petition of Mr. Hugh L. White again came up. The resolution offered on the previous day was read, and the mover thereof, Mr. Jackson, again addressed the House.

"Already," said he, "the rations found for the troops of this expedition have been paid for by the Secretary of War, and I can see no reasonable objection to the payment of the whole expense. As the troops were called out by a superior officer, they had no right to doubt his authority. Admit a contrary doctrine, and it will strike at the very root of subordination. It would be saying to soldiers, 'Before you obey the command of your superior officer, you have a right to inquire into the legality of the service upon which you are about to be employed, and until you are satisfied, you may refuse to take the field.' This, I believe, is a principle which cannot be acted upon. General Sevier was bound to obey the orders he had received to undertake the expedition. The officers under him were obliged to obey him. They went with full confidence that the United States would pay them, believing that the United States had appointed such officers as would not call them into the field without proper authority. If even the expedition had been unconstitutional, which I am far from believing, it ought not to affect the soldier, since he had no choice in the business, being obliged to obey his superior. Indeed, as the provisions have been paid for, and as the ration and pay rolls are always considered as a check upon each other, I hope no objection will be made to the resolution which I have moved."

A gentleman having remarked that he could see no connection between the resolution and the petition, Mr. Jackson explained:—"By referring to the report, it will be seen that the Secretary of War has stated that to allow the prayer of this petition would be to establish a principle that will apply to the whole of the militia in that expedition. If this petitioner's claim is a just one, therefore, the present petition ought to go to the whole, as it is unnecessary for every soldier employed on that expedition to apply personally to this House for compensation."

The question was debated at considerable length. Mr. James Madison spoke strongly on Jackson's side. The subject was finally referred to a select committee of five, Mr. A. Jackson chairman; who reported, of course, in favor of the petitioner, and recommended that the sum of twenty-two thousand eight hundred and sixteen dollars be appropriated for the payment of the troops, which was done (Parton, 1859).

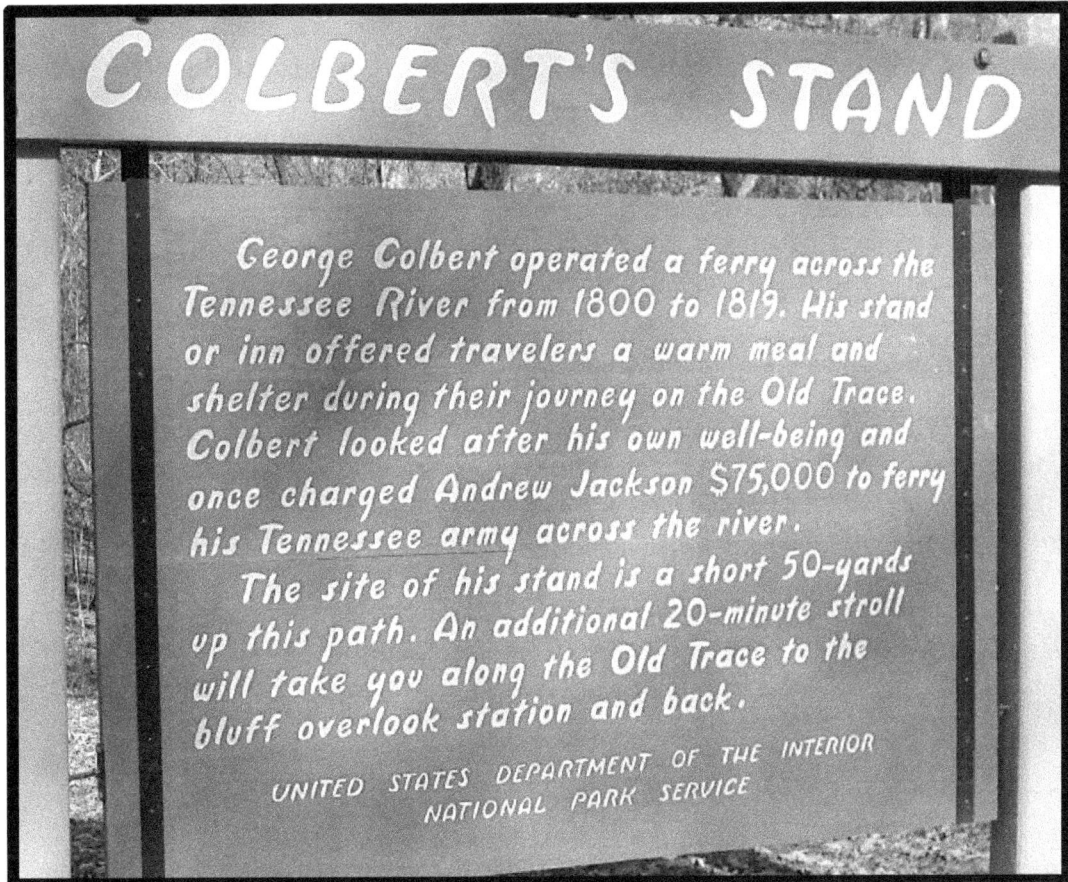

COLBERT'S STAND

George Colbert operated a ferry across the Tennessee River from 1800 to 1819. His stand or inn offered travelers a warm meal and shelter during their journey on the Old Trace. Colbert looked after his own well-being and once charged Andrew Jackson $75,000 to ferry his Tennessee army across the river.

The site of his stand is a short 50-yards up this path. An additional 20-minute stroll will take you along the Old Trace to the bluff overlook station and back.

UNITED STATES DEPARTMENT OF THE INTERIOR
NATIONAL PARK SERVICE

George Colbert's Ferry operation began in 1798 providing Natchez Trace traffic a means to cross the otherwise impassable river. George had virtually a monopoly for the river crossing, and he charged 50 cents per passenger and one dollar per horse and rider. Later reports suggest that Colbert once charged Andrew Jackson $75,000 to ferry his army across the river; but, Jackson's own records indicate the amount was only a few hundred dollars that was actually paid.

John Swaney—Mail or post rider John Swaney had the route from Nashville to Natchez and gave details about Colbert's Ferry as found in Jonathan Daniels' book, _The Devils Backbone_ (1985) as follows: _John Swaney the mail rider set out from Nashville on Saturday night. He carried a few newspapers, "letters and government dispatches" in his oil dressed deerskin mail pouch, and a "half bushel of corn for his horse, provisions for himself, an overcoat or blanket, and a tin trumpet". Riding hard, by midnight he reached the cabin of Tom Davis in the Big Branch of the Harpeth River._

Less than 25 miles from Nashville, this was the last white man's house. Beyond lay the wilderness.

On Sunday morning he reached the Duck River. There John Gordon, first postmaster at Nashville as Abijah Hunt was in Natchez, operated a ferry. Here man and horse ate breakfast before starting on the 80 miles to the Tennessee River. Already at that wide stream the Chickasaw Colberts, who had harbored the Natchez Refugees from the Spanish nearly twenty years before, took travelers across. "The Indians were contrary", the mail rider remembered in his old age. They would not come across the river for him if he failed to get to the landing before bedtime.

The Colberts were more than contrary. They were shrewd, strong, and had a Midus Touch for making money. And sometimes they seemed not too particular as to how they made it. Before Colonel Robertson, the Cumberland founder, made a treaty with them which lasted long and well, he called them "Pirates". Certainly the Spanish held to that idea. From the beginning, however, these Scotch Chickasaws were careful to avoid banditry. One story was that always they were traders with skins and meat to offer for coffee, cloth, powder, and guns. Still in this trading "it was an easy process from chaffering to disputing, from angry words to blows, from robbery to murders."

Certainly such charges were unjustified when Swaney crossed the river to spend the night with George Colbert. This Colbert then had been petted not only in Nashville. He had been to Philadelphia and seen George Washington. While Swaney rode, George Colbert was to help make the treaty for a better road over the Trace—and get a good cut for himself in the process. A few years later an informed traveler wrote that this Colbert's house looked "like a country palace with its abundance of glass in doors and windows." It was probably less pretentious when Swaney came. The mail rider apparently got along well with George Colbert, whose Indian name was Tootemastubbe. He was "an enemy of education, missions, and whiskey," which apparently he put together as menaces to the Indians.

From Colbert's house, Swaney rode 120 miles to the chief villages of the Chickasaws. On the way not a house or even an Indian hut interrupted the wilderness. Making a fire with his tinderbox, Swaney spent one night camping in the woods or canebrakes. At the end of this wilderness ride was the house of another Colbert. Whatever may have been its comforts or discomforts, Swaney always remembered the pretty half-breed—or even eighth breed—daughters of the household. So did others. Tired and dirty boatmen and well-accoutered gentlemen, too, stopped sometimes just to stare at girls who were described by turns as "the prettiest woman in Mississippi" or even as "the most beautiful woman on the continent."

Here Swaney made his first exchange of horses. In old-age recollection he exaggerated distances. Still it was 80 miles from Colbert's Ferry to the Chickasaw settlements near Tupelo. The Trace did not pass through the chief Choctaw settlements, but he road through their nation toward the smoother path to Natchez. The whole distance was about 500 miles (Daniels, 1985).

John Gordon—Swaney traveled south toward to Colbert's Ferry on the Natchez Trace and crossed the Duck River on a ferry ran by John Gordon. Gordon had an agreement with George Colbert of Colbert's Ferry on the Tennessee River to run the ferry on the Duck River and to share his profits with Colbert. By treaty George Colbert was given control of all ferries that operated in the Chickasaw Nation. The following is a short description of the life and times of John Gordon as given in *Touring the Middle Tennessee Backwoods*, by Robert Brandt (1995):

John Gordon's home on the Duck River

Travel on the Trace picked up following the governments' improvement of the road between 1801 and 1803. About that time, John Gordon, working in partnership

101

with Chickasaw Chief George Colbert, began operating a trading post and ferry here on the Duck River.

Gordon had come to the Cumberland settlements from Fredericksburg, Virginia, around 1786 and established himself as an accomplished Indian fighter. He served as Nashville's first postmaster. There is a marker in his honor on the grounds of the Customs House at Eighth and Broad in Nashville.

John Gordon moved his wife Dollie Cross, and their children here to his grant on the Duck River sometime after 1808. Gordon was a valuable Lieutenant to Andrew Jackson in his campaigns against the Creeks and Seminoles, spending much of his time working for Jackson as a spy. Gordon died while he was away in 1819 (Brandt, 1995).

Fort Mims Massacre—Colonel George Strother Gaines asked for a volunteer to ride to Nashville with news of the Red Stick Creek attack and destruction of Fort Mims on August 30, 1813. A young man at Fort Stephens by the name of Samuel A. Edmondson agreed to make the ride through Indian country to notify General Andrew Jackson at Nashville, Tennessee. Specifically noted in Colonel Gaines' letter is George Colbert's Ferry where Edmondson is to get a fresh horse and supplies. The following is the story as given by Colonel George S. Gaines account of Fort Mims:

In explanation it may be proper to state that Colonel George S. Gaines was United States Factor at Fort Stephens on the Alabama River. It was here that he received a letter containing an account of the fall of Fort Mims.

Extract from Gaines' Reminiscences in the Mobile (Alabama) Register, July 3, 1872:

It was late in the evening when I received the letter. I was in the citizens' fort at the time, and read the letter aloud for the information of those around me. I saw it created a panic, and remarked, if we could get General Jackson down with his 'Brigade of Mounted Volunteers,' the Creek Indians could soon be quieted.

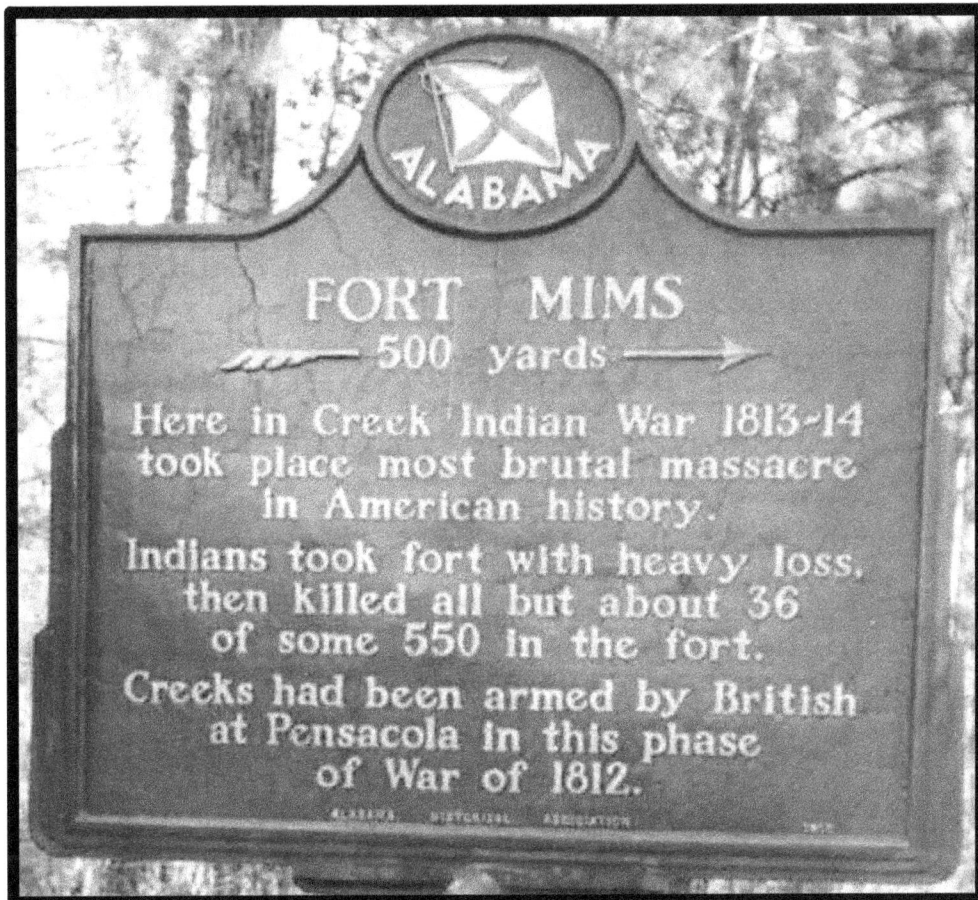

A young man named Edmondson, who was a guest in my family, was standing near, and looking at him, I remarked: If I could induce a cheerful man to go as express to Nashville, Tennessee, I have a fine horse ready and can manage by writing to persons I know on the path to have a fresh horse ready for him every day.' He said that he was willing to go. Mrs. Gaines said that she would prepare provisions for him. I immediately sat down and wrote letters to General Jackson and Governor Blount, communicating the massacre of Fort Mims and the defenseless condition of our frontier, appealing to General Jackson to march down with his brigade of mounted men and save the Tombigbee settlement and property in my charge. I was personally acquainted with the General, also Governor Blount. I wrote a letter to Charles Juzon and William Starnes at Oknoxubee; John Pitchlyn, mouth of Oktibbeha; George James, residing at or near the present Egypt (M. & O. R. A.); Jim Brown, Natchez road; **George Colbert, chief of the Chickasaws, Colbert's Ferry and others beyond the Tennessee river requesting them on the arrival of Mr. Edmundson to furnish him**

with their best horse and take care of the horse he would leave until his return from Nashville, then bring or send me their bills for payment. (Each of the persons named was in the habit of visiting the trading house for supplies of salt, coffee, sugar, etc.) This task occupied me nearly all night. In the morning, Mr. Edmondson, with provisions, a well filled purse, etc., set out for Nashville. It is perhaps needless to say, that in response to this urgent call, General Jackson moved promptly and inaugurated a campaign that completely crushed the Creeks.

General George Strother Gaines
5/1/1784-1/21/1873

But to our Lowndes County hero, Mr. Samuel A. Edmondson, he was born in Camden, South Carolina in 1794, and came to Mississippi Territory while quite a young man. After becoming a citizen of Lowndes County, he was married to Mrs. Jane Martin, by which union he reared two sons, Powhattan and Robert Tecumseh, and two daughters, Mrs. James M. Halbert and Mrs. Jerre Dowsing.

Mr. Edmondson died at the home of his son-in-law Mr. Halbert in 1869, and was buried at the Elllis grave yard in that vicinity. It is deemed a privilege, thus after a lapse of almost a century to be enabled to place upon record this brief account of Mr. Edmondson's valuable services to his country (Mississippi Historical Society, 1903).

Alexander Wilson—In 1810, Alexander Wilson got very angry after arriving at the Tennessee River in the afternoon because no one would come to the north side to ferry him across. The next morning Wilson was finally able to get across the Tennessee River on George Colbert's Ferry.

Alexander Wilson, born at Paisley, Scotland, was ten when his mother died. He left school at twelve years old to live with his older sister and her husband, William Duncan, who was a weaver; a trade Alexander learned. Wilson became dissatisfied with the oppression in Scotland and decided to seek a better life in America with his nephew William Duncan.

Wilson and Duncan arrived at New Castle, Delaware on July 14, 1794. Wilson began selling his woven goods and making observations about birds. In 1802, Wilson met William Bartram a naturalist who encouraged him to study birds which he did the rest of his life. He devoted his time to observing and painting birds; therefore, he became the Father of American Ornithology.

In 1805 he wrote to Thomas Jefferson asking to join an expedition so he could study birds in other parts of the country. Although Jefferson wrote back, he never mentioned anything about the expeditions. In May, 1810, Wilson had received word of Meriwether Lewis's death, just as was crossing through the Natchez Trace in Tennessee where Lewis died. Lewis and Wilson became acquainted due to a mutual friendship with President Jefferson and a common interest in Charles Wilson Peale's museum in Philadelphia. Wilson paid Mrs. Grinder, the wife of the innkeeper of the house where Lewis perished, to put a fence around Lewis's grave to keep out wild animals. (There is now a monument marking the spot.) He also interviewed Mrs. Grinder to better understand how Lewis died, and reported his findings in a letter to Alexander Lawson, and later in a poem and eulogy he published in the Port Folio. Wilson's book, American Ornithology, a nine volume set was published from 1808 to 1814. Wilson fell ill shortly thereafter and died 23 August 1813 from dysentery which he had contracted during his travels...the last two volumes were published posthumously by Wilson's friend and sometimes traveling companion George Ord, who also wrote the first biography of Wilson (Hunter, 1983).

The next morning, 7 May, Wilson rode 15 miles and stopped at an Indian's hut to feed his horse...Wilson noted that the Indians were amused by the parakeet. Wilson spent that night on the banks of the Tennessee River in present Lauderdale County, Alabama. During his travels through Mississippi, he passed through numerous swamps and lengthy cane thickets, suffered an attack of dysentery, and survived a tornado. He arrived at Natchez on 17 May, having traveled, according to his calculations, 478 miles in 14 days (Nicholson, 1986).

Alexander Wilson arrived at George Colbert's Ferry in the afternoon of May 7, 1810, but was unable to get anyone to come get him on the north side of the Tennessee River. He ranted and yelled to the top of his lungs trying to get someone to ferry him across the river, but failed to get help and had to spend the night on Lauderdale County side of the river.

Alexander Wilson
7/6/1766-8/23/1813

According to McDonald (2007), *"I was so enraged that had I not been cumbered with baggage I believe I should have ventured to swim it."* These were the impatient words of the ornithologist Alexander Wilson, as he recollected the trouble it *took to cross the Tennessee River about the year 1810. Traveling the Natchez Trace was difficult, but crossing at Colbert's Ferry was exasperating.*

Wilson arrived on the north bank late in the day and whooped and shouted until dark. He couldn't have known that George Colbert had a rule never to cross the river at night. The next morning, after an uneasy night on the swampy north bank, he continued his loud calls for the ferry boat. It wasn't until around 11:00 A.M. that Colbert's servants showed up to ferry Wilson across to the south bank (McDonald, 2007).

Lorenzo Dow—Dow was a traveling preacher that crossed the Tennessee River on George Colbert's Ferry on October 26, 1804. He did not seem to be very considerate of the Chickasaw people that he encountered along the Natchez Trace. There is no mention that Low tried to preach to the Indians; therefore, he probably considered them heathers or savages.

According to Wikipedia, *Lorenzo Dow (October 16, 1777-February 2, 1834) was an eccentric itinerant American preacher, said to have preached to more people than any other preacher of his era... Dow's enthusiasm sustained him through the incessant labors of more than 30 years, during which he preached in almost all parts of the United States...he attracted great crowds to hear and see him, and he was often persecuted as well as admired. Because the churches were closed to him, Lorenzo Dow preached in town halls, farmers' barns, and even in open fields. He would preach anyplace where he could assemble a crowd. He preached to Methodists, Baptists, Quakers, Catholics, and atheists alike. He liked to appear unexpectedly at public events, announcing in a loud voice that exactly one year from today, Lorenzo Dow would preach on this spot. He never disappointed his audiences; he always appeared exactly 365 days later at the appointed place, usually met by huge crowds. Dow's public speaking mannerisms were like nothing ever seen before among the typically conservative church goers of the time. He shouted, he screamed, he cried, he begged, he flattered, he insulted, he challenged people and their beliefs. He told stories and made jokes. It is recorded that Lorenzo Dow often preached before open-air assemblies of 10,000 people or more and held the audiences spellbound.*

Dow's fame spread, and so did his travels. He traveled on foot and occasionally on horseback (when someone would donate a horse) throughout what was then the United States...Dow's sermons were often unpopular in the southern United States, and he frequently was threatened with personal violence. He sometimes was forcibly ejected from towns, pelted with stones, eggs, and rotten vegetables. That never stopped him; he simply walked to the next town and gave the same sermon again.

Lorenzo Dow was personally unkempt. He did not practice personal hygiene and his long hair and beard were described as "never having met a comb." He usually owned one set of clothes: those that were on his back. When those clothes became so badly worn and full of holes that they were no longer capable of covering him, some person in the audience usually would donate a replacement. The donated clothes often were not the correct size for his skinny body. When he traveled, he carried no luggage other than a box of Bibles to be given away. Throughout most of his life, what little money he ever collected was either given away to the poor or used to purchase Bibles (Wikipedia, 2012).

Lorenzo Dow
10/16/1777-2/2/1834

According to McDonald, *Lorenzo Dow, the Methodist circuit rider, tells in his journal about using the ferry on October 26, 1804. He paid one dollar for each member of his party. This was the regular fee for man and horse. A man without a horse was half that amount. Post riders crossed at a special half fare. Colbert once complained that most white people who used his ferry were "Kaintucks". Many of them, he said, were poor and could not pay, and he carried them across free of charge. Most of his customers, though, were Indians, and George Colbert was never known to charge a blood brother* (McDonald, 2007).

The following is excerpts about crossing the Tennessee River at George Colbert's Ferry from the diary of Lorenzo Dow as written in October 1804 as follows:

October 24, 1804—Traveled about thirty five miles, and saw one company of Indians on the way.

October 25, 1804—The Post and a traveler passed us by early, but we overtook them, and continued together to Tennessee River; the wind was high, and none did cross except the Post and he with danger.

October 26, 1804—We crossed, paying a dollar each, where was a small garrison, and few half bred Indians.

October 27, 1804—We gained the suburbs of Big Town of the Chickasaws. I am now beside the fire, the company laying down to rest, and our horses feeding in a canebrake and provisions nearly out.

October 28, 1804—Sunday! Two of our horses were missing, but were returned early in the morning by a Negro and Indian, who, I suppose, had stolen them to get a reward. One of our company was for flogging the Negro, which I opposed lest it should raise an uproar, and endanger other travelers by the Indians…At length we came to another village where some whites lived, and one Mr. Gunn…We tarried two days in this settlement, held some meetings, and receiving gratis, necessaries for our journey, took our departure. Having a gun with us, we killed some turkeys, which were numerous in flocks: from what we saw, there were bears, and plenty of wolves and deer in the woods...

November 4, 1804--…arrived at the settlement of Natchez (Dow, 1814).

Phillip Buckner—There are two versions of Phillip Buckner crossing the Tennessee River on George Colbert's Ferry. The first account from William Lindsey McDonald (2007) says that a Phillip Buckner, who was a Virginian, crossed the Tennessee River in 1798 prior to the construction of the Natchez Trace. Buckner traveled along the old Mountain Leaders Trace to the Tennessee River where he crossed on George Colbert's Ferry when it was located at the mouth of Bear Creek. At this time, George Colbert was selling whiskey at his ferry crossing as seen in the account as follows: *"Got to Colburts at the ferry about 8 O'clock: got , seven quarts of whiskey at one Doll per Quart and four dried fish at seven pce apiece: Cross't the River. J. Owing swaim the River J. Green broke one of the bottles of whiskey: went three or* *four miles; Dined; Sam'l horse broke another bottle of whiskey; we then determined to drink the balance to save it; went on about 10 miles to a good run of water; Bell lost his coat behind him."*

The second account as given by Fred Stutzenberger (1999) says, Phillip Buckner was a traveler along the Natchez Trace in 1811 and described a crossing of the Tennessee on George Colbert's Ferry. *As the journey resumes, the Trace seems to be gaining altitude, with long, steep inclines and descents. Some areas cause the horses to puff and lather despite a rather leisurely pace. On the 23rd day, the Tennessee River comes into view. Christopher calls a halt and explains what is ahead. "It'll cost us ta cross this h'ar river. Thar's a ferry run by George Colbert. He sez he's a Chickasaw chief, but his Daddy come frum Scotland 'n wuz one o' tha furst white men in this country. He's Chickasaw alrite, 'cause he's a wily devil, but whin hit come ta bisniss, he's all Scotsman! Anyway, let's ride on in 'n find out jist how much the red scoundrel is gonna take us fur ta cross his ditch... Half a day later and three dollars apiece poorer, you and your companions are across the river with not so much as a moccasin getting wet. After camping for the night at Rock Springs, the Trace is mostly uphill, long even grades interspersed with winding stretches over which you can travel for hours and then look across to a section you passed miles ago* (Stutzenberger, 1999)

General James Wilkinson—General Wilkinson helped lay out the Natchez Trace at the suggestion of George Colbert. George Colbert's Ferry was moved from the lowlands on both sides of the Tennessee River at the mouth of Bear Creek upstream to the present location where Natchez Trace crosses the Tennessee River. According to McDonald (2007), Wilkinson's report addresses the change of location for the ferry as follows: *"I find, on inquiry and from observation, that the route by Bear Creek is an improper one, as the bottoms on both sides of the Tennessee River are inundated for a considerable distance during the floods, and the ground over which it passes is hilly and much broken. I am, at the same, informed by Major* (George) *Colbert that a good way, and a good crossing, may be found a little further to the eastward, which will shorten the distance."*

McDonald continues, *"The General* (Wilkinson) *was rather generous to* (George) *Colbert. He agreed to furnish a new ferryboat to replace the old one "worn out in the public service," as well as to build for Colbert the following structures: "Cabins for him, at such place as he may fix on, cabins for his own accommodations and that of travelers to include a kitchen and a small store house and stables, and be pleased to put up a strong pen. These buildings are not to cost more than the men's labor."*

General James Wilkinson was the Army Chief of Staff under President George Washington's administration, but after Wilkinson's death, he was proven to have committed treason against the United States. According to Wikipedia (2012), *Wilkinson was an American soldier and statesman, who served in the Continental Army during the American Revolutionary War. He was twice the Commanding General of the United States Army, appointed first Governor of the Louisiana Territory in 1805. After his death, he was discovered to have been a paid agent of the Spanish Crown...Dying on December 28, 1825 at the age of 68; he was buried in Mexico City, Mexico...*

General James Wilkinson
3/24/1757-12/28/1825

In April 1787, Wilkinson took a highly controversial trip to New Orleans, which was a colony of Spain. At that time, Americans were not allowed to trade in New Orleans. Wilkinson met with Spanish Governor Esteban Rodríguez Miró and managed to convince him to allow Kentucky to have a trading monopoly on the Mississippi River; in return he promised to promote Spanish interests in the west. On August 22, 1787, Wilkinson signed an expatriation declaration and swore allegiance to the King of Spain to satisfy his own commercial needs...

However, by 1788 Wilkinson had apparently lost the support of officials in the Spanish mainland. Miro was not to grant any of the proposed pensions and was forbidden from giving money to support a revolution in Kentucky. Furthermore, Wilkinson continued to secretly receive funds from Spain for many years...

General Mad Anthony Wayne had led the legion army against the Native Americans in the Battle of Fallen Timbers in August 1794. This battle was a huge victory for the United States, yet Wilkinson had criticized the General's actions during the battle simply to antagonize Wayne. Wilkinson proceeded to file formal complaints against the General Wayne and his decisions to the President. Upon finding out about the complaints against him, Wayne decided to fight back, launching an investigation into Wilkinson's history with the Spanish. During all of this time, Wilkinson had renewed his secret alliance with the Spanish government through the Governor of Louisiana Carondelet, alerting them to the actions of both the United States and the French occupancy in North America. When Spanish couriers were intercepted carrying Wilkinson's payments from the Spanish, Wayne's suspicions were confirmed and attempted to court martial Wilkinson for his treachery. However, Wayne developed a stomach ulcer and died on December 15, 1796. Despite of his nearly confirmed treason, upon Wayne's death, the President promoted Wilkinson to Major General of the Army...

Wilkinson was transferred to the southern frontier in 1798...Wilkinson remained senior officer of the United States Army under President Thomas Jefferson. Along with Governor William C. C. Claiborne, Wilkinson shared the honor of taking possession of the Louisiana Purchase on behalf of the United States in 1803. At this time, Wilkinson renewed his treasonous relationship with Spanish colonial officials, offering advice to them on how to contain American expansion in exchange for the restoration of his pension. Among other things, Wilkinson tipped off the Spanish to the object of the Lewis and Clark expedition...

In 1805, following the Louisiana Purchase, President Thomas Jefferson appointed Wilkinson governor of the northern Louisiana territory despite his high-ranking position in the military. This was unusual: Jefferson had given Wilkinson a startling amount of power and authority. Wilkinson then sent Zebulon Pike on expeditions to the Southwest in 1805 and 1806 to discover the source of the Mississippi River...

Wilkinson was commissioned a major general in the War of 1812. In March 1813, Wilkinson led the American force that occupied Mobile in Spanish West Florida...In 1821 Wilkinson visited Mexico in pursuit of a Texas land grant. While awaiting government approval of his Texas scheme, Wilkinson died in Mexico City, where he was buried...

Wilkinson's involvement with the Spanish, although widely suspected in his own day, was not proven until 1854, with Louisiana historian Charles Gayarré's publication of the American general's correspondence with Rodríguez Miró, the Spanish governor of Louisiana. Other historians would subsequently add to the catalog of Wilkinson's treasonous activities (Wikipedia, 2012).

Colonel John Doughty—John Doughty and the Tennessee Volunteers crossed the Tennessee River on George Colbert's Ferry in 1803. In December 1796, Andrew Jackson got George Colbert approved for $22,816.00 for supplies for the Tennessee Volunteers; however, on the occasion of the 1803 crossing of Colonel John Doughty, General James Robertson and Colonel Return J. Meigs were sent to George Colbert's home to investigate the charges. The amount due was reduced by Colbert, but it still took two years for Congress to pay the bill for Doughty's Tennessee Volunteers.

The amount charged and received for the 1803 crossing at Colbert's Ferry was not clear and neither were the charges for ferrying John Coffee's troops across the river in 1813; but for sure, George Colbert charged Andrew Jackson $75,000.00 for ferrying his troops across the Tennessee River in 1815. The reason George Colbert gave for the high charges was that the promises

Colonel John Doughty
7/25/1754-9/16/1826

made by General James Wilkinson in building improvements at Colbert's Ferry were not completed; and, he was trying to recover what was committed by the United States but not completed as had been agreed.

According to Wikipedia (2012), *John Doughty was an American military officer who briefly served as the senior officer of the United States Army in 1784...He was promoted to brevet major in September to which he became the Army's senior ranking officer following the discharge from the army of all but eighty men in June 1784 and was the senior officer of the United States Army from 20 June to 12 August 1784...He was dispatched by President Washington to the frontier to negotiate with the Choctaw Nation for trading post sites in 1789. He repelled with serious losses an attack by* (Chickamauga warriors) *Cherokee, Shawnee, and Creek Indians while leading a detachment up the Tennessee River on a negotiating mission to the Chickasaw Nation in 1790...In May 1800 Doughty resigned and returned to private life on his estate at Morristown, New Jersey, to engage in agriculture and pursue literary studies. He died there on September 16, 1826.*

William Richardson—According to McDonald (2007), *William Richardson of Boston, returning from New Orleans in 1815, arrived at the* (George Colbert's) *ferry while General Andrew Jackson's army was camped there. He wrote in his journal: I however, being as wet as I could be, searched every building and at last found a place where I tied my horse without permission from anyone. I left my friend to feed them and went to seek shelter for ourselves. In this I was, by way of bribing, very fortunate. I procured a little apartment for ourselves and retired from the N. O. that filled every other part of the house.*

Colbert's Tupelo Home

Saleechie ran an inn on the Natchez Trace in present-day Tupelo, Mississippi. After Tuskiahooto died in 1817, and after the United States mail route was officially changed to follow Jackson's Military Road through Florence in 1817, George closed his ferry operations on the Tennessee River. He moved to Tupelo, Mississippi and began his plantation activities. On November 20, 1817, the son of Return J. Meigs the Indian agent, who also had the same name and was the United States Postmaster General, issued an order that the United States mail from Nashville to New Orleans would go through Florence, Alabama as follows: *"Until further advised you can, agreeable to your letter of the 26th, pass the public ferry on the Tennessee instead of Colbert's*

Ferry." Therefore, because of the death of his principal wife Tuskiahooto, the loss of the government mail route, and the opening of the Gaines Trace, George closed the ferry on the Natchez Trace, moved to Tupelo, and began his very successful farming operations on his plantation.

William Henry Gates—Gates was the authority for the following statement: *"My father, William Gates, went to McNairy County, Tenn., and bought the running gear for two six-horse wagons, sold them to Colbert, and the latter moved to the nation in them."*

Edwin G. Thomas—Thomas says: *"In 1836, I attended the land sales at Pontotoc. The first night in the nation I stayed at Saleechie Colbert's four miles west of where Tupelo now stands. She was a woman well-fixed up, had a good house, and gave good fare."*

Alexander Duggar—*"In 1821 Alexander Dugger first became acquainted with the Indians at Cotton Gin. George Colbert... Pitman Colbert lived with his father on the same place. They were very wealthy, working 140 hands; had a large farm near Colbert's Ferry in Alabama"* (Warren, 1904).

Benjamin Hawkins—According to McDonald (2007), *Benjamin Hawkins, General Superintendent of Indian Affairs in the South during this period, made this observation: "These people (the Chickasaws) are out from their old towns and fencing their farms. They have within two years fenced nearly 150, and all the farms have a Stock of cattle or hogs. The men begin to attend seriously to labor. Major George Colbert who ranks high in the government of his nation and was the speaker at the treaty with us has labored during the past summer at the plough and with the hoe. This example has stimulated others."*

One thing that Hawkins failed to mention was the some 150 black slaves owned by Chickasaw Chief George Colbert. These were basically the labor that made the plantation of Chief Colbert very successful. Hawkins also had a large number of black slaves on his own plantation in Georgia.

Horatio Cushman—The following is the philosophy of George Colbert according to Horatio Cushman (1899). *Colonel George Colbert in the prosperous days of the Chickasaw people, lived three or four miles west of what is now known as the town of Tupelo, Mississippi, (Tupelo is a corruption of Tuhpulah—To call or shout). George Colbert became to be the most-wealthy of the four brothers and was, in his* *personal appearance and manners, very prepossessing. He did not act in any public capacity, yet he exerted a great personal influence as a private citizen. He was a true conservative in sentiment and in spirit. He regarded his people, the Chickasaws, uninfluenced by the Whites and uncontaminated by their vices, as having reached the point of national progress most favorable to virtue and earthly happiness; therefore, he opposed all innovations as an evil which wisdom, virtue and patriotism loudly disapproved; and seemingly with much justice, since the Chickasaws were a virtuous people before the Whites came and introduced their vices among them; therefore, he was an outspoken enemy to missions, to schools, to whiskey, in short, to all the good as well as the evils that were being imported into his then happy country, having learned by experience and observation that the evil introduced by the Whites counterbalanced the good in point of amount as five to one; yet he failed to shape the policy of his Nation in accordance with his views, for the missionaries came and introduced. Christianity and established it upon a firm basis in spite of the whiskey-traders and others who followed closely in their wake, with all their concomitant vices, who seemed to delight in thwarting the noble efforts of those devoted and self-sacrificing men of God (even as they do at the present day), that they might the more easily drag the Indians down to their own degraded level.*

To escape the demoralizing influences of such degraded characters, and not the missionaries, did George Colbert advocate the emigration of his people to the remote wilds of the west, where he hoped and believed the evil tide of innovation would be arrested which threatened to engulf his people, if they remained in their ancient domains, and sweep away in its mighty current of iniquity all the Chickasaw old land marks of their moral foundations. In that distant land, so remote (then considered) from the whites, he fondly cherished the belief that his nation would throw off the manners and customs of the whites which they had already adopted, and return to the old paths of that simplicity of life in which their progenitors had walked for ages unknown. But he was doomed to disappointment, for not only the missionaries went with his people to their new homes to be found in the west, but the whiskey peddler and his congenial spirits, not to be thus cheated out of their victims, soon, followed on their track with the zeal of their master, the devil, where they have been hovering around the outskirts of the Chickasaw Nation, and often sneaking within, from that day to this, as they have been doing around in the territories of all Indians; and though the Chickasaw people, alike with all their race, have had to fight the devil and his imps in an unequal contest, being hampered by the government of the United States in its laws regarding its worthy sons of freedom, whose proclivities lead them to indulge their "glorious independence" regardless of all laws and every principle of truth, justice and honor, in regard to whiskey in particular; yet the Chickasaws and Choctaws have made that wilderness, to which they were banished, blossom as the rose, while George Colbert sleeps beneath the soil under the shades of the forest trees in the present country of his noble people, the Chickasaws. He lived and died firmly adhering to the principles which he believed to be the greatest interest to his country. He was a true patriot, and loved the simple manners of the olden times, and could not yield them to give place to modern customs with their accompanying vices; and who can blame him? Alas! the Indians, everywhere on this North American continent, have been compelled to pay a higher price for the few crumbs of Christianity that they have been allowed to pick up and convert to the use of their starving souls than any race of people that ever lived, since the divine command of the world's Redeemer bade his apostles, "Go ye into all the world and preach my Gospel" (Cushman, 1899).

Missionary Visits the Colberts

During the year 1799, missionaries visited the Chickasaw Nation and recorded daily religious activities they had with members of George Colbert's family. The record provides a unique view of life among the Colberts and their religious beliefs and relationships prior to removal. The following diary is from The New York Missionary Magazine and Repository of Religious Intelligence by Cornelius Davis in 1800. The magazine contains the following extracts from Reverend Joseph Bullen, a Presbyterian Missionary from New York.

Our friends at Nashville informed us, that it was 270 miles to the Chickasaw towns; that there were several swimming waters to cross; that for us to go without guides would be very dangerous; and even added, that we could have but little rational hope of doing them good; that in one month we might get company, therefore they would have us stay with them for the present.

May 10th, 1799—Being weary with delay, and trusting in divine goodness to direct our way, we sat out by ourselves for the Indian country: our horses were so encumbered with baggage, that we could move but slowly on, and our situation was rather lonesome; but we had provided victuals, blankets, an axe, and gun, and were frequently met by people from Natchez, and Orleans, returning to Kentucky. Were impeded by rains—waters of Tennessee high.

General William Colbert—By the time the missionaries got to the Tennessee River the water was extremely high and probably caused a delay in their journey. The diary does not continue until nine days later when they wrote about meeting General

William Colbert. It is not sure how they crossed the Tennessee River, but at this time the George Colbert's Ferry had not been established at the Natchez Trace crossing.

May 19th, 1799—Lord's Day Met General William Colbert, a Chickasaw Chief, who gave us an introductory letter to his brother, Major George Colbert, and directed that our business be deferred till his return.

May 20th, 1799—We came to Big Town, weary, hungry, and myself much unwell. Here we got hominy with milk, and bad water. The Indians appear to be poor but kind. With these 1 held some talk by the help of a Negro who could interpret. Lodged in a warm house on a bear skin.

May 21st, 1799—Could get nothing for breakfast, unless it were thin drink and damaged meat. This town consists of two hundred houses, is situated on an eminence, has good air, and an agreeable prospect, but is badly watered; they are a people generally less in size and stature than the whites. Most of them appear to have the manners of ancient simplicity and labor is done by the women, hunting by the men: their visage differs but little from that of other Indians: their houses are made of poles, from three to five inches diameter, and plastered with mortar, are 16 feet by 22 on the ground, floored with earth, and covered by clabboards.

We went to Long-Town, five miles, where we expected to find George Colbert to whom we had a letter; in this we were disappointed, for though sent for he did not come, being on a visit with one of his wives. The Indians were together on account of a letter from the Cherokees on some national business; had some talks here, assisted by Joseph Colbert in which I endeavored to recommend the beloved speech, and make them know its contents; but my letters, and the design of our coming, we thought it our duty not to disclose as yet. The Indians are kind, and their best fare course, and I am much unwell, in a great measure owing to want of comfortable subsistence; we have a house to ourselves, but competent food is not to be had.

Joseph and Levi Colbert—The missionaries describe Big Town as having some 200 Chickasaw homes, but it appears the people are extremely poor. They left Big Town and went to Long Town some five miles away where they met Joseph Colbert, the son of James Logan Colbert. Joseph later conducted the missionaries to his brother's home, Levi Colbert.

May 22, 1799—Our Indian friends noticing our situation,-directed Joseph Colbert to conduct us to his brother Levi's; was but poorly able to ride; came to Levi's, who, with his two wives, appears to live comfortably: here we were politely received, well fed, and kindly treated; with him we were soon on terms of agreeable familiarity; to him the design of our mission was disclosed, with which he was evidently pleased.

May 23d, 1799—Employed in reading, writing, and in conversing with Levi and others. Taught Levi to write his name, made him and others acquainted with the history of the creation, apostasy, Noah's flood, and the confounding of the languages; learnt some Indian words. The Indians, though strangers to letters, have characters which they mark on trees, and, like Oriental people, they begin at the right hand, and write or read to the left; they also go the off side to mount a horse; their women: ride their feet the offside; they are a left-handed people.

May 24th, 1799—Found myself in better health than when we came. The Chickasaws are without any kind of religious observance, and without temple and priest, except that a few of their enchanters have images, the use of which is little understood by the nation in general; were assisted in conversing with the Indians, by Joseph Colbert who speaks both languages. My son teaches them reading, to which they attend with apparent delight. Close application does not consist with their indolent habits.

May 25th, 1799—This day became acquainted with the history of the nation, as given Colbert by his mother: " We are only a family from a great rich nation towards the sun setting, as far as Indians could travel during two moons; our fathers dreamed, that away towards the sun rising was land of life; that people know more than Indian, and above want; from them our children learn good things. Our fathers then sat out, travel, come where we now live, here land of life. Our great Father's white children know more than Indian, Chickasaw no hurt any of them. By and by we learn of them things make us glad."

Malcolm McGee—The group meets Malcolm McGee, a Scots-Irish interpreter who married into the Colbert family. McGee moved to the Chickasaw Nation where he married into the tribe and stayed for the rest of his life. He is gracious to the missionaries and tries to be of assistance in helping them spread the gospel. McGee also introduces the missionaries to the Chickasaw leader Wolf's Friend; and, McGee tries to explain the gospel to Wolf's Friend as taught by the missionaries. It is easy to see that McGee goes out of his way to be of assistance to these religious people preaching the gospel to the Chickasaws.

May 26th, 1799—Went to McGee's, the interpreter; was kindly received and hospitably entertained. Delivered him a letter from the Secretary of State; found him kindly disposed, but a stranger to everything of religion. So I read and explained to him several things in the Bible; he gave attention, and promised me every aid in his power in making known the good things, but added, that his ignorance of the gospel was such, that, at present, he could not interpret it; he could not read, and had never heard a sermon. McGee's wife and slaves, who all understand English; are fond of hearing, so that the time is agreeably, and, I hope, usefully spent.

May 27th, 1799—On consulting McGee, he told me that the white men, half-breeds and slaves, who all speak English, have great influence with the Indians; he therefore advised, that to effect the good proposed by our mission, we begin with these, who, he says, as they learn, will have good talks to the Indians, and so the knowledge and practice of these things will soon become national: the counsel I think good, and shall endeavor to follow it. McGee was born in the city of New York.

John McIntosh—Prior to 1770, John McIntosh was originally assigned as a British agent for the Choctaws. Later he established a Chickasaw town for mixed-bloods and whites known as McIntoshville. When the war was ended, McIntosh stayed with the Chickasaws and married a Chickasaw woman and became a person of importance among the Indians. He found the whole Chickasaw Nation residing in one big village and persuaded them to scatter out more. He planted a colony south of Pontotoc at a place called "Tocshish," put down on old maps as "McIntoshville." The town became the favorite residence of the renegade white men and half-breeds.

McIntoshville was on the Old Natchez Trace 12 miles south of Tupelo, Mississippi, and was called Tockshish, named for a Chickasaw word meaning "tree root". The community was made up of white men and Indians built up around the home of the British Indian agent, John McIntosh. When the Natchez Trace was established as a national road in 1801, Tockshish became a relay station where post riders carrying mail between Nashville and Natchez could exchange weary horses for fresh ones. McIntosh's was made the second post office between Nashville and Natchez. After an exchange of horses, a short rest, and food, the post riders would then ride on with their mail bags. Traveling north along Natchez Trace was a five days journey from there to Nashville, Tennessee; and, traveling south along the Natchez Trace was a seven days ride to Natchez, Mississippi.

There was a higher civilization, more wealth and intelligence in the Tocshish settlement than in any other part of the Chickasaw Nation. McIntosh established a stock farm at Toccopola, where, for some years, his crop was destroyed by herds of buffalo. He visited Hot Springs, Arkansas about 1816 to recover his health where he died at a very advanced age and was buried there.

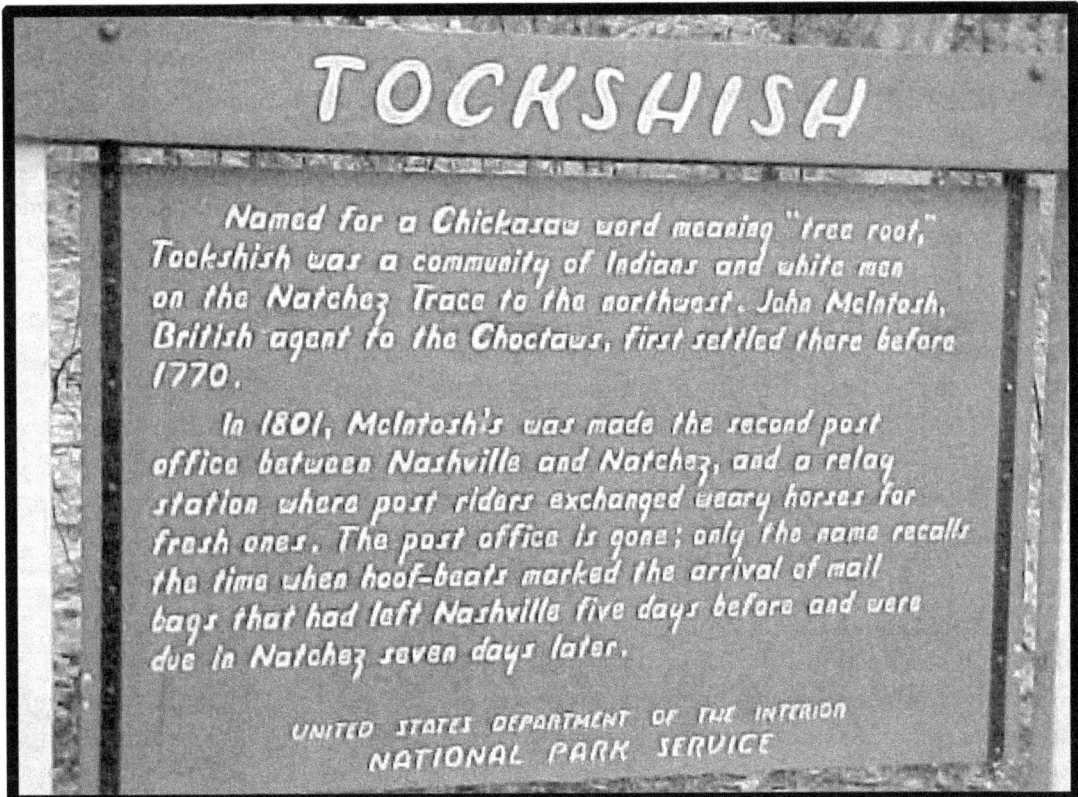

TOCKSHISH

Named for a Chickasaw word meaning "tree root," Tockshish was a community of Indians and white men on the Natchez Trace to the northwest. John McIntosh, British agent to the Choctaws, first settled there before 1770.

In 1801, McIntosh's was made the second post office between Nashville and Natchez, and a relay station where post riders exchanged weary horses for fresh ones. The post office is gone; only the name recalls the time when hoof-beats marked the arrival of mail bags that had left Nashville five days before and were due in Natchez seven days later.

UNITED STATES DEPARTMENT OF THE INTERIOR
NATIONAL PARK SERVICE

This day we came to Mr. McIntosh's, who talked in a discouraging manner, and deems it a weakness in any man to think of making Christians of Indians. I told him that I was of the same opinion, but believed God is able to make them good Christians, and that we wish for the honor of being workers together with God. On being further acquainted with this man, we found him an honest, agreeable man, and useful, as he talks good Indian, in helping me to hold good talks to the Indians, who continually frequent this place, and wish to know the beloved speech.

William Mizle—William Mizle, half Indian and half French, was married to a daughter of Piomingo. He had lived among the Chickasaws for many years and was a trader with the Spanish in Pensacola, Florida. By 1803, he opened a trading post at the Chickasaw Bluffs where Memphis now stands, soon after the Spaniards gave up their claim to the lower Mississippi Valley. Mizle kept a record of sales to Indians from the

121

main villages in Lee, Pontotoc and Chickasaw Counties in Mississippi. He bought corn whiskey from the flatboats coming down the Mississippi River from Ohio, Kentucky, and Indiana; and, he sold whiskey at his trading post.

May 28th, 1799—This day became acquainted with William Mizle, long resident in this nation, and sometime interpreter at the Bluffs. From him I learnt something of the customs and language of the Chickasaws: he says the method of healing in this nation is to take water, soak roots in it, blow in it with a pipe, and say over it a number of words by way of charm, and wash the body of the sick with this preparation. This is performed by people they call witches, who are initiated as follows. The preceptor takes the candidate for this dignity, in, summer weather, shuts him in a hot-house four days, to live on amber, a strong drink made of tobacco and water, then sets him to air, gives him gruel, heats the house anew, shuts him in four days more; he is then suffered to come out emaciated; he must then for twelve moons abstain from women, meat, fat, and strong drink, and is then a complete witch; can make storms or fair weather; can cause or cure diseases; foretell future events, and give good or ill success to any undertaking. Thus far Mizle, This day had conversation with numbers. My son teaches the youth to read, and gives them books: we hope some good may be done here.

Chickasaw Customs—The missionaries identify some of the customs of the Chickasaw practiced in 1799. One particular Chickasaw ceremony explained by the missionaries was the marriage between an Indian man and an Indian woman. Another tradition among the Chickasaws described by the missionaries was burial of the dead.

May 29th, 1799—My employment was reading, writing, and improving opportunities, which continually presented, for conversation. Several people here wish to understand the doctrines and duties of Christianity. On mentioning marriage among Christians, was informed of their usages in such cases. When an Indian wishes a young or single woman to become his wife, he sends her a small present of clothes or trinkets, which, if she accepts, (he becomes his wife, and, from that time, there devolves on her the duty of keeping fire, raising corn and other vegetables for the family, and supporting the children. The man's only business is hunting and war. A man may have any number of wives: marriage is only during the pleasure of both parties: in case of separation, the children all belong to the mother.

When a person dies, a grave is dug in the house nine feet deep, the body is washed and dressed in its best clothes, and then interred; if a man of account, a pipe, tobacco, rifle-gun, ammunition, feed, corn, and such, are buried with him. Boards are laid six inches below the surface, then a covering of mortar levels the grave with .the floor; then women are called to mourning and those skillful at lamentation to wailing. This continues twelve moons, about two hours in a day. When a person expires, they shoot three guns, as they say, to keep off evil spirits.

Thomas Love—Thomas Love was the Scots-Irish husband of Sally Colbert, daughter of James Logan Colbert. Thomas love fathered some thirteen children from his two wives. The Love family became about as large and wide spread as the Colbert family, even though they were related by marriage.

May 30th, 1799—Unwell, propose riding out. Here a Mr. Shepherd accompanied us to a Thomas Love's, where our reception was cordial, and treatment kind; though wet with a shower on the way, yet I feel in better health. I am like to have an opportunity to preach next Sabbath at this house.

May 31st, 1799—In conversation endeavored to show the evil of a practice among Indians, of bringing up their boys without work or restraint. Levi, Kemp, and Love's children begin to learn reading and other good things.

June 1st, 1799—Strong drink has overcome several of my Indians, others are conversible, and wish to learn. I wish they may learn to fear God, and receive everything as from him; part of each day is spent in learning their language.

June 2d, 1799—Preached the first sermon in the Chickasaw Nation; read and explained the first chapter of Genesis. These people attended with the utmost seriousness and solemnity; they expressed great joy that they had an opportunity to worship God, and hear of things concerning Jesus Christ. After sermon there came to me an old man, who, fifty years ago, had heard preaching; he told me it was the most delightful season of worship he had ever experienced; to me, indeed, it was a happy day.

June 3d, 1799—Had an interview with Colonel McKee, agent for the Choctaws, who appeared disposed to encourage our exertions, and withed similar endeavors might be used with the nation to which he is going. My week-day employments are reading, and such when retired; and with this people, conversation. My own leanness, and the indolent habits of the Indians are discouraging considerations, but I hope, in God's goodness, to carry on his own work. If but a barley loaf fall into the host of Midian, it is enough. God will work for his own name, .though the instrument be a poor worthless worm. When Philistia is to be smitten, it shall be effected, though a dry bone be the weapon.

Colonel John McKee—The Choctaw agent John McKee (1771-1832) a native of Virginia, was appointed in 1792 by Governor William Blount of the Southwest Territory to negotiate a boundary settlement with the Cherokee. He served as temporary agent to the Cherokee in 1794 and as Choctaw agent from 1799 until Silas Dinsmoor's appointment in 1802.

McKee once again was appointed United States agent to the Choctaws replacing Dinsmoor in April 1814. McKee then recruited both Choctaw and Chickasaw warriors to fight with Jackson against the British. McKee and Gaines negotiated a cessation agreement with the Choctaw in December 1815 to locate a new federal trading house near the site of the Old Spanish Fort Confederation. McKee, along with John Coffee and John Rhea, negotiated the Choctaw Treaty of October 24, 1816, which required the tribe to cede 10,000 acres east of the Tombigbee River to the United States. He resigned in 1821 to enter politics, serving three consecutive terms (1823-29) as United States Congressman from the Tuscaloosa District. McKee's plantation, Hill of Hoath, was in present-day Boligee, Green County, Alabama and served as his home until death.

Colonel John McKee
1771-8/12/1832

June 4th and 5th, 1799—Numbers attended on us to learn reading, writing, catechism, & c.

June 6th, 1799—*In conversation with some Indians, who had sundry scruples to solve, two of which were as follow: On being informed, that the great Father above maketh all things, knoweth all things, governeth all things,— the Indians say, Great Father above make all things! How come he make rattle-snake, make thunder and lightning? The other I shall mention is, on hearing one of us teach them the ten commandments, that clause in, the second, visiting the iniquities of the fathers upon the children, and such, railed a scruple how it could be just to punish children for wrong done by fathers. I considered I had cause to bless God for the attention among them which would induce such inquiries, and was enabled to give such solutions as appeared fully satisfactory to them.*

June 7th and 8th, 1799—*Returned to McIntosh's, who received, and kindly treated us: my son teaches the young people. I am endeavoring to learn the language, and to translate the Lord's Prayer and the commandments into Indian.*

June 9th, 1799—*Preached from Romans vi. 23. " For the wages of sin is death." .The design was to show the grievous destruction sin has brought on us, and the fullness, freeness, and efficacy of that remedy provided in Jesus Christ. The hearers were numerous, serious, and attentive to this service, read and explained the 2d chapter of Genesis.*

James B. Allen—James B. Allen married Susan Colbert, the youngest daughter of James Logan Colbert. Susan was only a quarter blood Chickasaw. James B. Allen was of Scots-Irish ancestry from North Carolina and had moved to Nashville to practice as a lawyer; however, for some reason he moved south into the Chickasaw Nation and married Susan Colbert.

June 10th, 1799—*Employed as usual, James Allen undertook to teach his wife reading and catechism.*

June 11th, 1799—*Returned back to Levi's; were kindly received, and had such talks as we hope will do good.*

June 12th, 1799—*Weary with the fatigues of yesterday one of Levi's wives from home, the other lies out; they have times of separation like the ancient Hebrew women in this nation they have great faith in dreams; they believe there is a great Father above, but pay him no kind of religious homage; am laboring to show them the nature and propriety of devotion; their want of words to express several important ideas is a great inconvenience.*

June 14th, 1799—Am this day three months from home, and long after my own house; I think as arutntly as Jacob did for his father's: the inconvenience is trifling, if the good proposed can but be affected,

June 15t, 1799—I had notice of the return of the Chief Colbert and a prospect of a public talk. The Lord grant everything may be so conducted as mall be for his own glory.

June 16th, 1799—A beautiful morning, but the season dry; expect this day an, interview with, the Chief Colbert who has sent for me; went to his house, accompanied by Levi and my son; were very politely received and attended to, had some talks upon righteousness, temperance, and a coming judgment. In the afternoon the Indians went off to Big-Town; would have us stay till to-morrow, and then come, because they said we should get nothing to eat in town. Here the slaves dressed themselves, met together, requested my son that I would preach to them; they are about twenty in number, were admitted into my apartment; we prayed together. I read to them several passages in the New Testament, explained to them the character and great love of Christ, that he loves poor blacks as well as others; told them how we should love Christ, and how a poor woman washed his feet with tears. It was a happy season; the parade of a royal palace would be nothing to it.

June 17th, 1799—Went to Big-Town, expecting a talk with the nation; in this I was disappointed: here we were made acquainted with a family of the name of Underwood, who showed us no small kindness; with these we held some good talks.

Ball Play—The missionaries witnessed a ball play at Big Town in the Chickasaw Nation and explained how the Chickasaws played stickball. This is an eyewitness account of preparations to begin a stickball game.

June 18 th, 1799—At Big-Town they had a ball play; they spent the last night in frolic; on the ball-ground they divide into two parties, the ladies who attend sing and dance; the mysteries are conducted by one of those witches heretofore mentioned for each party. At each end of the play-ground they erect two poles, five yards high, one yard asunder; four yards behind them they set up an image, the likeness of a man, with a painted face, one yard high, and decorated with a raven's skin and feathers; the leader in the mysteries is in a manner naked, his head adorned with a pair of buffalo horns, his face and body painted of different hues; to his left arm hangs the wing of a crow ; he is often falling down before the image, muttering and taking a strong physic, which these people believe has great influence in the success of the game. While the singing and dancing was performed by the ladies, a drum, made of a cypress tree, was beating, and the young beaus, about eighty in number, who were to play ball, beautified with vermilion, bear's oil, lamp-black, and white clay, their heads with feathers, red binding, & c. jewels in their noses and ears, thence awhile, then utter a hideous yell, and run round ft circle they have round the place of the mysteries, which may not be passed unless by the performers. My son and I had well-nigh spoiled the whole by entering the holy ground, but being beckoned to we went round. As they pass this, they yell with all apparent zeal, then return and repeat the singing, yelling, running, and such. These pious ceremonies being ended, the play begins; the charms used by the witches had no effect, or an equal effect, for neither party prevailed. The Chickasaw women appear to be meek, modest, and temperate; the men are more virtuous than one would think, considering they, are brought up to no business but hunting, and to little or no restraint; at evening we came away, and lodged at Long-Town.

June 19th, 1799—Returned to Levi's; the people are very attentive, but there has been yet no national talk with us or act for receiving us, we even think of leaving the nation.

June 20th, 1799—The heat intense; these Indians are wanting to learn, so we are not idle; they do not know their age, and but little of distances.

June 21st, 1799—Left my son to teach in this part, and went myself to McIntosh's, 26 miles; things look doubtful here; these deluded people will get drunk, and we can yet-have no public talk, though Levi says we shall soon have one.

June 22d, 1799—Have noticed ever since I came here, that when appearances are discouraging one day, they are encouraging the next; it is so now; have become acquainted with James Colbert a native of this country, who has been baptized, reads and writes, is a man of property; one quarter Indian; is a sober man; knows something of religion, wishes his nation to know and observe the same; believes his soul is immortal; hopes he shall regard its good; is disposed to explain the beloved speech, and my talks to the nation: had also good talks to-day with McGee and others.

Wolf's Friend—The missionaries meet Wolf's Friend who is held in high regard in the Chickasaw Nation. Wolf's Friend is very receptive to the missionaries and wants them to return with their families and settle on Chickasaw land. Wolf's Friend competed with Piomingo for tribal leadership of the Chickasaw Nation and probably achieved the status of chief for a short period after Piomingo's death. Even though Wolf's Friend signed a treaty with the Spanish at Mobile in 1784, Piomingo signed a treaty and alliance with the United States at Hopewell, South Carolina in 1786. Wolf's Friend met with President John Adams in Philadelphia in October 1798. His visit was encouraged by General James Robertson, and he was accompanied by George Colbert and his half-brother William Colbert. Chickasaw interpreter Malcolm McGee said that Wolf's Friend shot and killed himself shortly after his visit with President Adams. McGee also stated that Wolf's Friend suffered from the gravel (kidney stones); however, according to the diary kept by Reverend Joseph Bullen, Wolf's Friend was still alive on July 29, 1799, just prior to Bullen leaving the Chickasaw Nation.

June 23rd, 1799—Had this morning, by McGee's help, a good long talk with Wolfe's Friend, head man of this nation, informed him of the creation, and how that all men are brothers—of sin—of redemption—of the promise to all nations—of the good rules in the beloved speech—of the great love, the council at New-York have for the Chickasaws, and of the good-will of his great father the President, expressed in a letter from the Secretary at War. He looked pleased, and said, it made him very glad to hear these things, that he wished to hear more, and in about four days we will have big talk. Preached at James Colbert's; read the ninth Psalm; labored to show the folly and sin of forgetting God, and to persuade my hearers to realize his presence; they were seriously attentive; was mightily encouraged: this was a happy day. After service, one James Gunn, a white man, came to me, and said, I am glad—it is good to be in the presence of the Lord; I pray that I and my house may serve the Lord.

James Gunn—James Gunn was a refugee Loyalists who lived among the Chickasaws at a location that later became known as Gunn Town in Lee County, Mississippi, near present-day Tupelo. He found an asylum and a Chickasaw wife, Molly Colbert the daughter of General William Colbert, after the Revolution. James Gunn's new home became the Chickasaw Nation and he and Molly Colbert had one daughter Rhoda Gunn. James was a native of Virginia, but fought for King George III. He first settled in what was afterwards Pontotoc County, near Tocshish. He became wealthy and owned many Negro slaves, but allowed no idleness or fun on his premises on the 4th of July. To the end of his long life he celebrated the birthday of King George III. He died in 1826. For a number of years some of his descendants lived near Gunn Town, and many of them still live in that part of the State.

June 24th, 1799—Being requested, I preached again. I now love to be here: James and Susannah Colbert consent to the marriage covenant, and are declared husband and wife. Charles, their only child, and Peggy Allen, daughter of Colbert's sister, were baptized, and also Mary, Hannah, James, and Margaret, children of James and Jane McKim. An aged negro woman, property of William Colbert has come 30 miles to hear sermon, and said, me live long in heathen land, am very glad to hear the blessed gospel."

James Colbert—The missionaries meet James Colbert, who is one quarter Chickasaw and the youngest son of James Logan Colbert. James Colbert marries Susannah James, daughter of Benjamin James. The missionaries states that Peggy Allen, the daughter of James' sister Susan, was baptized; therefore, it appears from the missionary diary written in 1799, that Susan Colbert is indeed the daughter of James Logan Colbert and not the daughter of General William Colbert as some have suggested.

June 25th, 1799—Went to McGee's, read and explained to him out of the sermon on the Mount. Mr. McGee and I were invited to Wolfe's Friend's to dine to-morrow; the day after we are to have a great national talk.

June 26th, 1799—Went with McGee to the friends, who received us very politely; explained to him more fully our business. P. M. went to Levi Colbert's, in order to get things ready for the talk.

June 27th, 1799—Returned; find everything prepared for the talk. A large parade, a standard erected 30 feet high, a white cloth flying in token (McGee says) of love and peace. The Indians are fast coming together; it is a clear hot day; an agreeable shade and seats were fixed for the head men; I was seated next to the principal chief, and the interpreter on the other side; they were dressed neat and clean, and the most of them very fine. I began with reading a letter from Captain Pike, announcing the safe arrival of their presents at the Bluffs. I then added that I was glad that their presents were come, hoped they would do them good, and brighten the chain of friendship between the two nations; then told them, I had yet better news to tell them, that I had come to bring them the word of life; read to them the letters of the Missionary Society, and from the heads of departments; explained, as fully as I could, the Christian religion; gave them a Bible in the name of the Society, explained to them the benefits of learning; informed them that the Great Father above had given white people the knowledge of 26 characters, that knowing these, when they look in one book they can see how they can have the Great Father above to be their friend, do them good, and keep them in the right way. Look in another book, it will tell how to do all sorts of work; also gave the two chiefs and interpreter each a Testament. After consulting among themselves, and a good talk to them from their head man, I was informed they were very glad to hear these things, were thankful to the council of New York for their love to them, a people they had never seen, and to me and my son that we had come such a long journey to teach them good things; that we were received as their own people; they would have me bring my wife and children, and come and live with them; that the land is before me, to settle where I please, but that if I had come from the adjacent states, I should not have been received ; but now they would have me to do whatever I think best to make their people know good things, that we may depend on kind treatment. After the talks, we all partook of a plentiful repast, provided at the expense of Wolfe's Friend.

July 26th, 1799—Disappointed of an interpreter to go with me to Wolfe's friend and Big-Town, went' to McIntosh's, Colbert's, and Gun's.

George Colbert—The missionaries meet George Colbert, son of James Logan Colbert. George let the missionaries know that he and his brother did not care about whiskey, wanted to learn about good things, and to be good farmers of corn, cotton, cattle, and hogs.

July 29th, 1799—George Colbert, a Chickasaw Chief, called in a decent dress, and lodged here. He informed me how he and his brother Levi had labored to further the pious and benevolent designs of the Society; that he, Levi, and a number of others, wish to learn good things: no get drunk, but work, make corn, cotton, cattle, hogs & c. Wolfe's Friend made out his talks to-day; he says, head men and warriors all wish us to come back, if possible, by April next. He also appointed two chief men to accompany us as far as Knoxville, and wished we might be in the holy keeping of the Great Father above.

July 30th, 1799—Removed from Pontotok to Levi Colbert's; have left some books with friends Gun, Colbert and Oxbury, who, I expect, will have good talks with the Indians.

July 31st, 1799—At Levi Colbert's; somewhat out of health; labored to explain and enforce on their minds the truth and importance of revealed religion, to which they attended: September 1. Had no public service; had an opportunity to impress on their minds a sense of the truth and necessity of religion, and of the sanctity of the Sabbath. This people have no songs or poetry.

August 2d, 1799—Waiting for Mr. Lewis and our guides to the Cherokees, Mr. Lewis called on us; we took one talk to the Secretary at war, and one to Dr. Rodgers, from the Colbert's.

August 3d, 1799—Went to Billy Colbert's and Long-Town; was unwell; my Indian guides will be ready tomorrow; had good talks at Long-Town, assisted by Joseph Underwood, a half-breed.

August 4th, 1799—Sat out for the Cherokees, in company with Captains George and Chagniby, camped by a creek, and slept comfortably (Davis, 1800).

George Colbert Visits President Washington

Many of the Southeastern Indian leaders were summoned to meet with President George Washington to sign peace treaties which were usually designed to acquire more Indian lands for white settlement. In addition, the Indian chiefs were looking to the United States for aid in military supplies to fight their enemies, farm implements, and food especially during bad crop years. George Colbert made the trip with Piomingo to meet with President Washington in the company of other Chickasaw leaders.

Some two years prior to the meeting of Piomingo and George Colbert with President George Washington, the Chickasaws are sent a letter from the Secretary of War inviting them to come to Philadelphia as follows:

"Message from the Secretary of War to the Chickasaw Nation, dated 17th February 1792.

Brothers: Your father, General Washington, the great chief and president of the United States, has commanded me to send you this talk. Receive it, therefore, as an evidence of his affection, and the affection of the United States towards the Chickasaw Nation.

He heartily thanks Piomingo and the other Chickasaw warriors for joining our troops the last season. The President of the United States is very desirous to reward the attachment of Piomingo and the warriors who were with him at Fort Washington (Now the City of Cincinnati, Ohio), and he now sends to Piomingo and two other principal chiefs great silver metals, and each a suit of rich uniform clothes; and further, he has ordered presents to be sent from Fort Washington to the Chickasaw Nation generally, of such articles as shall be useful to them.

The Chickasaws must send a message to the commanding officer at Fort Washington, giving him sufficient notice of the time when and the place where they will receive the goods. These goods are sent as presents and as an evidence of the attachment of the United States to the Chickasaws, and a reward for their friendship.

If Piomingo should, with other chiefs, choose to join their arms with ours in the cause of the next campaign, let them repair to Fort Washington by the first of June next, where they shall be well armed, well fed, and, also, after the campaign, well rewarded for their services in money or goods, as they shall best like it.

After the next campaign, our beloved chief, General Washington, invites Piomingo and three other great chiefs to repair to Philadelphia. He wishes to convince them by a personal interview how desirous he is of promoting the happiness of the Chickasaws.

The Chiefs who shall come forward shall be kindly received, well treated, and returned to their own country enriched with presents. Given at the City of Philadelphia, ect" (Malone, 1922). Sculptor of Piomingo was William N. Beckwith.

The above letter was sent two years before the meeting below finally occurred in Philadelphia with President George Washington. According to the following article by Richard Green (2009) in The Chickasaw Times, *at noon on July 11, 1794, a group of Chickasaws, including Chiefs Piomingo and George Colbert, arrived at the President's House in Philadelphia for*

Chief Piomingo
Before 1750?-1799

a welcoming ceremony hosted by President George Washington. At the time, Philadelphia was the United States capital 1790-1800 while Washington, D.C. was under construction.

The President's House was on Market Street one block north of Independence Hall, where the Declaration of Independence was adopted in 1776 and the U.S. Constitution was drafted and signed in 1787. The house was demolished in the 1830s, about the time that the Chickasaws were being removed to Indian Territory.

Inside the three-story residence, Lawler said, Washington typically greeted important guests in the State Dining Room which he recently had improved for that purpose with the addition of a large semi-circular bow window. Washington would greet visitors standing with his back to the bow window, thus backlighting him, at six feet two, in rather a commanding manner.

Following the presidential greeting, ceremonial smoking likely was held in an even more elegantly appointed and impressive space, the Hall. Because it was framed on one end by a magnificent two-tiered mahogany staircase, the room's ceiling towered an estimated 38 feet above the floor. With the President were almost certainly Secretary of War Henry Knox (who was responsible for Indian affairs), and 28-year-old John Quincy Adams, the son of Vice President John Adams. The up-and-coming young diplomat and future United States President had been invited by President Washington to attend the reception and meeting with the Chickasaws. It is lucky for us that young Adams attended because he wrote an unusually descriptive account (for the 18th century) of the meeting...(Green, 2009). Portrait of John Quincy Adams was by John Singleton Copley in 1796.

**John Quincy Adams
7/11/1767-2/23/1848**

In the summer of 1781, James Logan Colbert, the father of George, had attacked the Americans at Fort Jefferson over five or six days because it had been built on Chickasaw land without their permission. Shortly after the siege by Colbert and the Chickasaws, the fort was abandoned in August 1782 and signed a peace agreement was signed by the

Chickasaws and Americans. Also in 1782, Piomingo met with General James Robertson and agreed to peace; however, Green (2009) goes into great detail describing the background information leading to the meeting with President George Washington in the following:

In the 1780s, Chickasaws were divided over whether to ally with the Spanish colonialists or the fledgling United States. Chief Piomingo signed a treaty of alliance with the United States at Hopewell, S.C., in 1786 while another strong and well-respected chief, known variously as Ugulayacabe or "Wolf's Friend," signed a treaty with Spain at Mobile in 1784.

For a time, both chiefs also did business with their apparent adversaries, in what was probably a strategy of playing one nation against the other to enhance trade deals to benefit the tribe. But by the late 1780s, Piomingo was resolutely pro-American and anti-Spanish. Part of his resolve stemmed from the fact that Spain's staunchest ally and America's fiercest foe was the principal chief of the Creeks, the mixed blood Alexander McGillivray.

In 1787, McGillivray demanded that the Chickasaws expel American agents. When that didn't happen, the chief sent raiding parties to harass or kill Chickasaws and their American guests. One such raiding party in 1789 killed Piomingo's brother and nephew, who were carrying a message from Piomingo to the recently inaugurated President George Washington (Green, 2009).

It should be noted that prior to the death of Captain James Logan Colbert on January 7, 1784, that Creek Chief Alexander McGillivray and the Chickasaws under Colbert's leadership were friends and allies against the Spanish and the American settlers. James Logan Colbert had been on a visit to McGillivray's home to consult with him and to get McGillivray's advice. On his return home, Colbert was thrown from his horse and killed. McGillivray and Colbert had worked together with Doublehead's Chickamauga Confederacy supplied by the British and fighting against the American government. After the American Revolution, both the Creeks and Chickasaws sought the assistance of Spain; however, the Spanish decided to refuse to help the Chickasaws, thus the Creeks became allied with the Spain and Chickasaws became allied with the United States. The difference in their loyalty brought conflict between the Chickasaws and Creeks.

Green (2009) continues an excellent description of the relationship of the Chickasaws and the United States government leading to the meeting with President George Washington.

Unable to retaliate because of a shortage of ammunition, Piomingo asked the Spanish for arms. When Spain refused, Piomingo sought to meet with Washington in New York City. Bad weather or perhaps an unfavorable sign from the spirit world prevented the trip there, so Piomingo turned to the state of Virginia, which complied with the request that permitted the Chickasaws to strike back against the Creeks.

Meanwhile, President Washington had been unresponsive to Chickasaw requests for more aid until Piomingo and fifty warriors volunteered in 1791 to help the young republic deal with several tribes of northern Indians who wanted to keep the United States off their lands.

While it may seem ironic that Chickasaws would be aiding the United States to invade sovereign tribal land, Piomingo felt he had no choice. To defend themselves from Creek attacks, Chickasaws needed shipments of arms from the Americans, and the only way to secure them, Piomingo believed, was to demonstrate loyalty to the Americans. Furthermore, some of the northern tribes had been enemies of the Chickasaws through much of the 18th century.

Loyalty mattered to Washington, who showered gifts on Piomingo and the warriors who accompanied him. In 1792, the Americans invited the Southern tribes to a council and peace treaty signing in Nashville. Tennessee territorial governor William Blount told the assemblage of tribes that Spain would demand land cessions but that the U.S. would not. "The United States have lands enough," Blount said, in one of the earliest and most erroneous predictions in American history.

Moreover, the Chickasaws were told that their blood and the blood of the Americans "was the same," meaning one would always defend against attacks made on the other. And in fact, the Chickasaws had struck against the Creeks when they had attacked American settlers in the Cumberland Valley.

That same year, Spain invited the Southern tribes to New Orleans to receive gifts and sign a peace treaty. One of the attendees was the Chickasaw king, Taski Etoka, who began receiving a Spanish retainer. McGillivray again signed with Spain and Creek raids on the Chickasaw increased. This time, when Piomingo asked for more American aid, it was promptly shipped to Chickasaw Bluffs (today's Memphis, TN). As a result, the pro-American Chickasaws launched successful counterattacks on the Creeks, who were further disadvantaged when the chronically ill McGillivray suddenly died in February 1793. The pro-Spanish Chickasaws and other tribes, meanwhile, signed the Treaty of Nogales with Spain late that year. It was an offensive/defensive alliance and provided for annual gifts and permanent Spanish Indian agents.

Through Governor Blount in April 1793, Piomingo asked the President for arms, ammunition, and corn to offset a series of crop failures due to drought. Blount said yes, but no delivery date was included, so Piomingo decided to make his request in person during the late summer of 1793. His party set off, probably from his home in Chukafalaya (Long Town), intending to remind Washington of the promises made to the tribe at Nashville in 1792 by Secretary Knox. However, the Chickasaws met Governor Blount, who induced them to return home as deadly fevers were sweeping through Philadelphia.

In 1794, Piomingo felt even more urgency to see the President and made another request. Ugulaycabe had given the Spanish permission to build a fort on the Mississippi River at Chickasaw Bluffs, which had long been an important military position in Chickasaw country. Then, Ugulayacabe built a settlement nearby from which they could protect the Spanish from Piomingo's faction should those warriors attack.

President George Washington
2/22/1732-12/14/1799

Realizing the seriousness of the situation, Governor Blount was authorized to notify Piomingo that Washington would see him. Piomingo, George Colbert, and other unnamed chiefs and warriors set off and arrived in Nashville in June. In July, the Piomingo contingent arrived in Philadelphia — the largest American city with a population of about 35,000.

In the following, Green (2009) gives the written history of the meeting as recorded by John Quincy Adams. *Published historical accounts of the meeting are perfunctory, recording the gist of President Washington's brief speech. But, apparently unknown to those historians, John Quincy Adams had taken quill in hand and recorded observations in his diary.*

Chickasaw Party—*He wrote that the Chickasaw party included five chiefs, seven warriors, four boys, and an interpreter. Judging from the size of previous traveling parties to Philadelphia or New York, there were probably others who, for reasons of space, were not present in the room. Adams identified only Piomingo, about age 47, by name, but there is good reason to believe that long-time tribal interpreter and confidant Malcolm McGee was present, as was 30-year-old Chief George Colbert, also known as Tootemastubee. It is likely that mixed blood chief William Glover and Mucklesa Mingo were also present, as both had attended the Nashville Conference of 1792 (Green, 2009).*

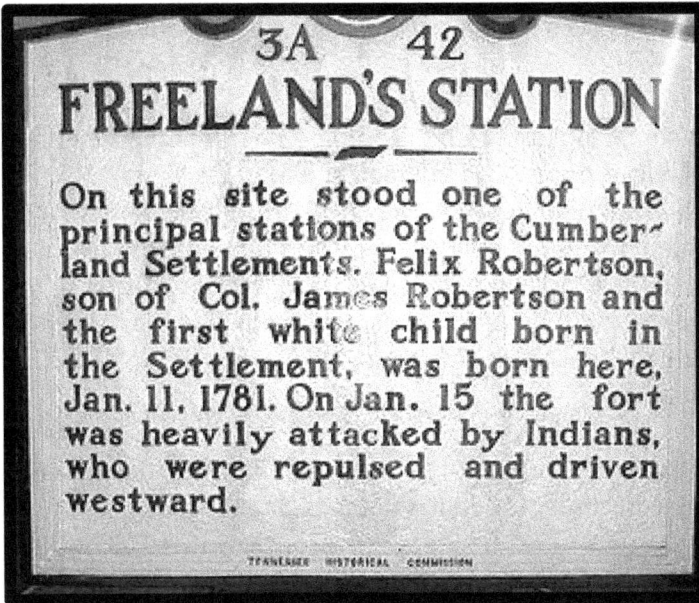

3A   42
FREELAND'S STATION

On this site stood one of the principal stations of the Cumberland Settlements. Felix Robertson, son of Col. James Robertson and the first white child born in the Settlement, was born here, Jan. 11, 1781. On Jan. 15 the fort was heavily attacked by Indians, who were repulsed and driven westward.

TENNESSEE HISTORICAL COMMISSION

Other historians describe Piomingo as being much older than 47 in the early 1780's. Shortly after the attack on Freeland's Station on January 15, 1781, General James Robertson had a meeting with Chickasaw Chief Piomingo and both agreed to terms of peace. The Chickasaws had participated in several prior attacks, but after the meeting with Robertson, the Chickasaw alliance was broken with the Chickamauga. The Chickasaws actually became allied with Robertson and the Cumberland settlers. It is worthy to give the description of the old chief Piomingo as described by Edward Albright in *Early History of Middle Tennessee* as follows:

"Piomingo was a striking figure among the noted Indian rulers of his day. He is described as having been of medium height, well-proportioned in body, and as possessing a face of unusual intelligence. Though at the time of his visit to Bledsoe's

Lick, more than a hundred years old, he strode the earth with the grace of a youth. His dress was of white buckskin, and his hair, which he wore, hanging down his back in the form of a scalp lock, was, by reason of his great age, as white as snow. This was clasped round about on top of his head by a set of silver combs" (Albright, 1909).

The assault on Freeland's Station was the last engagement the settlers had with the Chickasaws, though the latter, before they retired, united with a party of Cherokees and did much damage to the stock and plantations on the Cumberland. Our historians say that Colonel Robertson made peace with them in 1782, but I do not find any evidence of such a treaty. Peace was restored by the removal of the original cause of irritation (Goodpasture, 1918).

At the meeting with Robertson, Chickasaw Chief Piomingo became the first of his tribe to officially abandon the Chickamauga Confederacy and to break from Doublehead's alliance. Note when Piomingo met with General James Robertson in 1781, his hair was white as snow which would indicate that he was quite old at the time of the peace conference at Bledsoe's Lick. Eventually in 1795, Doublehead himself would also forsake the Creek faction of the Chickamauga Confederacy that was his most powerful force and ally. The Creeks would continue attacks on settlers until the Battle of Horse Shoe Bend in March 1814.

Green (2009) continues with his description of the party of Chickasaws meeting with President George Washington as recorded by John Quincy Adams.

This blend of full bloods and mixed bloods reflected the transition of tribal leadership. In less than five years, the transition would be accelerated with the death of Piomingo. At a time of increasing contact with Americans, the Colbert brothers, George, William, and James, the sons of a white man (James Colbert) would become the leading chiefs of the tribe.

The Chickasaw boys Adams mentioned probably were the sons of chiefs selected by their families to be taught English by Americans. Washington made the offer during the meeting, but it isn't known if these boys remained behind to begin their education.

Despite the summer heat, the chiefs must have felt the need to demonstrate their loyalty graphically. Adams wrote that some were dressed in "coarse jackets and trousers, and some in the uniform of the United States." Some of the party had shirts,

138

others had none. No one, he noted, was "painted or scarified" and four or five had "rings in their noses."

He also noticed that one or two had large plates [gorgets], apparently of silver, hanging upon the breast... Piomingo and George Colbert had received peace medals in 1792 from Washington through Secretary Knox, so these might have been them. But if these were peace medals, Adams probably would have identified them as such.

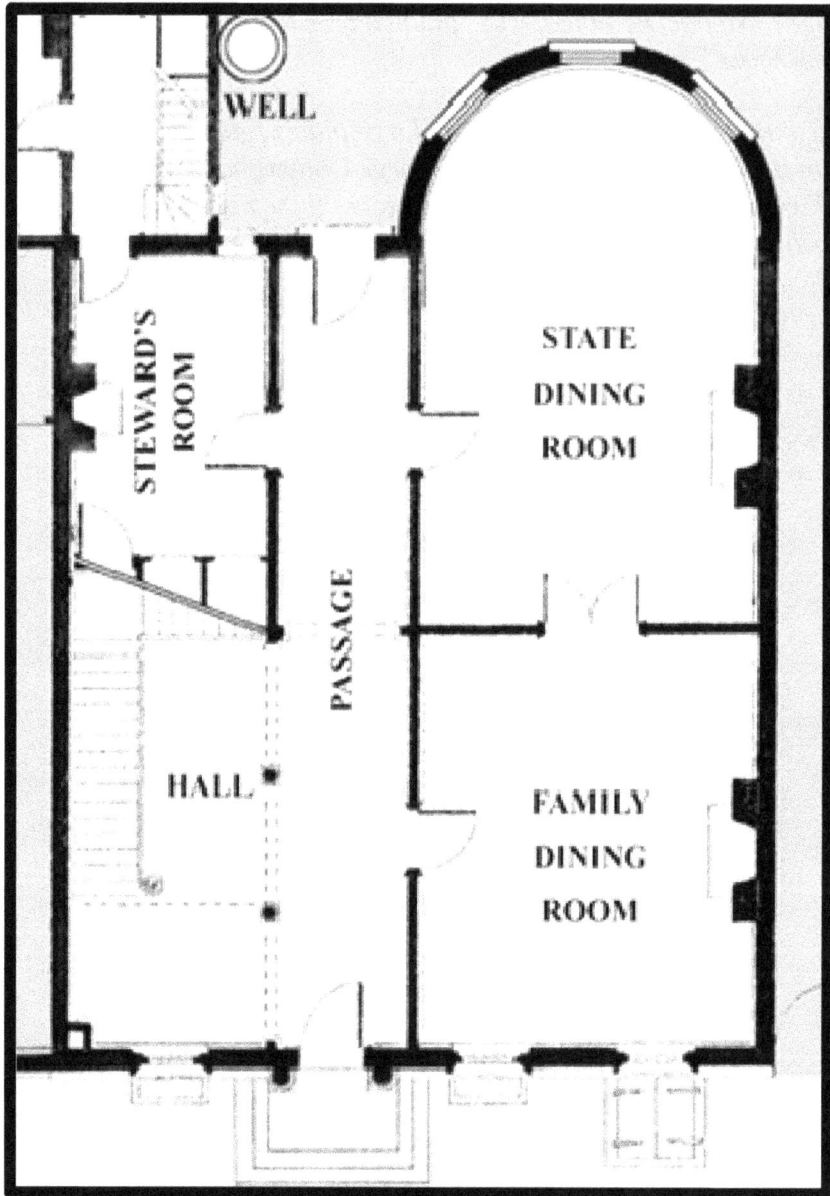

Conjectural floor plan ©2001-2009 Edward Lawler, Jr.

Washington probably greeted the Chickasaws while standing in the Bow Window of the State Dining Room. The delegation, Washington, and John Quincy Adams smoked the ceremonial pipe in the Hall. Refreshments probably were served in the Family Dining Room.

The ceremonial smoking of a peace pipe featured a decidedly odd twist. Instead of the usual clay or stone hand-held variety used by Chickasaws and most Indians, this one, according to Adams, was of "East Indian" origin, made of leather and was a gargantuan 12 to 15 feet in length. Washington took a couple of puffs, and then passed the "tube" to Piomingo and so on around the circle.

Adams noted that the Chickasaws "looked as if they were submitting to a process in compliance with our custom. Some of them ... smiled with expressions that reflected "novelty" and even "frivolity," as if the "ceremony struck them ... as ridiculous."

President Washington then read his speech, which probably had been written by Secretary Knox. Adams noted that Washington stopped at the end of each sentence for the translation. And Adams wrote that following each translation, the translator would repeat the same word twice, which he wrote sounded like "Tshkyer!" The five chiefs would then utter a sound that "resembled a horse's neighing" and that it would be faint or strong according to the "degree of satisfaction..."

The President's speech is part of his official papers that are housed at the Library of Congress. Washington told the Chickasaws that their actions in support of the American Army against the hostile tribes northwest of the Ohio [in 1791] are the "strongest evidence of your friendship." If the Chickasaws "will join their arms with ours" the United States will "defray all the expenses upon a liberal scale." He said to communicate tribal needs "to the Secretary of War who will furnish you with Goods for your nation, your families and yourselves."

As added inducements, Washington told them if they wanted to continue on to see New York City, he would make the arrangements for their accommodations. And as noted, Washington said the United States would also provide for the education of willing Chickasaw boys. Meanwhile, he told them "to consider yourselves as at home."

This suggests that they might have been accommodated at the President's House at least for the night. But Ed Lawler believes it is unlikely: "I've never found references to guests other than family and close friends staying overnight at the President's House during Washington's administration. The upstairs' rooms were mainly occupied by family and staff, he said. On the other hand, the main house was approximately 9,000 square feet in size, and contained several rooms on the second and third floors that had been used as bedrooms, according to Lawler.

Adams continued by reporting that after Washington concluded his speech, Piomingo announced that he wasn't feeling up to speaking, but promised to do so in the next few days. Those meetings, Lawler said, would typically have been conducted at the offices of the war department in a recently constructed building aptly called the New Hall, which still stands today.

Finally, as wine, punch, and cake were served probably in the Family Dining Room, Adams heard Washington tell a group of the Chickasaws that they had always been "sincere and faithful friends" and that the U.S. valued them "most highly." Washington waited for a response, but according to Adams, they "made no answer to the President's compliment."

Meetings were held periodically over the next 10 days, but no details are known. A final meeting was held between the President and Chickasaw chiefs at 11 a.m. on July 21. Henry Knox submitted a farewell speech for Washington's review, but no copy of it is known to exist. Nevertheless, we do know that at that meeting President Washington commissioned one of the chiefs as a captain in the militia and gave the delegation many gifts.

Secretary of War Henry Knox
1785-1794

The information comes via Ugulayacabe, who wasn't there but discussed the trip with some of the participants when they returned home. The gifts included either $600 or $1,000 (that's $12,000 to $20,000 in today's money) to Piomingo (the sum was in dispute), clothing and boots for everyone, and presents for their families and for persons named by Piomingo but who were not present. Each Chickasaw received $30 to use for purchases in Philadelphia stores.

At the request of the Chickasaw chiefs, Washington gave Piomingo a written document, setting forth the boundaries of the Chickasaw territory. These coincided exactly with those expressed by Piomingo at the conference in Nashville in 1792. The document stated that the Chickasaw territory was under the protection of the United States and included a warning to its citizens.

It is likely that New Hall is where the Chickasaws and Secretary of War Henry Knox negotiated their treaty.

They were forbidden to trespass on, injure, or molest Chickasaw persons, lands, hunting grounds, or other rights or property. They were also forbidden to purchase or treat (trade) with the Chickasaws for the title or occupation of any lands held or claimed by them. Washington also said he would "call upon all appropriate citizens to aid and assist in the prosecution and punishment, according to law, of all persons who shall be found offending in the premises."

New Hall, Philadelphia

Piomingo probably couldn't have worded it any better. But in five years, Piomingo and George Washington were both dead and five years after that the Chickasaws were forced to make their first substantial land cession to the United States. It was a slice of land, which became western Tennessee, northwest Alabama, and western Kentucky.

Chief George Colbert, who had been with Piomingo and George Washington at the meetings in 1794, signed the land cession treaty as the Chickasaw's principal chief. John Quincy Adams was a member of the U.S. Senate, which ratified the treaty in 1807 (Green 2009).

War Department Papers

The following is the records of the United States War Department identifying important dates concerning the Chickasaw Nation. These records start with the United States recognizing the land claims of the Chickasaws at Hopewell, South Carolina on January 10, 1786.

January 10, 1786--<u>*Articles of a Treaty with the Chickasaw Nation*</u> *–The treaty was concluded at Hopewell, on the Keowee River, near Seneca Old Town, between Commissioners Plenipotentiary of the United States of America and the Chickasaw Nation. The treaty contained 11 Articles and established the boundaries of the Chickasaw Nation.*

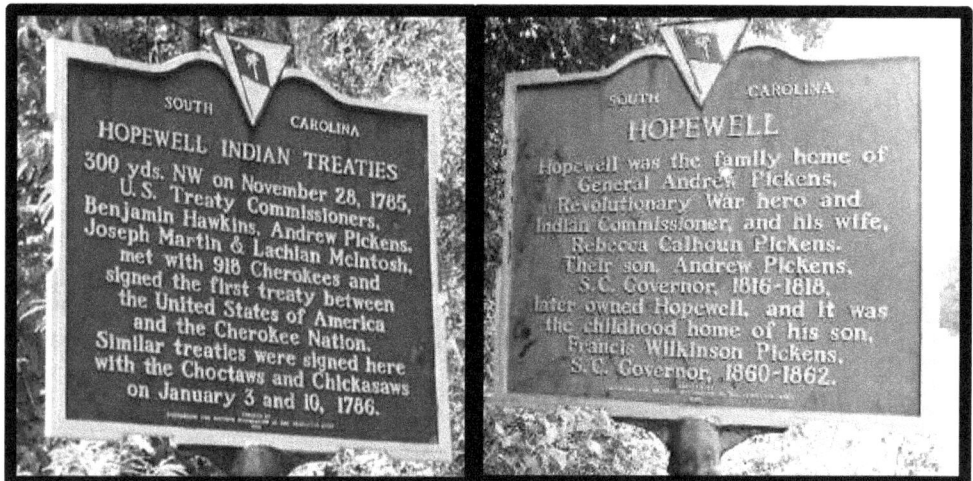

Hopewell Indian Treaties Historical Marker

The above historical marker is located on United States Highway 76 at Old Stone Church (almost 1 mile above Anderson-Pickens County line, South Carolina), turn left on South Carolina Section Road 22 and travel about 0.7 of a mile, then turn left on South Carolina Section Road 149; the marker is about 1 mile. The front side of the marker states: *Hopewell was the family home of General Andrew Pickens, Revolutionary War hero and Indian commissioner, and his wife, Rebecca Calhoun Pickens. The son, Andrew Pickens, South Carolina governor, 1816-1818, later owned Hopewell, and it was the childhood home of his son, Francis Wilkinson Pickens, South Carolina governor, 1860-1862.* The reverse side of the marker states: *Hopewell Indian Treaties, Three hundred yards northwest on November 28, 1785, U.S. treaty commissioners, Benjamin Hawkins, Andrew Pickens, Joseph Martin, and Lachlan McIntosh, met with 918 Cherokees and signed the first treaty between the United States of America and the Cherokee Nation. Similar treaties were signed here with the Choctaws and Chickasaws on January 3 and 10, 1786.* The January 10, 1786, treaty with the Chickasaws recognized the boundaries of Chickasaw lands.

Benjamin Hawkins represented the United States in many treaties negotiated with the Chickasaws and other Southeastern Indian tribes. The following is a summary of the life of Benjamin Hawkins as given in *Wikipedia: The Free Encyclopedia,* 2012.

Benjamin Hawkins
8/15/1754-6/6/1816

Benjamin Hawkin—
Benjamin Hawkins (August 15, 1754– June 6, 1816) was an American planter, statesman, and United States Indian agent. He was a delegate to the Continental Congress and a United States Senator from North Carolina, having grown up among the planter elite. Appointed by George Washington as General Superintendent for Indian Affairs (1796–1818), he had responsibility for the territory of the Southeast south of the Ohio River, and was principal Indian agent to the Creek Indians.

Hawkins established the Creek Agency and his plantation in present-day Georgia, where he lived in what became Crawford County. He learned the Muscogee language, was adopted by the tribe and married Lavinia Downs, a Creek woman, with whom he had seven children. He wrote extensively about the Creek and other Southeast tribes: the Choctaw, Cherokee, and Chickasaw. He eventually built a large complex with African slave labor, including mills, and raised considerable livestock in cattle and hogs.

Hawkins was born to Philemon and Delia Martin Hawkins on August 15, 1754, the third of four sons. The family farmed and operated a plantation in what was then Granville County, North Carolina, but is now Warren County. He attended the College of New Jersey, later to become Princeton, but left in his last year to join the Continental Army. Hawkins was commissioned a Colonel and served for several years on George Washington's staff as his main interpreter of French.

Hawkins was released from federal service late in 1777, as Washington learned to rely on la Fayette for dealing with the French. He returned home, where he was elected to the North Carolina House of Representatives in 1778. He served there until 1779, and again in 1784. The Carolina Assembly sent him to the Continental Congress as their delegate from 1781 to 1783, and again in 1787.

1805 painting, Benjamin Hawkins teaches Creeks to use European technology

In 1789, Hawkins was a delegate to the North Carolina convention that ratified the United States Constitution. He was elected to the first U.S. Senate, where he served from 1789 to 1795. Although the Senate did not have organized political parties at the time, Hawkins' views aligned with different groups. Early in his Senate career, he was counted in the ranks of those senators viewed as pro-Administration, but by the third congress, he generally sided with senators of the Republican or Anti-Administration Party.

In 1785, Hawkins had served as a representative for the Congress in negotiations over land with the Creek Indians of the Southeast. He was generally successful, and convinced the tribe to lessen their raids for several years, although he could not conclude a formal treaty. The Creek wanted to deal with the 'head man'. They finally signed the Treaty of New York after Hawkins convinced George Washington to become involved.

In 1786, Hawkins and fellow Indian agents Andrew Pickens and Joseph Martin concluded a treaty with the Choctaw nation at Seneca Old Town, today's Hopewell, South Carolina. They set out the boundaries for the Choctaw lands as well as provisions for relations between the tribe and the U.S. government.

In 1796, Washington appointed Benjamin Hawkins as General Superintendent of Indian Affairs, dealing with all tribes south of the Ohio River. As principal agent to the Creek tribe, Hawkins soon moved to present-day Crawford County in Georgia where he established his home and the Creek Agency. He studied the language and was adopted by the Creek. He wrote extensively about them and the other southeast tribes.

He made a common law marriage for years with Lavinia Downs, a Creek woman. They had a total of six daughters: Georgia, Muscogee, Cherokee, Carolina, Virginia, and Jeffersonia, and one son, Madison Hawkins. In 1812, thinking he was on his death bed, Hawkins married Lavinia formally in the European-American style to make their children legitimate in United States society. Jeffersonia was born after this marriage. As the Creek had a matrilineal system, all the children were born into their mother's clan, and gained their Creek status from her.

Hawkins was close to his nephew William Hawkins of North Carolina, whom he made an executor of his estate along with his wife; he bequeathed him a share of his estate, reputed to be quite large. This bequest became a source of contention among his heirs, especially as he had not altered his will to include his last daughter Jeffersonia Hawkins.

Hawkins began to teach European-American agricultural practices to the Creek, and started a farm at his and Lavina's home on the Flint River. In time, he purchased enslaved Africans and hired other workers to clear several hundred acres for his plantation. They built a sawmill, gristmill, and a trading post for the agency. Hawkins expanded his operation to include more than 1,000 head of cattle and a large number of hogs. For years, he met with chiefs on his porch and discussed matters there. His personal hard work and open-handed generosity won him such respect that reports say that he never lost an animal to Indian raiders.

He was responsible for 19 years of peace between the settlers and the tribe, the longest such period during European-American settlement. When in 1806 the government built a fort at the fall line of the Ocmulgee River, to protect expanding settlements just east of modern Macon, Georgia, the government named it Fort Benjamin Hawkins in his honor.

Hawkins saw much of his work to preserve peace destroyed in 1812. A group of Upper Creek (who became known as the Red Sticks) were working to revive traditional ways, and they opposed the assimilation of the Lower Creek (with whom Hawkins worked closely) and continuing encroachment by European Americans. They allied with the Shawnee chief Tecumseh of the Western Confederacy to resist increasing settlement by European Americans. During the War of 1812, the British encouraged the Red Stick resistance. Although Hawkins was not attacked, he was dismayed by the damage to the Creek people from their civil war, with the White Sticks and Red Sticks at odds.

During the Creek War of 1813-1814, Hawkins organized the friendly Lower Creek under Major William McIntosh, a chief, to aid Georgia and Tennessee militias in their forays against the Red Sticks. General Andrew Jackson led the defeat of the Red Sticks at the Battle of Horseshoe Bend in present-day Alabama. Hawkins was unable to attend negotiations of the Treaty of Fort Jackson in August 1814, which required the Creek to cede most of their territory and give up their way of life. Hawkins later organized friendly Creek warriors against a British force on the Apalachicola River; they had threatened to rally the scattered Red Sticks and reignite the war on the Georgia frontier. After the British withdrew in 1815, Hawkins was organizing a force to secure the area when he died from a sudden illness in June 1816.

Hawkins never recovered from the shock of the Creek civil war. He tried to resign his post and return from the Georgia wilderness, but his resignation was refused *by every president after Washington. He remained Superintendent until his death on June 6, 1816. At the end of his life, he formally married Lavina Downs in a European-American ceremony, making their children legitimate in United States society. They already belonged to Downs' clan among the Creek, as they had a matrilineal system; this gave them status in the tribe.*

Benjamin Hawkins was buried 32°40'0.61"N 84 5'45.73"W at the Creek Agency near the Flint River and Roberta, Georgia. Fort Hawkins was built overlooking the ancient site since designated as the Ocmulgee National Monument. Revealing 17,000 years of human habitation, it is a National Historic Landmark and has been sacred for centuries to the Creek. It has massive earthwork mounds built nearly 1,000 years ago as expressions of the religious and political world of the Mississippian culture, the ancestors to the Creek (Wikipedia, 2012).

July 7, 1789—<u>Report on the Chickasaws and Choctaws</u>--Henry Knox, George Washington, and Knox views the substantial distance of the Chickasaws and Choctaws from frontier settlements as the principle reason that few complaints regarding white encroachments have thus far been lodged. Knox notes that Chickasaws and Choctaws are "represented as candid, generous, brave, and honest" and have placed themselves under the protection of the United States and no other sovereign.

September 13, 1789—<u>A message to the Chickasaw nation of Indians, from the commissioners plenipotentiary for restoring and establishing peace and amity between the United States of America and all the Indian nations situated within the limits of the said States, southward of the river Ohio</u>--Commissioners for Treating with the Indians South of the Ohio- A message to the Chickasaw nation of Indians, from the commissioners plenipotentiary for restoring and establishing peace and amity between the United States of America and all the Indian nations situated within the limits of the said States, southward of the river Ohio. They make reference to Mr. Bennett Ballew and express friendship. Make reference to Treaty at Hopewell.

November 21, 1789—<u>McGillivray's Mischief, Etc.</u>--Arthur Campbell to Henry Knox- Campbell warns that intelligence from Indian Country shows that [Alexander] McGillivray has sent a deputation of Creek headmen to the Wabash Indians to encourage hostilities against American western settlements. It appears also that the supply of ammunition delivered to the Chickasaw chief in Richmond is in danger of being intercepted. Discussed land claims in Virginia, the Carolinas, and...

December 24, 1789—<u>*Gun Powder and Lead for Chickasaws*</u>*--Henry Knox, Thomas Holt- Deliver to Governor Randolph gun powder and lead to be furnished to Chickasaw Nation.*

December 30, 1790—<u>*The President to Piomingo and Chickasaw Nation*</u>*-- George Washington-Notes that Major Doughty was sent to brighten the chain of friendship with United States and to assure of firm adherence to Treaty of Hopewell. United States does not want any Chickasaw lands. Mr. Vigo, the bearer, will bring goods conformably to the Treaty of Hopewell.*

February 17, 1792—<u>*Affection for the Chickasaw Nation*</u>*--Henry Knox, Chickasaw Nation of Indians- Knox assures the Chickasaws of the affection of President Washington for the Chickasaw Nation and enlists their aid as allies in the campaign against the northern Indians.* This letter is included in the above text at the beginning of the chapter; George Colbert visits President George Washington.

July 29, 1792—<u>*Observations from Travels to Chickasaw and Choctaw Nations*</u>*-- Anthony Forster, William Blount, Related sentiments of councils held at both Chickasaw and Chocktaw villages in relation to politics, peace, and war between the whites people (U.S) and the Indians. Discussed names, points of view, and events in detail.*

August 11, 1792—<u>*Proceedings of Governor Blount and the Chickasaws & Choctaws*</u>*--William Blount, A copy of speeches given by the headmen and warriors of the Chickasaw and Choctaw nations and Governor Blount regarding land disputes, boundary lines, and peace. Many maps and boundaries are described.*

February 13, 1793—<u>*Proposed War with the Creeks*</u>*--Chiefs of the Chickasaw Nation, General Robertson-The Chickasaw chiefs blame the Creeks for the violence in the southwest and ask for the guns, ammunition, supplies, and food to go to war with them.*

March 23, 1793—<u>*War Between the Chickasaws and Creeks*</u>*--William Blount, Henry Knox- Following the brutal murder of a Chickasaw brave by a party of Creeks, Blount assesses the potential for war between the two southern tribes.*

April 27, 1793—<u>*Secretary of War addresses the Chickasaw Nation*</u>*--Henry Knox, Chiefs of the Chickasaw Nation, Mentions meeting in Sandusky for peace treaty.*

Notified Chickasaws that they can obtain wanted arms, ammunition, and corn from the General of the Army at Fort Washington.

April 27, 1793—Message to the Chickasaw Nation from Secretary at War-- Henry Knox, Chiefs of the Chickasaw Nation- Knox speaks on behalf of President Washington to the Chickasaw Nation.

*April 29, 1793—Large Army of Creeks Coming Against This Nation--*Piomingo, General Robertson- Piomingo alerts General Robertson that his Chickasaws will soon be attacked by a Creek army. He hopes that the general will recall past promises of assistance to his nation in dire circumstances such as these.

May 28, 1793—Frontier People Exasperated by the Injuries They Receive-- William Blount, Henry Knox- Blount describes the burial of a murdered Chickasaw man and reports on the general turmoil on the southwestern frontier. The white settlers constantly complain about the depredations committed by the Cherokees and Creeks though the Chickasaws are well regarded. Blount feels that his responses to the needs of the settlers are inadequate.

Governor William Blount
4/6/1749-3/21/1800

William Blount—William Blount served as governor of Southwest Territory the area south of the Ohio River and west of the Appalachians and was appointed to the position by President George Washington in 1790. Blount worked with all the Southeastern Indian tribes including the Chickasaws to develop friendly relations with the United States. The following about Blount as given in Wikipedia (2012): *Blount governed from the home of William Cobb, Rocky Mount, located in current Piney Flats, Tennessee. After concluding the Treaty of Holston, he announced that the territorial capital would move to newly founded Knoxville. Blount named Knoxville after the first Secretary of War, Henry Knox. After moving to Knoxville, construction began on his mansion, known as Blount*

Mansion, in 1792. The mansion still stands in downtown Knoxville and is a popular museum...In 1792, while governor of the Southwest Territory, Blount built the William Blount Mansion in Knoxville. The mansion is a National Historic Landmark. Blount County, Tennessee, is named after Blount, as is the town of Blountville, Tennessee. Grainger County, Tennessee, and Maryville, Tennessee, are both named after his wife, Mary Grainger Blount.

*   **June 4, 1793**—<u>Intimidate the Indians as well as Kill Them</u>--William Blount, Henry Knox, Blount discusses the measures he has taken to prevent further depredations by parties of marauding Creek Indians. The Cherokee chiefs have announced their peaceful disposition and the Chickasaws, having joined in the war against the Creeks, are not joined by the Choctaws who fear the loss of Spanish trade if they do not remain neutral.*

*   **August 1, 1793**—<u>Goods Needed Annually for the Chickasaw and Choctaw Indians</u>--Andrew Pickens, [not available], "Estimate of goods necessary to be furnished the Chickasaw and Choctaw Indians annually."*

*   **September 3, 1793**—<u>James Seagrove Creek Indian Agent, to Secretary of War Henry Knox on how Georgia inhabitants view peace efforts with Creek Nation, attempts to meet with Georgia Governor Telfair, proposal for meeting of Creek Chiefs at Philadelphia, and rumors of whites and Chickasaws planning to attack Creeks</u>--James Seagrove, Henry Knox- Seagrove reports that he is waiting at Augusta to meet with Georgia Governor Telfair. While there he is also attempting to ascertain the prospects for peace with the Creeks, based on newspaper accounts, current reports, and based on the measures being taken by the Governor. Reports that Governor Telfair is making plans for large-scale military operations against Creek Nation, but says this will...*

*   **October 28, 1793**—<u>Treaty between Spanish and Indians</u>--King of Spain, Creeks, Choctaw, Chickasaw, Cherokee Indians, Head of a treaty between the King of Spain and the Creek, Chickasaw, and Cherokee Indians.*

*   **April 16, 1794**—<u>Attaching Chickasaws to the United States</u>--General James Robertson, Anthony Wayne- Robertson has engaged Robert Thompson, a Chickasaw who speaks some English, to accompany the three Chickasaw warriors who will visit Wayne's camp. Their nation is powerful and it will be useful to attach them to the interests of the United States. They want good guns to go to war with but will return them when the campaign is over. Robertson's brother Elijah will pilot them as far as Governor Shelby.*

July 11, 1794—Speech to the Chickasaw Indians--Henry Knox, George Washington- Secretary Knox submits a draft of a speech to the chiefs and warriors of the Chickasaw Nation of Indians. The speech starts out by expressing gratitude in the Chickasaws joining with the United States Army in combating the "hostile tribes northwest of the Ohio," who allegedly had been "deaf to the voice of reason and peace."

July 31, 1794—Equipage for the Chickasaw Chiefs--Tench Francis, Samuel Hodgdon, [Partly illegible] Hodgdon is asked to pack up [?] to be transported to the Chickasaw Chiefs.

November 3, 1794—Notification of Clothing Delivery to the Chickasaws-- William Blount, Chiefs of the Chickasaw Nation, Chief Opoia Mingo has been given clothing by General Washington to deliver to the people of the Chickasaw nation as a token of friendship. The Chickasaws are commended for encouraging their warriors to support General Wayne's army.

November 7, 1794—Southwest Indian relations--General James Robertson, William Blount-General James Robertson tells Governor William Blount of Southwest Territory that he does not believe that any enemy Indians are in or around settlements, although some have taken off with horses. His son, Jonathan, had his horse stolen. According to the Chickasaws, the Indians lately on the borders of the white settlements have been Creeks.

November 8, 1794—Aggression by Creek Indians--General James Robertson, William Blount- General Robertson comments on the murder of Colonel Isaac Fitzworth and his family by Creek Indians, along the waters of Red River. Seven persons total were killed and scalped. This, along with other expressions of aggression, proves the information given us by the Chickasaws, that the Creeks had declared publicly their intensions of distressing this district, or, if able, to extirpate it...

December 28, 1794—Certificate of Indian Boundaries from the President-- Outlines laws governing boundary between Cumberland and Chickasaw Nation.

January 13, 1795—Support and Supplies to Fight Creeks--General James Robertson, William Blount- Robertson writes Governor Blount on behalf of the Chickasaws who seek support and supplies as they endeavor to fight the Creeks, citing treaty b/w Chickasaws and U.S. stating the Indians are now citizens of the U.S.

January 20, 1795—<u>*How to Handle Murder of Creeks by Colbert and His Party*</u>*-*
-William Blount, General James Robertson- Blount expressed pleasure in the murder of
five Creeks by Chickasaws, but believed if the United States did not support the
Chickasaws in their inevitable war with the Creeks, the United States would lose
friendship with Chickasaws. Believed war between nations may be delayed due to
season, and the type of deliberations that happen before Indian Nations go to war.
Request guidance on how to instruct Colbert and his warriors...

May 9, 1795—<u>*Indian Goods*</u>*--Timothy Pickering, General James Robertson-*
Quoted speech made by the Secretary of War to Chickasaw chiefs in Philadelphia
regarding Indian goods given to promote/negotiate lasting peace.

May 12, 1795—<u>*Chickasaw Goods from Pittsburgh to Nashville*</u>*--Timothy*
Pickering, Samuel Hodgdon-The interim Secretary of War requests information from
the Commissary of Military Stores regarding the carriage of Chickasaw goods from
Pittsburgh to Nashville,
specifically the weight.

Timothy Pickering—
Timothy Pickering served as fourth quartermaster of the United States and the third Secretary of State until May 12, 1800. He worked to win the confidence of the Chickasaw Nation and was responsible for providing goods and services to the Chickasaws in return for their support of the United States. In 1783, Pickering went into the business of a mercantile partnership with his friend Samuel Hodgdon that lasted some two years. Notice that Hodgdon became involved with Pickering in delivering goods to the Chickasaw people.

Timothy Pickering
7/17/1745-1/29/1829

June 10, 1795—Talk from the Choctaw Nation to the Creek Nation--Choctaws, Creek Chiefs, Friendship between nations of Indians after peace talk and smoking of tobacco. Noted conspiracy of Americans selling land and Indian people. Proposed alliance against Americans. Seeks peace with Cherokees, requests Chickasaws talk with Cherokees to sway them towards peace with Choctaws.

July 4, 1795—Supply of Troops and Discussion of Treaty with Great Britain--Timothy Pickering, Anthony Wayne-Transmitted letter pertaining to family of officer held prisoner by Indian tribe. Enclosed copy of newspaper containing treaty negotiated with British by Mr. Jay. Chickasaw and Choctaw chiefs arrived at War Office seeking protection from Creek Nation and possibly seeking supplies from United States government. Discussed usability of hats provided by military for troops, has submitted for additional...

July 9, 1795—Spanish at Chickasaw Bluff--General James Robertson, William Blount, Extract of letter from General James Robertson to William Blount, Governor of the Southwest Territory. The Governor reports that the Spanish Government has erected cannons and other works at the Chickasaw Bluff on the east bank of the Mississippi River.

July 12, 1795—Spanish at Chickasaw Bluff--William Glover, General James Robertson, Extract of letter from William Glover to General James Robertson concerning the Spanish Governor erecting a fort in the Chickasaw region.

July 17, 1795—Forwarding the Chickasaw Goods--Isaac Craig, Samuel Hodgdon- In addition to requesting a barrel of muscavado sugar, Major Isaac Craig notes that the Quartermaster General thought that it would be advisable to send the Chickasaw goods directly from Pittsburgh rather than routing them through Fort Washington. All the goods from the treaty have already been sent forward. $3000 is required to expedite the business at Presq'isle.

August 6, 1795—Offer to Chickasaw Nation--Major George Colbert will not communicate with Chickasaws until he hears directly from the President regarding an offer to be made to the Indian Nation. Draft of ratification of treaty, requests instructions.

August 16, 1795—Offer to Chickasaw Nation--Timothy Pickering, George Washington, Maj. Colbert will not communicate with Chickasaws until he hears directly *from the President regarding an offer to be made to the Indian Nation. Draft of ratification of treaty, requests instructions.*

August 26, 1795—Account of Robert Hays--William Simmons, Timothy Pickering, Simmons certifies that $58.46 is due Robert Hays, being the expenses of Major William Colbert, William McGillivray (Chickasaw chief) and John Brown, two other Chickasaws, and Malcolm McGee, Interpreter from Knoxville to and at Philadelphia.

September 11, 1795—Proposed Peace between Creek and Chickasaw Nations, Timothy Pickering, George Washington, Southwestern Territory is at peace according to letter from Governor Blount. Notification that General Robertson will go to Chickasaw Nation and notify them of Creeks intention of peace and request for prisoner exchange. Governor Blount will meet with the Creeks at the Tellico Blockhouse.

Samuel Hodgdon—After the Revolutionary War, Samuel Hodgdon served under Brigadier General Henry Knox, who fourteen years later, was Secretary of War when Hodgdon was appointed Quartermaster General. Hodgdon apparently carried out the duties of field commissary satisfactorily, and served as an assistant to the Quartermaster General Thomas Pickering. Hodgdon was nominated for the position of Quartermaster General by President Washington and confirmed by the Senate, becoming the first appointed by the president. He also was the first civilian to be named to the post. On March 4, 1791, he became Quartermaster of the army being raised for General St. Clair's expedition into the Western frontier.

September 18, 1795—Peace Between Creek and Chickasaw Nation-- George Washington, Timothy Pickering-

Samuel Hodgdon
9/3/1745-6/9/1824

156

Pleased with summary of dispatches from Governor Blount rather than having to read complete transcripts, believed this method should be employed in the future. Glad to hear of proposed peace between the Creeks and Chickasaws, believed Governor Blount should immediately facilitate this agreement. Advised not holding militia troops in service longer than necessary.

October 2, 1795—*Receipt from Pickering for State of Virginia to defray expenses of transporting and supplying Chickasaw and Choctaws from Richmond to Knoxville--Jaquelin Ambler, [not available], Ambler received $1000 by hands of Edward Carrington Supervisor of Virginia to reimburse Commonwealth Virginia like sum advanced John Chisholm by Governor Brooke to defray expenses of transporting goods for Chickasaw, Choctaw, and supporting Indians from Richmond to Knoxville.*

October 7, 1795—*Receipt of William McClish--William McClish- Money received for job of interpreter to Chickasaw Indians.*

November 12, 1795—*Spanish Treaty with Chickasaw on United States Land-- Anthony Wayne, Timothy Pickering- Enclosed a copy of Spanish treaty with Chickasaw Nation allowing them to build a fortification in the south western territory (U.S. territory), believed this was contrary to the Spaniards official position of peace with United States. Enclosed letter and affidavit of Governor St. Clair that supports aggressive intentions of Spanish. Wayne advised Governor Manuel Gayose de Lemos to immediately remove...*

June 7, 1796—*[A talk from the Mad Dog to the Chickasaw Nation]--Mad Dog, [not available], Talks received with happy hearts, Mad Dog's tribe now sends its strength to the Chickasaws.*

September 3, 1796—*Goods for the Chickasaw Indians--Nathan Jones, Samuel Hodgdon- Mr. Francis has been directed to purchase and deliver to Hodgdon three thousand dollars-worth of goods for the Chickasaw Indians. The Secretary of War requests those goods forwarded to Major Craig at Pittsburgh where they will remain until Craig receives further orders.*

December 1796—*Secretary of War McHenry to Chickasaw Chiefs on Boundary Disputes and Presents--James McHenry- Representatives of the Chickasaw nation (who presumably have traveled to Philadelphia) are reassured about the efforts of their "Father" (the President, George Washington) to see to their interests amid a boundary dispute between the United States and Spain. Also refers to adjudication of* *land/property disputes between the Chickasaws and various individuals and the state of South Carolina.*

December 9, 1796—*Intelligence report on Chief Red Pole and the Chickasaws--James McHenry, Intelligence report on Chief Red Pole and Chickasaws.*

Colonel James McHenry—James McHenry was born into a Scots-Irish family in County Antrim, Ireland in 1753. After migrating to the United States, he served as Secretary of War in 1796 where he provided assistance to the Chickasaw Nation. He was good friends with Timothy Pickering. He eventually sends a personal letter to Chickasaw Chief George Colbert concerning a payment to Colbert and Malcolm McGee.

December 15, 1796—*Protest Against U.S. Encroachment of Territory at Chickasaw Bluffs--Chiefs of the Chickasaw Nation, James McHenry- Chickasaw delegation continues to protest the United States plans to install a garrison at Chickasaw Bluffs after the Spanish garrison is evacuated from that place. Submits documentation that proves U.S. promises regarding Chickasaw land, and asks if the Indians are now being trifled with in disregard for these promises. Says they desire the continued goodwill of the U.S. and a reaffirmation from the...*

Colonel James McHenry
11/16/1753-5/3/1818

February 21, 1797—
Concerning the preparation of Indian annuities--James McHenry, John Harris-McHenry's response to Harris's request for early attention to be given to packing up the goods necessary for Indian annuities in the present year. McHenry encloses a statement

of the sums due, noting that there are reductions for the Chickasaw and Cherokee Nations.

March 30, 1797—<u>*Delivery of annuities to the Chickasaw Nation*</u>*, James McHenry, John Harris, Requests the delivery of annuities to Samuel Hodgdon for transportation to the Chickasaw Nation.*

May 21, 1797—<u>*Chickasaw Nation of Indians*</u>*--The author discusses his plans for boundary surveys, the rejection of an application of a trader, a letter from Piomingo to General Robertson complaining that the Creeks were stealing horses from the Chickasaws, and the claim of George Colbert against the Cherokees regarding payment for "his negroes."*

June 4, 1797—<u>*Report from the Cumberland*</u>*--Benjamin Hawkins, James McHenry, Hawkins reports on various affairs on the frontier, the current attitude of the Indian nations in the region, and the progress of his survey of the Cherokee and Chickasaw border lines.*

July 22, 1797—<u>*Chickasaw chief's response to white encroachment*</u>*--James McHenry, John Adams, Transcribes a discussion between a Chickasaw chief and American. The chief insists that his people are aware that whites will stop at nothing to take their lands and reminds the American that they remember the terms of past treaties. The Chickasaw then says that he has been informed by Spanish Louisiana Governo Gayoso that Americans want to take possession of their lands and demands an answer to…*

July 24, 1797—<u>*Presents for the Chickasaws, Etc.*</u>*--Unknown Author, James McHenry, Among a number of matters, the author discusses the distribution of presents to the Chickasaws at Chickasaw Bluffs. He apologizes for his late communication which is due to a violent intermittent which has attacked him and affected to such an extent that he is barely able to hold his pen.*

September 22, 1797—<u>*Regarding the Spanish presence at Chickasaw Bluff*</u>*-- James McHenry- Regarding the Spanish presence at Chickasaw Bluff - located in Tennessee - and Spanish intentions to reoccupy a post in clear violation of Pinckney's Treaty, which placed the Chickasaws under United States territory.*

September 22, 1797—<u>*Diplomatic relations with Chickasaws and Spanish on the western frontier*</u>*--James McHenry, Oliver Wolcott, Jr.-McHenry expresses frustration at* *conflicting orders out west in relation to the Chickasaws and Spanish in Tennessee. Alludes to the Spanish breaking the terms of Pinckney's Treaty of 1795, which placed the Chickasaws under United States territory. McHenry also reports that he has recently been attacked by a case of the fever.*

September 22, 1797—Information Regarding Diplomatic Situation Surrounding Enforcement of Treaty of Madrid (U.S.-Spanish Florida Border)--James McHenry, Isaac Guion James McHenry expresses hope that Isaac Guion has distributed annual presents to the Chickasaws; notes that Spanish officers have obstructed enforcement of the treaty in the U.S.-Spanish Florida border region, but opines that they have been doing so out of fear of a British invasion down the Mississippi. Reiterates that the President and Secretary of War have issued orders to Guion and Wilkinson...

September 29, 1797—Establishment of runners for the Chickasaw and Choctaw nations--James McHenry, Isaac Guion, James McHenry informs Isaac Guion that Benjamin Hawkins' principal resident agent for the southwestern Indians has established runners for the Chickasaw and Choctaw nations.

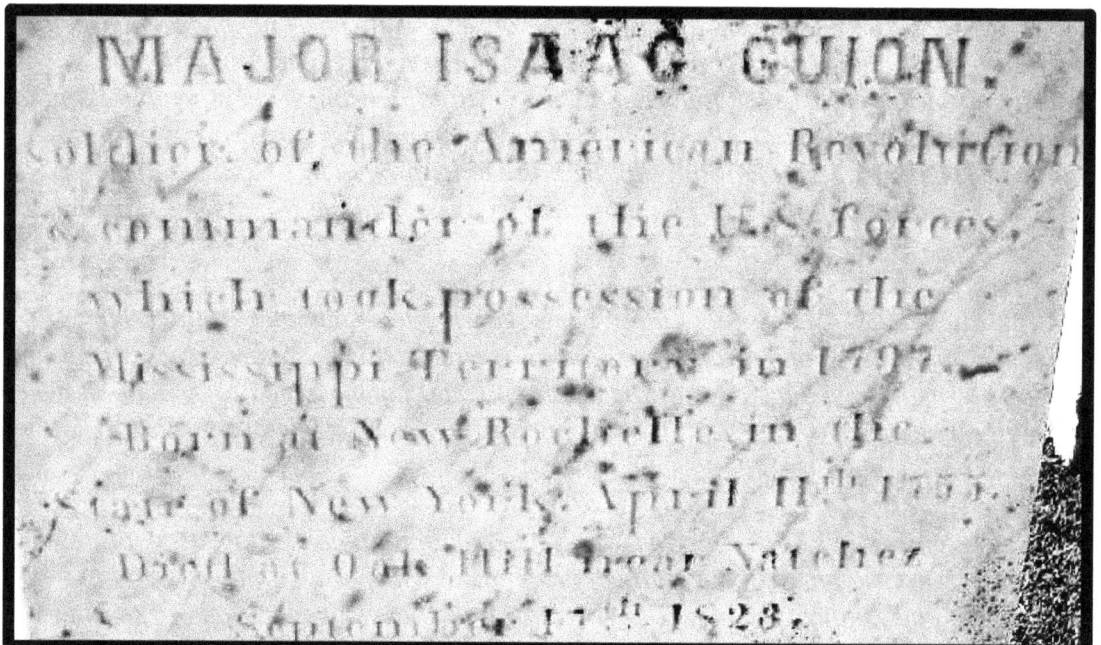

Major Isaac Guion
4/11/1755-9/17/1823

Major Isaac Guion—Isaac Guion was born April 11, 1755, in New Rochelle, Westchester County, New York. He died in Adams County, Mississippi on September 11, 1823. Guion served as a Captain in the Revolutionary War, and fought with Wolf and Montgomery's troops in the Capture of Quebec. During the war, he was promoted to the rank of Major. Major Guion moved to Mississippi around 1797, and was stationed at Chickasaw Bluffs. Major Guion worked to insure the Chickasaws were represented by the United States. He was honorably discharged from the army on June 1, 1802. His children were as follows: Lieutenant Frederick Lewis Guion, 1800-1824; Judge John Isaac Guion, 1802-1855; and, Judge George Seth Guion, 1806-1861.

October 22, 1797—Causes of the Delay in the Chief's Arrival, Etc.--Isaac Guion, James McHenry- Among other matters, Captain Guion discusses the delay of the chiefs in arriving at Fort Adams to receive their annuities. The delay is due to several causes including Piomingo's having to stay at home to defend his town against the Creek Indians who, it was reported, were planning an attack on the Chickasaws.

March 30, 1798—Annual Supply for the Chickasaw Nation of Indians--James McHenry, Samuel Hodgdon, Enclosed is an order on the Storekeeper to deliver the annual supply to the Chickasaw Nation of Indians. It should be transported to Major Craig at Pittsburgh and forwarded to Fort Washington to be deposited there in the care of the commanding officer pending further orders.

May 25, 1798—Receipt of Chickasaw Goods, Etc.--Isaac Craig, Samuel Hodgdon- Major Craig forwards vouchers for issues of stores to Samuel Hodgdon. Craig acknowledges receipt of Chickasaw Indian goods. The galley "President Adams" is launched.

October 10, 1798—Certification of payments; Francis Mentges, Inspector of Troops and Garrisons, for disbursements made for clothing and board of James Underwood, Chickasaw Indian, and his interpreter--William Simmons, James McHenry, Certification of payments; $78,000 to Francis Mentges, Inspector of Troops and Garrisons, for disbursements made for clothing and board of James Underwood, Chickasaw Indian, and his interpreter.

November 15, 1798—Horses delivered to Chickasaw chiefs--David Henley, Samuel Hodgdon, Encloses the register of five horses delivered to Chickasaw chiefs. Adds that he has no invoice of the public clothing for Colonel Butler, requesting that it be sent immediately.

November 16, 1798—Purchase of a horse for a Chickasaw chief--David Henley, Samuel Hodgdon, The Agent for the War Department at Knoxville, Tennessee bought a horse costing $45 for a Chickasaw chief setting off that evening.

January 27, 1799—Stipends, Dividends & Gift Sums to Indian Nations--James McHenry, John Adams, In return for Indian friendship, General Wilkinson has promised an annual stipend to a Chickasaw chief, Wolf's Friend, who is now in Philadelphia. Considers different points on the wisdom of filling such a request, including: that Wolf's Friend comes from a faction of Chickasaw not yet closely allied to the U.S.; no individual chief has ever been given a stipend, only part of the sum for the...

February 7, 1799—Encloses Copies of Speeches--James McHenry, John Adams, Submits speech to Bloody Fellow, Wolf Pound, and George Colbert. Will call upon the President in the morning for further instructions.

February 25, 1799—Warrant for defraying expenses of George Colbert--Malcolm McGhee received $300 to defray expenses of himself, George Colbert, a chief of the Chickasaws, his wife and two other Indians from Philadelphia to Knoxville, to be settled with David Henley, agent for War Department.

May 31, 1799—Payment of Accounts and Indian Annuities--Isaac Craig, James McHenry-Notification that the Quartermaster has no control or superintendence over

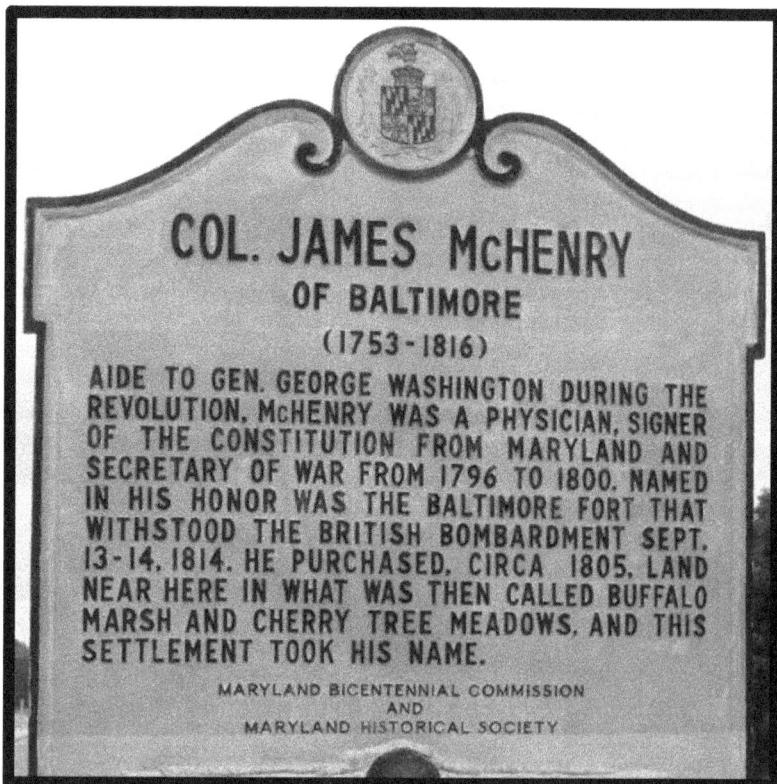

COL. JAMES McHENRY
OF BALTIMORE
(1753-1816)
AIDE TO GEN. GEORGE WASHINGTON DURING THE REVOLUTION, McHENRY WAS A PHYSICIAN, SIGNER OF THE CONSTITUTION FROM MARYLAND AND SECRETARY OF WAR FROM 1796 TO 1800. NAMED IN HIS HONOR WAS THE BALTIMORE FORT THAT WITHSTOOD THE BRITISH BOMBARDMENT SEPT. 13-14, 1814. HE PURCHASED, CIRCA 1805, LAND NEAR HERE IN WHAT WAS THEN CALLED BUFFALO MARSH AND CHERRY TREE MEADOWS, AND THIS SETTLEMENT TOOK HIS NAME.
MARYLAND BICENTENNIAL COMMISSION
AND
MARYLAND HISTORICAL SOCIETY

Hospital or Ordnance Departments therefore he will not admit charges from these departments to the Quartermaster's Department. Account of armorer suspended until Craig attends to it. Flat bottomed boat with all Chickasaw annuities sent forward. Doctors transported on same boat. Lyman and Turner's companies have been...

July 11, 1799—Complaint Against the Chickasaw--Chiefs of the Shawnees, Arthur St. Clair, The Chiefs of the Shawnee complain to St. Clair about the behavior of the Chickasaw. They claim that the Chickasaw are breaking the peace and troubling the Shawnee chiefs, women, and children. They ask St. Clair to defend them and stop any possible mischief.

November 21, 1799—Delivery of Medicine and Hospital Stores--James McHenry, John Harris, Letter, directs purchase of medicines and hospital stores and subsequent delivery for transportation to Massac and Chickasaw Bluffs.

December 23, 1799—Certification of payment; Francis Mentges, for clothing, boarding and for presents for Chickasaw, Cherokee and Catawba Indians--William Simmons, James McHenry, Certification of payment; $189.66 to Francis Mentges, for clothing, boarding, attending and for presents for Chickasaw, Cherokee and Catawba Indians.

August 15, 1800—Payment to George D. Blackmore--James Winchester, Samuel Dexter, Winchester paid $2000 to George D. Blackmore for ascertaining the boundary line between the United States and the Chickasaw Nation of Indians.

Chickasaw Land

Originally the Chickasaw people claimed the land from western Kentucky to the Ohio River, the west portion of the State of Tennessee to the Mississippi River, northern portion of the State of Mississippi and south to the Choctaw boundary, and the northern portion of the State of Alabama all the way east to the Flint River near present-day Huntsville, Alabama. Little by little the Chickasaw lands were taken by treaties with the United States until they were finally removed from their eastern homelands by 1837.

Piomingo—At the 1792 Nashville Conference, Chief Piomingo described the boundaries of the Chickasaw tribal lands: *"It begins on the Ohio at the ridge which divides the waters of Tennessee and Cumberland, and extends with that ridge eastwardly as far as the most eastern waters of Elk River; thence to the Tennessee, at* *an old field, where a part of the Chickasaws formerly lived, this line to be so run as to include all the waters of Elk River, thence across the Tennessee and a neck of land to Tenchacunda Creek, a southern branch of the Tennessee, and up the same to its source; then to the waters of Tombigby, that is, to the west fork of Long Leaf Pine Creek, and down it to the line of the Chickasaws and Choctaws, a little below the trading post"* (Malone, 1922).

At the beginning of the mid 1770's, the Chickasaw were a major faction of Doublehead's Chickamauga confederacy. James Logan Colbert led an attack on Fort Jefferson, which was an American outpost near the junction of the Ohio and Mississippi Rivers. The Chickamauga was on friendly terms because Chickasaw Chief George Colbert married two of Doublehead's oldest daughters. George Colbert claimed that Doublehead was living at the Muscle Shoals by his permission.

Letters concerning land claims

Chinubbee King of the Chickasaws—King Chinubbee was an ally of Spain and a staunch supporter of the Chickasaw-Spanish clan and its leader, Wolf's Friend. He granted Spain the right to establish military bases in the Chickasaw Nation and, in 1795, the post San Fernando de las Barrancas was constructed. The Spanish influence among the Chickasaws was halted by the Treaty of San Lorenzo. Chinubbee went on to sign treaties with the United States on behalf of the Chickasaw Nation. His mark appears on the treaties of 1801 and 1805. His death around 1819 opened the way for the ascendancy of the Colberts in dominating tribal affairs

January 25, 1805, Chennabe, King of the Chickasaws, Letter—The following letter is from Chennabe, King of the Chickasaws, from the Chickasaw Nation, on January 25, 1805. The letter is directed at government officials and tells them that the Chickasaws do not want to sell any more lands. The letter is in response to a letter sent to George Colbert and is as follows:

Sir:—

I received your letter sent to Major George Colbert, and have listened to your talk—and you stated to us to know whether we would sell the land on the north side of the Tennessee. My friend you know very well that land is very expensive. If we were disposed to sell that land we would not sell it by the wholesale—when we are disposed to sell that land we will have it surveyed and have so much an acre for it the same as the white people does to one another with these lands. We cannot sell these lands. It is true the game is scarce and partly gone. That is the only place that my children and warriors have to hunt and get their livings on at present. I hope will not think it any harm because we deny selling our lands—You mentioned to me that the Cherokees and my people were joined in war with the Shawanesse. It is not so. We never were. when the Shawanesse first came they came up the Tennessee and then up Bear Creek about thirty miles, and there left their canoes and came to war with the Chickasaws and killed several of our people—The Chiefs and warriors of my Nation turned out against them, and drove them off. From thence they went to the Creeks and lived there a while, and then they returned back, and crossed at the Chickasaw old fields, above the Muscle Shoals, from thence they went on to Duck River and Cumberland river, and settled there, and the Chickasaws found them out, and two of our principal Chiefs in those days one named Opio Metihah and Ponshey Metahah, which in that day were the two principal chiefs of our Nation, they raised their warriors and went against the Shawanesse and defeated them, and took all their horses, and brought into the Nation, and the Cherokees had no hand in the war, with us. We drove them ourselves without any assistance from any red people. My friend you mentioned to us that if we were not disposed to sell to let you know fully, so that Congress need not put themselves to the trouble and expense of calling a treaty. We are not disposed to sell now. But I have no doubt it will be the case one day or another, if so we can tell you. We have killed some game on that land yet and we cannot sell at present. Some years past General Wilkinson, Col. Hawkins and General Pickens called a treaty with us at the Chickasaw Bluffs. They requested a road through our country, we granted that request. The said commissioners said that Congress would not ask us to sell any of our lands—that it was not their request to ask any further favors of us after we granted them the favor of a road through our nation. My friend once the British lead us into darkness and gave us very fine talks, for us to join them against the Spaniards, and we did thinking they would always remain in this country. After they had lost their country and went off over the big water, we began to find our error—After the Spaniards got possession of West Florida, they wanted us to kill Americans and we would not—The Cherokees and Creeks did, and that caused them to lose the best part of their country and now they want to claim our land. If they had behaved as well as we have, their country would not as well as ready that they were killing your women and children and spoiling them. I am your friend and brother,

CHENNABE—*King of the Chickasaws*

Major George Colbert

April 26, 1805, General James Robertson Letter—The following letter is from General James Robertson from Nashville, Tennessee on April 26, 1805, appears to be directed to the Cherokees. Robertson states that he had met with George Colbert and another Chickasaw chief concerning their land claims. In the letter, Robertson identifies Flint Creek on the south side of the Tennessee River just a few miles east of present-day Decatur, Alabama as a boundary line of the Cherokee, Chickasaw, and Creek Nations and is as follows:

My Friend:

I had hopes of seeing you this spring or summer at such place as your people should think proper to meet the Commissioners of the United States to Confirm the session of land named last fall and as it struck me found the price a good one but other business will prevent me I have supposed when the Nation considered them in truth, that if the Commissioners would give them in perpotion to the price offered at Tellico Block house, that the Cherokees would relinquish thare clame to all the waters of Duck River, beleaving it would be thare interest so to do and as it will give our commissioners and government much pleasure to remove so much of the difficulty which they doubt may be caused by the clame of the Cherokees and Chickasaws to that country. Since I saw you I have had a copy of the parchment given the Chickasaws by President Washington to thare clame of land North of Tennessee, and I have seen **George Colbert** *and another Chickasaw chief who gave me the grounds for their clame, which I now think much better and stronger than I formerly had vewed it I will give you a sketch of thare clame. They say one of thare chiefs which has not been dead thirty years was the second in command in thare Nation and one that negotiated the business of the Cherokees in the case of thare boundarys, which begins on the Ohio at a point dividing the waters of the Tennessee river from the Cumberland so as to include all the waters of Duck and Elk rivers and then a direct course to the mouth of a creek empting into the Tennessee River on the South side which is called the* **flint creek** *and up that naming places between the Chickasaws and creeks, the ground of thare clame is as follows: they the Chickasaws say that when the Shawnoes lived on Cumberland and Duck rivers that war broke out between them and the Chicasaws that the Chickasaws drove them the shawnoes from those two rivers that the Shawnoes went to the North and that shortly after there was war between the Chickasaws and Cherokees, that at the construction of peace between those two nations they agreed on the boundary above mentioned—that at that time the grate body of the Cherokee Nation lived on the East of the big mountain and had a very extensive country, on the Eastern waters and the heads of the western rivers—from river to tombigby—that from those repeated wars they the Cherokees had fell back and encroached on the lands of the Chickasaws. George*

Colbert asserts that Doublehead settled at the Shoals by his permition. I assure sir that it is from true friendship I bare to you that I am so particular in giving you information and nothing can render me more satisfaction than to be of service to you or the Cherokee Nation. A matter has turned up which I did not in the least expect when I last saw you. I am with Mr. Dinsmoor appointed a Commissioner to the treaty which I suppose will commence in the month of May next. Our instructions are to push all the Chickasaw clame on the North of the Tennessee River by the instructions from the Secretary of War. The government is very anxious to prevent any disturbance between the two nations Cherokees and Chickasaws—it will give me infinite pleasure to be any ways instrumental in uniting or preventing any discord taking place between these two nations of people and I think from the acquaintance you have with Mr. Dinsmoor, you will not doubt his assistance in effecting so desirable an end. I shall sir be happy to hear from you at all times while I am

> *your sincere friend and humble Servant,*
> JAMES ROBERTSON

Ps-I expect the Cherokee Nation will send a deputation to Col. Meigs when they git reconsiled to thare one interest as expressed in thare last talk respecting the sail of land. I know that no person on earth can have a stronger desire to reconsile the disputes which are between the Cherokees and Chickasaw tribes Respecting thare clame clashing.

August 25, 1808, Chinubbee and Colberts Letter—After Doublehead's death on August 9, 1807, John D. Chisholm continued to act as an advisor to Doublehead's nephew Tahlonteskee Benge in Arkansas. He went west with the Cherokees in 1809 under the authority of President Thomas Jefferson. The Chickasaws wanted the United States Government, not only to remove all the white settlers and intruders on Doublehead's Reserve, but also remove John D. Chisholm from their country. Their formal request for Chisholm's removal is found in microcopy 208, roll 4, and number 2130. The letter from King Henderson of the Chickasaw Nation is dated August 25, 1808, is addressed to Henry Dearborn, Secretary of War, and is as follows:

We are informed that the Cherokees in 1805 sold part of our country north of the Tennessee River opposite to Muscle Shoals to the United States. We went to Muscle Shoals to meet Doublehead and his friends but they were not there as Colonel Meigs had summoned Doublehead, John D. Chisholm, and all his friends to Highwassee.

Since Doublehead's death, Chisholm acts as [agent] for Doublehead-Meigs too. When Major Thomas Lewis was agent to Cherokees, John D. Chisholm was banished from the country and went to the Creeks, Colonel Hawkins moved him from thence and he come back to the Cherokees, he then found a friend in Doublehead and he supported him till his death.

"We request as a particular favor, that you will be so good as to remove John D. Chisholm out of the Indian country. We have no doubt but government has been informed of Chisholm's character. If the government does not choose to make Chisholm quit the red peoples land, please to give us leave and we will take him out of it.

Relying on the Government of United States to remove bad white men from the red peoples country, we have not attempted to remove Chisholm , depending on the government to have done it for us – otherwise we should have done it long since."

Signed By:
Chinnabbe King et, George, William, James Colbert, and 28 others

Tennessee Land Claims

State of Tennessee—The State of Tennessee makes a complicated argument over the southern boundary of the state along the 35th latitude. Evidently, Tennessee feels it has a conflict with the Chickasaw Nation and does not have complete legal jurisdiction over their southern boundary as follows:

The next subject which presents itself for consideration, arising out of the nature of the resolution, is the right and policy of the State of Tennessee to extend her jurisdiction to the true southern boundary line of the State, as herein reported. In the disquisition of this proposition, the committee feels happy that the principle in the dubious and complicated question existing between the State of Georgia and the Cherokee Indians will not be implicated, and but for the erroneous survey and marking of a southern boundary of this State, the justness and propriety of the adoption of the measure would be most clear and manifest. If, as has been assumed in the discussion, and fully demonstrated, the true southern boundary of the State of Tennessee extends to latitude 35, then, to justify and legalize the extension of the jurisdiction of the State of Tennessee to the point, it is only necessary to establish the extinguishment of any and every prior and co-existing right, not strictly subordinate to the jurisdiction of the State of Tennessee. Previously to 1818, the tribe of Indians denominated the Chickasaws, held the usufructuary possession of the territory, now the subject-matter of action, in *obedience to the existing treaties and ordinances of the Congress of the United States. Upon the 19th October, of the year 1818, the Chickasaw nation, in council, by their chiefs, stipulated with the United States, by their commissioners Isaac Shelby and Andrew Jackson, and by solemn treaty ceded to the United States all claim or title which the said nation had to the land lying north of the boundary of the State of Tennessee, which is bounded south by the 35th degree of north latitude, and which land so ceded lies within the following boundaries: "Beginning on the Tennessee river, about thirty-five miles by water below **Colonel George Colbert's ferry**, where the 35th degree of north latitude strikes the same; thence, due west with said degree of north latitude, to where it cuts the Mississippi river, at or near the Chickasaw bluffs; thence up the said Mississippi river to the mouth of the Ohio; thence up the Ohio to the mouth of Tennessee; thence up the Tennessee river to the place of beginning."*

In the 5th article of the treaty, the two contracting parties covenanted and agreed that the line of the south boundary of the State of Tennessee, as described in the second article of this treaty, shall be ascertained and marked by commissioners appointed by the President of the United States. It is further agreed by the commissioners, that all improvements actually made by said Chickasaw Nation, which shall be found within the lands ceded by this treaty that a fair and reasonable compensation shall be paid therefor to the respective individuals having made or owned the same.

In pursuance of said article a commissioner under the appointment of the President of the United States, proceeded to mark and run said line, which line is made to run from three to four miles north of the true line, based and run upon the correct ascertainment of the true degree of the 35th degree of north latitude.

The question then presents itself, to which of the lines shall the treaty be located, in its legitimate and legal interpretation? It is covenanted, that the commissioner shall run the line, as described in the second article of the treaty;- if the same be differently run than therein authorized, it is a departure from, and a violation of the covenant, and not obligatory upon either party. To ascertain that fact, reference to the words employed, the objects described, and the legal import of those words, together with the controlling power of the objects described in the section, must be considered; and, in that consideration, the intention of the parties must have unlimited influence. At the formation of the treaty, the State of Tennessee was a member of the Union, with certain specified boundaries, circumscribing her territory, among which a line running from the Tennessee River, upon the 35th degree of north latitude, constituted her south boundary line. At the same time, and long previous, the policy of the general *government, in conformity with the interest and desire of the States in whose chartered limits were abiding Indians, was and had been to procure from such Indians a relinquishment of their title to land within the limits of those States; and, at that time, the Chickasaw Indians, one of the contracting parties, were residing within the limits of the State of Tennessee, claiming title to, and in possession of the soil. What, then, it is asked, was the intention of the contracting parties in making said treaty? Certainly, on the part of the United States, to obtain from the Indians their title to all the land lying within the limits of the State of Tennessee, and on the part of the Indians, to cede and convey all such title. In confirmation of this, a recital of a part of the second section, verbatim, is sufficient, which reads as follows: "The Chickasaw Nation of Indians cede to the United States of America, all claim or title which the said nation has to the land lying north of the south boundary of the State of Tennessee, which is bounded south by the 35th degree of north latitude." And if the section terminated here, no -doubt could arise, but that the treaty, in its construction, must be confined to the line constituting the south boundary of the State of Tennessee, whenever run according to the 35th degree of north latitude, truly ascertained. The after description of the boundaries, in the same section, it is contended, makes valid the line run and marked by Winchester. A refutation the State of Tennessee, whenever run according to the 35th descriptive words and objects used in the section, which are as follows: "Beginning on the Tennessee river, about thirty-five miles by water below **Colonel George Colbert's ferry,** where the 35th degree of north latitude strikes the same; thence due west, with said degree of north latitude, to where it cuts the Mississippi river, at or near the Chickasaw Bluff."*

*Now, here the beginning corner is located, not upon the Tennessee River at **Colonel George Colbert's Ferry**, nor at a point thirty-five miles below said ferry, but at a point upon said river, and below said ferry, where the 35th degree of north latitude strikes said river. Upon the locality and identity of this corner, no disputation can arise. From this corner, so fixed and ascertained, the line is to run due west with the said degree of north latitude, to where it cuts the Mississippi River, at or near the Chickasaw Bluffs. What are the controlling objects in the description of this line? The point of commencement being fixed upon the Tennessee River, at the place where the 35th degree of north latitude strikes the same, it is most clear, the continuation of said line, in obedience to the description, must be run due west from that point, with the said degree of latitude, to where it cuts the Mississippi River, irrespective of the Chickasaw bluffs, which call is deemed superfluous. By this construction, the object of the treaty is attained in the full satisfaction of the contracting parties, and reciprocal justice awarded. If then the Indians, from the terms of said treaty, have ceded to the United States all their interest and title within the limits of the State of Tennessee, the objection arising from their right to the extent of the municipal jurisdiction of the State over the*

170

land, ceases to operate. At the time of executing the treaty, the south line of the State had not been extended further west than the Tennessee, by actual survey; but its certainty and fixidity was such, to the Mississippi River, that in law its potential existence would operate to control the construction of the treaty, in the location of its line, and, by consequence, when the south boundary line of the State should be extended by correct admeasurement and survey, and actually established, it would be the true base line of the treaty. Nor will the influence of the principle lose its efficiency, because, posterior to the ratification of the treaty, and anterior to the enactment of the laws of Congress of 1818, and of the State of Tennessee of 1819, a demarkation of the line by an agent of the United States, predicated upon an erroneous survey and an incorrect latitude, fixed the boundary line from three to four miles north of the true latitudinal line. For if so, then by parity of reason and principle, notwithstanding the treaty called for and was predicated upon the 35th degree of north latitude, as the southern line of the State of Tennessee, had the same agent of the United States run and marked the line a degree south of the true degree. Tennessee would be entitled to all the land north of that degree.

It is conceived, however, as a self-evident proposition, that if the true dividing line between the States of Mississippi and Tennessee was the 35th degree of north latitude, any departure from that point in the location of the line, by an agent in whose appointment and subsequent action they had no agency or concurrence, cannot operate to change its true position, and more especially as the consequence would be to increase or diminish the constitutionally fixed dimensions of the two States. And if so, it is conceived as an equally clear, self-evident proposition, that the United States, in appropriating the soil, in satisfaction and fulfillment of the treaty of 1834, with the Chickasaw nation, cannot act upon the incorrectly surveyed line, denominated the Winchester line, but are compelled in justice to the State of Tennessee, to fix the base line for operations at the true degree of the 35th degree of north latitude. For if the 35th degree of north latitude was the true boundary line when the State of Tennessee, in her pupilage, constituted a part of the State of North Carolina, and if in the cession act of 1780, North Carolina ceded the soil to the United States, reserving to herself the power and right to have full and complete satisfaction made of all the land claims specified in the treaty, then, as the necessary and legal consequence of the treaty, the United States is inhibited from making any disposition of the soil repugnant to, or destructive of those reserved rights. Then the case presents itself, of a section of country to which an original and ultimately abiding title has been demonstrated to exist in the State of Tennessee, and to which the usufructuary title of the Indians has, for a full and valuable consideration, been obtained, and from which, by an amicable adjustment, they have voluntarily moved. And the question is propounded, can the State *of Tennessee properly take and exercise jurisdiction over said district of country encompassed in her chartered limits? To which the committee reply, that the extension of the jursidiction of the State of Tennessee over the specified territory, is in accordance with, and approvement of the fundamental principles of the federal association* (Garrett, et.al., 1900).

Other Chickasaw Land Claims

Bear Creek—In 1774 the Chickasaws refused the Henderson Land Company access to the mouth of Occochapo Creek (present day Bear Creek). After the treaty of 1816, most of the Chickasaws land was ceded to the United States. *Several Indian towns, known as Bear Creek Villages, are on the creek of that name in the western part of the county as early as the first part of the eighteenth century. Some students identify them as Cherokee, but their tribal relation is not known with certainty.*

All that part of Colbert County lying east of Big Bear Creek was claimed both by the Chickasaws and the Cherokees. By the treaty of September 14, 1816, the Cherokees ceded to the United States all their territory south of the Tennessee River extending as far west as Big Bear Creek. Six days afterwards, September 20, the Chickasaws ceded all the lands claimed by them south of the Tennessee River and east of Caney Creek, which is in Colbert County. The two Indian tribal claims thus overlapped each other. As there were no Chickasaw settlements at that time east of Caney Creek, it must have been regarded by the Chickasaws as their eastern boundary, and regardless of the Cherokee cession, this Chickasaw ownership of the territory west of Caney Creek was admitted by the United States, and their title to it was finally extinguished by the treaty of Pontotoc Creek, October 20, 1832 (Owen, 1921).

Tennessee River—After the conflict with the Shawnees ended, the Chickasaws moved east to the Chickasaw Old Fields on Chickasaw Island in the Tennessee River south of present-day Huntsville, Alabama. According to Professor Henry Sale Halbert (January 14, 1837-May 8, 1916), "*around the mid 1700's, the Chickasaw's formed the settlement in the Chickasaw Old Fields, which angered the Cherokees very much against their former allies. A great battle was fought in the Chickasaw village in 1769, in which the Chickasaw were victors, but their victory was gained at such a great loss that they retreated from the country, but the Chickasaw's continued their claims to lands on both sides of the Tennessee River.*"

According to Owen (1921), *the Cherokees formed no settlements on the Tennessee River until about 1770. There were four Cherokee villages in Colbert County during the last quarter of the eighteenth century. Beginning on the river, the first was Doublehead's Village, founded about 1790, and situated a short distance above the place where Geoprge Colbert subsequently established his ferry. A large spring, still known as Doublehead's Spring marks the site of this village. The second, was Oka Kapassa, founded about 1780, the site of which is ineluded in the present city of Tuscumbia. Oka Kapassa signifies "cold water" in the Choctaw-Chickasaw language, and was evidently the name given to the large spring in Tuscumbia. The name shows that the locality was well known to the Chickasaws, who may have had a village or hunting camp there prior to Cherokee occupancy. The third was a small village located at the foot of Muscle Shoals. The fourth was a larger village, or settlement, at the mouth of Town Creek extending for a mile and a half up and down the Tennessee River, and about the same distance southward from the river. It was from this village that Town Creek derived its name.*

A large mound near the lock on Colbert Shoals Canal, Tennessee River, near Riverton, survives, originally one of a group of three. One was removed by the Northern Alabama Rail Road and the other by Confederate troops during the War, in order to mount batteries there. At the mouth of Colbert Creek on Tennessee River, are two town sites, and a small burial mound. One mile below the mouth of the creek is another site. Some few earthenware vessels of a character differing from those found elsewhere have been discovered here. A town-site and cemetery near the mouth of Cane Creek, on property of R. M. Garner, show burials of a flexed type, but differing from any heretofore met with in the State. The Cherokees claimed to be the very first settlers in the Tennessee Valley, and the mounds and remains above are doubtless to be ascribed to them.

Natchez Trace—*George Colbert and Levi Colbert, for whom the county was named, both lived in Colbert County on the Natchez Trace, which crossed the Tennessee River at Colbert's Ferry. However, George Colbert did not live continuously at the ferry, but spent the greater part of his time at his other home, on Wolf Creek, four miles west of Booneville, Mississippi. Levi Colbert's home was on the Natchez Trace, at the crossing on Big Bear Creek. These two Colbert brothers were not real Chickasaw chiefs. On account of their knowledge of English and their superior intelligence they were appointed by the Chickasaw King to act as principal chiefs in all matters connected with the United States Government. George Colbert died in 1839, in the Chickasaw Nation west; Levi died at Buzzard Roost in the spring of 1834, while on his* way to Washington City on some official business. *Another brother, James Colbert, lived 30 or 40 miles further down the Tennessee* (Owen, 1921).

Boundary Treaties—In the Chickasaw Boundary Treaty of January 10, 1786, the government established a boundary they viewed as belonging to the Chickasaw people; however, according to Phil Hawkins, Jr., the Chickasaws and Cherokees did not have clearly defined borders in the area along the Muscle Shoals: *In the treaty of this date with the Chickasaws the lands allotted them eastwardly shall be the lands allotted to the Choctaws and Cherokees to live and hunt on. In the conference which took place between the commissioners of the United States and the Chickasaws and Cherokees, it was apparent that their claims conflicted with each other on the ridge dividing the waters of Cumberland from those of Duck River and around to the Chickasaw Old Town Creek on Tennessee, thence southwardly, leaving the mountains above the Muscle Shoals on the south side of the river, and to a large stone or flat rock, where the Choctaw line joined with the Chickasaws. The journal of occurrences at the time was lodged with the papers of the old Congress, and probably was transferred to the office of Secretary of State.*

On the 7th of January, 1806, in a convention between the United States and Cherokees, on the part of the former by Mr. Dearborn, the United States engaged to use their best endeavors to fix a boundary between the Cherokees and Chickasaws, beginning at the mouth of Caney Creek, near the lower part of the Muscle Shoals, and to run up the said creek to its head, and in a direct line from thence to the flat stone or rock, the old corner boundary, the line between the Creeks and Cherokees east of Coosa River (Powell, et. al., 1887). The Chickasaws did not recognize the 1806 boundary and, at the death of Doublehead, demanded that the intruders on their lands at the Muscle Shoals be removed.

The Chickasaw stronghold was the upper Tombigbee River towns in northeastern Mississippi where they had defeated French incursions into their territory on three separate occasions by the mid 1700's. The stronghold of the Chickasaw in the upper Tombigbee River Valley lasted from the time before Desoto in 1540 all the way to Chickasaw removal in 1837.

Shortly after the fight with the Cherokee in 1769, the Chickasaws moved west from the Chickasaw Old Fields beyond Caney Creek in the western portion of present-day Colbert County, Alabama. As the Chickasaws moved down the Tennessee River toward Mississippi, Doublehead and his followers moved into and occupied the Muscle Shoals. After conflicts over the Muscle Shoals ceased, the newly established United

States government recognized the Chickasaw land claims east to Chickasaw Island in the middle of the river and north along the Flint River into the State of Tennessee encompassing the upper drainage of Elk River. From the Chickasaw Old Fields in the Tennessee River to the south, the Chickasaw claims followed the Huntsville Meridian to the Tennessee Divide, and then west along the High Town Path to Haleyville, Alabama. The boundary line then ran south along the Byler Ridge that separates the waters of the Warrior River to the east and the waters of the Tombigbee River Drainage to the west, and then due west into Mississippi as authorized by the Chickasaw Boundary Treaty of January 10, 1786, as seen in the map above; however, Doublehead and his Chickamauga warriors also claimed the area by occupation.

The Chickasaw were the first tribe of the Great Bend to abandon the Chickamauga confederacy in January 1781. At this time, the great Chickasaw Chief Piomingo and General James Robertson of the Cumberland settlements agreed to terms of peace. However, a few Chickasaws remained loyal to the Chickamauga confederacy and lived at Doublehead's Town near Brown's Ferry. These loyal Chickasaws continued to make raids with Doublehead and the Chickamauga.

Chickasaw Treaties

The following treaties were compiled and edited by Charles J. Kappler for the Government Printing Office in Washington, D.C. Note that references to the sons of James Logan Colbert are identified in bold print.

1786—The 1786 treaty with the Chickasaws recognizes the land claims of the Chickasaw Nation and is the only one that does not mention the Colberts. At the time of the treaty, Piomingo was the chief of the Chickasaws and signed the treaty; but after his death George Colbert and some of his brothers are found on the treaties.

Treaty with the Chickasaw, 1786

a.k.a Treaty of Hopewell, January 10, 1786, 7 Stat. 24.

Articles of a treaty, concluded at Hopewell, on the Keowee River, near Seneca Old Town, between Benjamin Hawkins, Andrew Pickens, and Joseph Martin, Commissioners Plenipotentiary of the United States of America, of the one Part; and Piomingo, Head Warrior and First Minister of the Chickasaw Nation; Mingatushka,

one of the leading Chiefs; and; Latopoia, first beloved Man of the said Nation,
Commissioners Plenipotentiary of all the Chickasaws, of the other Part.

The Commissioners Plenipotentiary of the United States of America gives peace to the Chickasaw Nation, and receives them into the favor and protection of the said States, on the following conditions:

ARTICLE I

The Commissioners Plenipotentiary of the Chickasaw Nation shall restore all the prisoners, citizens of the United States, to their entire liberty, if any there be in the Chickasaw Nation. They shall also restore all the Negroes, and all other property taken during the late war from the citizens, if any there be in the Chickasaw Nation, to such person, and at such time and place, as the Commissioners of the United States of America shall appoint.

ARTICLE II

The Commissioners Plenipotentiary of the Chickasaws, do hereby acknowledge the tribes and the towns of the Chickasaw Nation, to be under the protection of the United States of America, and of no other sovereign whosoever.

ARTICLE III

The boundary of the lands hereby allotted to the Chickasaw Nation to live and hunt on, within the limits of the United States of America, is, and shall be the following. viz. Beginning on the ridge that divides the waters running into the Cumberland, from those running into the Tennessee, at a point in a line to be run north-east, which shall strike the Tennessee at the mouth of Duck River; thence running westerly along the said ridge, till it shall strike the Ohio; thence down the southern banks thereof to the Mississippi; thence down the same, to the Choctaw line or Natchez district; thence along the said line, or the line of the district eastwardly as far as the Chickasaws claimed, and lived and hunted on, the twenty-ninth of November, one thousand seven hundred and eighty-two.

Thence the said boundary eastwardly, shall be the lands allotted to the Choctaws and Cherokees to live and hunt on, and the lands at present in the possession of the Creeks; saving and reserving for the establishment of a trading post, a tract or parcel of land to be laid out at the lower port of the Muscle Shoals, at the mouth of Ocochappo, in a circle, the diameter of which shall be five miles on the _____ river, which post, and the lands annexed thereto, shall be to the use and under the government of the United States of America.

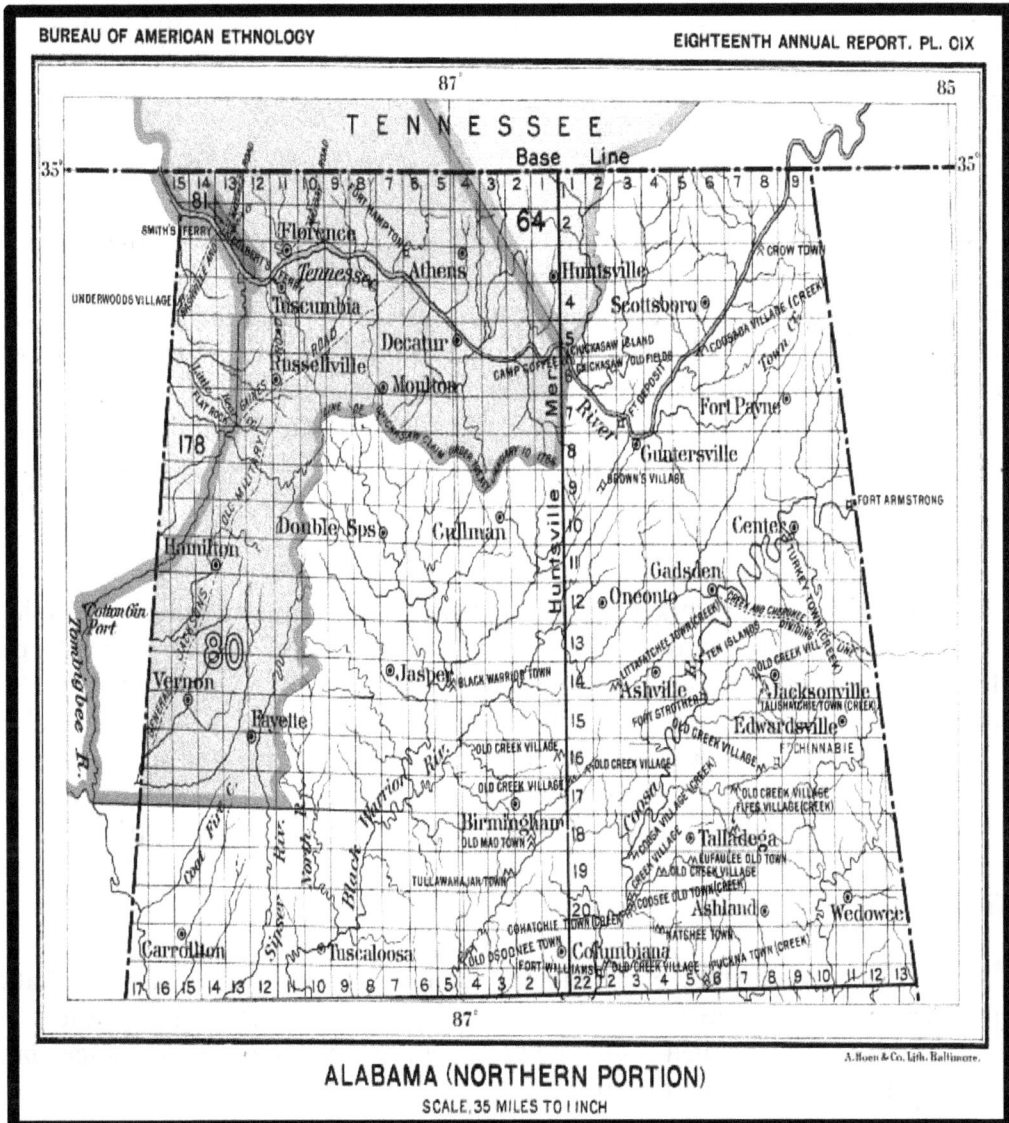

Boundaries of the Chickasaw Nation
Northwest Alabama (shaded area)
January 10, 1786

ARTICLE IV

If any citizen of the United States, or other person not being an Indian, shall attempt to settle on any of the lands hereby allotted to the Chickasaws to live and hunt on, such person shall forfeit the protection of the United States of America, and the Chickasaws may punish him or not as they please.

ARTICLE V

If any Indian or Indians, or persons residing among them, or who shall take refuge in their nation, shall commit a robbery or murder, or other capital crime, on any citizen of the United States, or person under their protection, the tribe to which such offender or offenders may belong, or the nation, shall be bound to deliver him or them up to be punished according to the ordinances of the United States in Congress assembled: Provided, that the punishment shall not be greater, than if the robbery or murder, or other capital crime, had been committed by a citizen on a citizen.

ARTICLE VI

If any citizen of the United States of America, or person under their protection shall commit a robbery or murder, or other capital crime, on any Indian, such offender or offenders shall be punished in the same manner as if the robbery or murder or other capital crime had been committed on a citizen of the United States of America; and the punishment shall be in presence of some of the Chickasaws, if any will attend at the time and place, and that they may have an opportunity so to do, due notice, if practicable of such intended punishment, shall be sent to some one of the tribes.

ARTICLE VII

It is understood that the punishment of the innocent under the idea of retaliation is unjust, and shall not be practiced on either side, except where there is a manifest violation of this treaty; and then it shall be preceded, first by a demand of justice, and if refused, then by a declaration of hostilities.

ARTICLE VIII

For the benefit and comfort of the Indians, and for the prevention of injuries or oppressions on the part of the citizens or Indians, the (The name of the river is not in the original.) United States in Congress assembled shall have the sole and exclusive right of regulating the trade with the Indians, and managing all their affairs in such manner as they think proper.

ARTICLE IX

Until the pleasure of Congress is known respecting the eighth article, all traders, citizens of the United States, shall have liberty to go to any of the tribes or towns of the Chickasaws to trade with them, and they shall be protected in their persons and property, and kindly treated.

ARTICLE X

The said Indians shall give notice to the citizens of the United States of America, of any designs which they may know or suspect to be formed in any neighboring tribe or by any person whosoever, against the peace, trade or interests of the United States of America.

ARTICLE XI

The hatchet shall be forever buried, and the peace given by the United States of America, and friendship re-established between the said States on the one part, and the Chickasaw Nation on the other part shall be universal, and the contracting parties shall use their utmost endeavors to maintain the peace given as aforesaid, and friendship re-established. In witness of all and every-thing herein contained, between the said States and Chickasaws, we, their underwritten commissioners, by virtue of our full powers, have signed this definitive treaty, and have caused our seals to be hereunto affixed.

Done at Hopewell, on the Keowee, this tenth day of January, in the year of our Lord one thousand seven hundred and eighty-six.

Benjamin Hawkins, [L. S.]
And'w. Pickens, [L. S.]
Jos. Martin, [L. S.]
Piomingo, his x mark, [L. S.]
Mingatushka, his x mark, [L. S.]
Latopoia, his x mark. [L. S.]

Witness:
Wm. Blount,
Wm. Hazard,
Sam. Taylor,
James Cole, Sworn Interpreter

1801—In the treaty of 1801, both George Colbert and William Colbert signed the document; notably absent was Piomingo. The treaty actually authorizes the Natchez Trace and provides for the Chickasaws to operate ferrys along the route. George Colbert got the right to operate the ferry at the Natchez Trace crossing of the Tennessee River; he also received the oversight of the Duck River Ferry that was actually operated by John Gordon.

Treaty with the Chickasaw, 1801

October 24, 1801. 7 Stat. 65. Ratified, May 1, 1802. Proclaimed, May 4, 1802.

A treaty, of reciprocal advantages and mutual convenience between the United States of America and the Chickasaws.

The President of the United States of America, by James Wilkinson brigadier general in the service of the United States, Benjamin Hawkins of North Carolina and Andrew Pickens, of South Carolina, commissioners of the United States, who are vested with full powers, and the Mingo, principal men and warriors of the Chickasaw Nation, representing the said nation, have agreed to the following articles.

ARTICLE 1

The Mingo, principal men and warriors of the Chickasaw Nation of Indians, give leave and permission to the President of the United States of America, to lay out, open and make a convenient wagon road through their land between the settlements of Mero District in the State of Tennessee, and those of Natchez in the Mississippi Territory, in such way and manner as he may deem proper; and the same shall be a high way for the citizens of the United States, and the Chickasaws. The Chickasaws shall appoint two discreet men to serve as assistants, guides or pilots, during the time of laying out and opening the road, under the direction of the officer charged with that duty, who shall have a reasonable compensation for their service: Provided always, that the necessary ferries over the water courses crossed by the said road shall be held and deemed to be the property of the Chickasaw Nation.

ARTICLE 2

The commissioners of the United States give to the Mingo of the Chickasaws, and the deputation of that nation, goods to the value of seven hundred dollars, to compensate him and them and their attendants for the expense and inconvenience they may have sustained by their respectful and friendly attention to the President of the United States of America, and to the request made to them in his name to permit the opening of the road. And as the persons, towns, villages, lands, hunting grounds, and other rights and property of the Chickasaws, as set forth in the treaties or stipulations heretofore entered into between the contracting parties, more especially in and by a certificate of the President of the United States of America, under their seal of the first of July 1794, are in the peace and under the protection of the United States, the commissioners of the United States do hereby further agree, that the President of the United States of America, shall take such measures from time to time, as he may deem proper, to assist the Chickasaws to preserve entire all their rights against the encroachments of unjust neighbors, of which he shall be the judge, and also to preserve and perpetuate friendship and brotherhood between the white people and the Chickasaws.

ARTICLE 3

The commissioners of the United States may, if they deem it advisable, proceed immediately to carry the first article into operation; and the treaty shall take effect and be obligatory on the contracting parties, as soon as the same shall have been ratified by the President of the United States of America, by and with the advice and consent of the Senate of the United States.

In testimony whereof, we, the plenipotentiaries, have hereunto subscribed our names and affixed our seals, at Chickasaw Bluffs, the twenty-fourth of October, 1801.

James Wilkinson, Brigadier General, [L. S.]	*Opiehoomuh, his x mark, [L. S.]*
	Olohtohopoie, his x mark, [L. S.]
Benjamin Hawkins, [L. S.]	*Minkenattauhau, his x mark, [L. S.]*
And. Pickens, [L. S.]	*Tuskkoopoie, his x mark, [L. S.]*
Chinmimbe Mingo, his x mark, [L. S.]	*William Glover, his x mark, [L. S.]*
Immuttauhaw, his x mark, [L. S.]	*Thomas Brown, his x mark, [L. S.]*
Chumaube, his x mark, [L. S.]	**William Colbert**, *W. C. [L. S.]*
George Colbert, *his x mark, [L. S.]*	*Mooklushopoie, his x mark, [L. S.]*
William Mcgillivray, his x mark, [L. S.]	*Opoieolauhtau, his x mark, [L. S.]*

Teschoolauhtau, his x mark, [L. S.]
Teschoolauptau, his x mark, [L. S.]
James Underwood, his x mark, [L. S.]
Samuel Mitchell, agent to the
Chickasaws,
Malcolm McGee, his x signature,
interpreter to the Chickasaws,

William R. Bootes, captain Third
regiment and aid de camp,
J. B. Wallach, lieutenant and aid de
camp,
Jn. Wilson, lieutenant Third Regiment

1805—In the 1805 treaty, the Chickasaws agree to give up a large tract of land in order to pay their debts; George Colbert receives $1,000.00 for services rendered to the Chickasaw Nation. Both George and Levi Colbert signed the treaty of 1805; for some reason, William Colbert did not sign this treaty.

Treaty with the Chickasaw, 1805

July 23, 1805, 7 Stat., 89, Ratified May 22, 1807, Proclaimed May 23, 1807.

Articles of arrangement made and concluded in the Chickasaw country, between James Robertson and Silas Dinsmoor, commissioners of the United States of the one part, and the Mingo chiefs and warriors of the Chickasaw Nation of Indians on the other part.

ARTICLE 1

WHEREAS the Chickasaw Nation of Indians have been for some time embarrassed by heavy debts due to their merchants and traders, and being destitute of funds to effect important improvements in their country, they have agreed and do hereby agree to cede to the United States, and forever quit claim to the tract of country included within the following bounds, to wit: beginning on the left bank of Ohio, at the point where the present Indian boundary adjoins the same, thence down the left bank of Ohio to the Tennessee River, thence up the main channel of the Tennessee River to the mouth of Duck River; thence up the left bank of Duck River to the Columbian highway or road leading from Nashville to Natchez, thence along the said road to the ridge dividing the waters running into Duck River from those running into Buffalo River, thence easterly along the said ridge to the great ridge dividing the waters running into the main Tennessee River from those running into Buffalo River near the main source of Buffalo River, thence in a direct line to the Great Tennessee River near the

Chickasaw old fields or eastern point of the Chickasaw claim on that river; thence northwardly to the great ridge dividing the waters running into the Tennessee from those running into Cumberland River, so as to include all the waters running into Elk River, thence along the top of the said great ridge to the place of beginning: reserving a tract of one mile square adjoining to, and below the mouth of Duck River on the Tennessee, for the use of the chief O'Koy or Tishumastubbee.

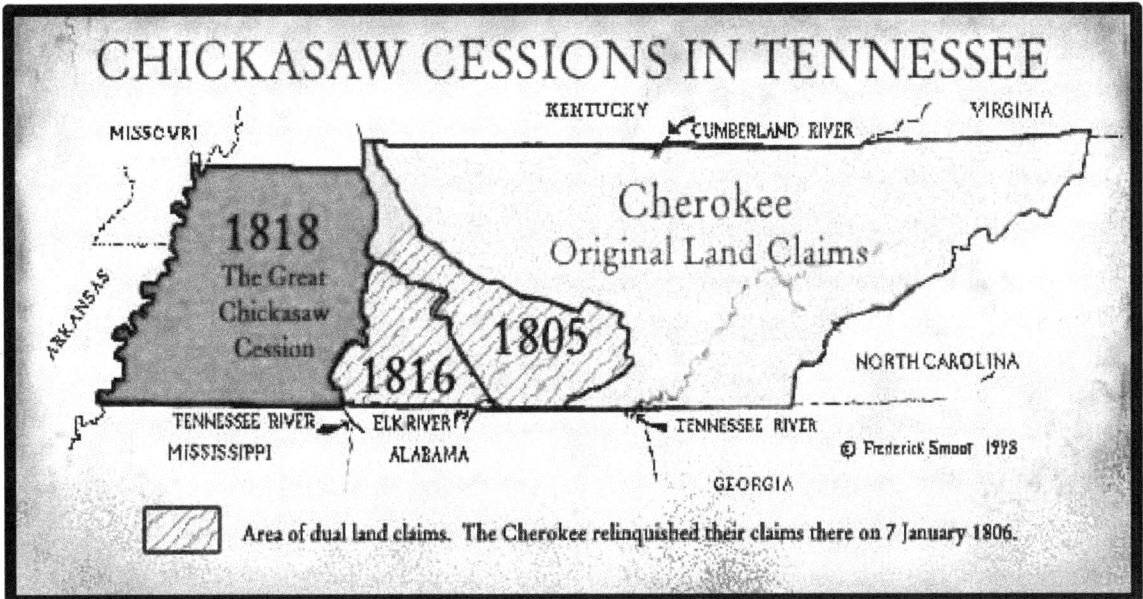

CHICKASAW CESSIONS IN TENNESSEE

ARTICLE 2

The United States on their part, and in consideration of the above cession, agree to make the following payments, to wit: Twenty thousand dollars for the use of the nation at large, and for the payment of the debts due to their merchants and traders; and to **George Colbert** and O'Koy two thousand dollars, that is, to each one thousand dollars. This sum is granted to them at the request of the national council for services rendered their nation, and is to be subject to their individual order, witnessed by the resident agent; also to Chinubbee Mingo, the king of the nation, an annuity of one hundred dollars, during his natural life, granted as a testimony of his personal worth and friendly disposition. All the above payments are to be made in specie.

ARTICLE 3

In order to preclude forever all disputes relative to the boundary mentioned in the first section, it is hereby stipulated, that the same shall be ascertained and marked by a commissioner or commissioners on the part of the United States, accompanied by such person as the Chickasaws may choose, so soon as the Chickasaws shall have thirty days' notice of the time and place, at which the operation is to commence: and the United States will pay the person appointed on the part of the Chickasaws two dollars per day during his actual attendance on that service.

ARTICLE 4

It is hereby agreed on the part of the United States, that from and after the ratification of these articles, no settlement shall be made by any citizen, or permitted by the government of the United States, on that part of the present cession included between the present Indian boundary and the Tennessee, and between the Ohio and a line drawn due north from the mouth of Buffalo to the ridge dividing the waters of Cumberland from those of the Tennessee River, to the term of three years.

ARTICLE 5

The articles now stipulated will be considered as permanent additions to the treaties now in force between the contracting parties, as soon as they shall have been ratified by the President of the United States of America, by and with the advice and consent of the Senate of the said United States.

In witness of all and everything herein determined, the parties have hereunto interchangeably set their hands and seals, in the Chickasaw country, this twenty-third day of July, in the year of our Lord one thousand eight hundred and five, and of the independence of the United States of America the thirtieth.

Commissioners:
James Robertson [L. S.]
Silas Dinsmoor, [L. S.]
Chiefs and warriors:
Chenubbee Mingo, the king, his mark,[L. S.]
George Colbert, *his x mark, [L. S.]*
O Koy, his x mark, [L. S.]

Tiphu Mashtubbee, his x mark, [L. S.]
Choomobbee, his x mark, [L. S.]
Mingo Mattaha, his x mark, [L. S.]
E. Mattaha Meko, his x mark, [L. S.]
Wm. McGillivry, his x mark, [L. S.]
Tisshoo Hooluhta, his x mark, [L. S.]
Levi Colbert, *his x mark, [L. S.]*

Signed, sealed, and interchanged, in presence of *Thomas Augustine Claiborne, secretary to the commissioners, Samuel Mitchell, United States agent to the Chickasaw Nation, John McKee, R. Chamberlin, second lieutenant Second Regiment Infantry, W. P. Anderson, of Tennessee.*

Sworn interpreters
Malcolm McGee, his x mark,   *Christopher Olney,*
John Pitchlynn,   *Wm. Tyrrell,*

1816—In the Turkey Town Treaty of 1816, the Chickasaws give up claims to a large tract of land in Tennessee and Alabama; the Alabama section includes land east of Caney Creek, south to Cotton Gin Port, and then to the Choctaw boundary. The Chickasaws were paid $120, 000.00 for the land while the Cherokees got $60,000.00 due to overlapping claims. Levi Colbert who lived at Cotton Gin Port received $4,500.00 for improvements made on the land. George and Levi Colbert got land set aside for their particular use; the land was to go to the heirs of the Colberts. Levi received $150.00, George and James Colbert received $100.00, and William Colbert received $100.00 annuity for life. All four Colbert brothers mentioned above signed the treaty.

Treaty with the Chickasaw, 1816

September 20, 1816, 7 Stat., 150 Proclamation, Dec. 30. 1816

To settle all territorial controversies, and to perpetuate that peace and harmony which has long happily subsisted between the United States and Chickasaw Nation, the president of the United States of America, by major general Andrew Jackson, general David Meriwether, and Jesse Franklin, esquire on the one part, and the whole Chickasaw Nation, in council assembled, on the other, have agreed on the following articles, which when ratified by the president, with the advice and consent of the senate of the United States, shall be binding on all parties:

ARTICLE 1

Peace and friendship are hereby firmly established, and perpetuated, between the United States of America and Chickasaw Nation.

ARTICLE 2

The Chickasaw Nation cede to the United States (with the exception of such reservations as shall hereafter be specified) all right or title to lands on the north side of the Tennessee River, and relinquish all claim to territory on the south side of said river, and east of a line commencing at the mouth of Caney creek running up said creek to its source, thence a due south course to the ridge path, or commonly called Gaines's Road, along said road southwestwardly to a point on the Tombigby River, well known by the name of the Cotton Gin port, and down the west bank of the Tombigby to the Choctaw boundary.

ARTICLE 3

In consideration of the relinquishment of claim, and cession of lands, made in the preceding article, the commissioners agree to allow the Chickasaw Nation twelve thousand dollars per annum for ten successive years, and four thousand five hundred dollars to be paid in sixty days after the ratification of this treaty into the hands of **Levi Colbert**, as a compensation for any improvements which individuals of the Chickasaw Nation may have had on the lands surrendered; that is to say, two thousand dollars for improvements on the east side of the Tombigby, and two thousand five hundred dollars for improvements on the north side of the Tennessee River.

Chickasaw Land Claims after 1816 Turkey Town Treaty

ARTICLE 4

The commissioners agree that the following tracts of land shall be reserved to the Chickasaw Nation:

1. One tract of land for the use of **Colonel George Colbert** and heirs, and which is thus described by said Colbert: "Beginning on the north bank of the Tennessee River, at a point that, running north four miles, will include a big spring, about half way between his ferry and the mouth of Cypress, it being a spring that a large cow-path crosses its branch near where a cypress tree is cut down; thence westwardly to a point, four miles from the Tennessee river, and standing due north of a point on the north bank of the river, three [four] miles below his ferry on the Tennessee River, and up the meanders of said river to the beginning point."

2. A tract of land two miles square on the north bank of 'the Tennessee River, and at its junction with Beach creek, for the use of Appassan Tubby and heirs.

3. A tract of land one mile square, on the north side of the Tennessee river, for the use of John McCleish and heirs, the said tract to be so run as to include the said McCleish's settlement and improvements on the north side of Buffalo Creek.

4. Two tracts of land, containing forty acres each, on the south side of the Tennessee River, and about two and a half miles below the Cotton Gin port, on the Tombigby River, which tracts of land will be pointed out by **Major Levi Colbert**, and for the use of said Colbert and heirs.

It is stipulated that the above reservations shall appertain to the Chickasaw nation only so long as they shall be occupied, cultivated, or used, by the present proprietors or heirs and in the event of all or either of said tracts of land, so reserved, being abandoned by the present proprietors or heirs, each tract or tracts of land, so abandoned, shall revert to the United States as a portion of that territory ceded by the second article of this treaty.

ARTICLE 5

The two contracting parties covenant and agree that the line on the south side of the Tennessee River, as described in the second article of this treaty, shall be ascertained and marked by commissioners to be appointed by the president of the United States; that the marks shall be bold; trees to be blazed on both sides of the line, and the fore and aft trees to be marked with the letters U. S. That the commissioners shall be attended by two persons to be designated by the Chickasaw Nation, and that the said nation shall have due and seasonable notice when said operation is to be commenced.

ARTICLE 6

In consideration of the conciliatory disposition evinced, during the negotiation of this treaty, by the Chickasaw chiefs and warriors, but more particularly as a manifestation of the friendship and liberality of the president of the United States, the commissioners agree to give, on the ratification of this treaty, to Chinnubby, king of the Chickasaws, to Tishshominco, William McGilvery, Arpasarshtubby, Samuel Scely, James Brown, **Levi Colbert**, Ickaryoucullaha, George Pettygrove, Immartarharmicko, Chickasaw chiefs, and to Malcolm M'Gee, interpreter, one hundred and fifty dollars each, in goods or cash, as may be preferred and to major William Glover, **C**olonel **George Colbert**, capt. Rabbitt, Hoparyeahoummar, Immoukeloursharhoparyea, Hoparyea, Houllartir, Tushkerhopoyyea, Hoparyreahoummar, jun. Immoukelusharhopoyyea, **James Colbert**, Coweamarthlar, and Iilnachouwarhopoyyea, military leaders, one hundred dollars each; and, as a particular mark of distinction and favor for his long services and faithful adherence to the United States government, the commissioners agree to allow to **General William Colbert** an annuity of one hundred dollars for and during his life.

ARTICLE 7

"Whereas the chiefs and warriors of the Chickasaw Nation have found, from experience, that the crowd of peddlers, who are constantly traversing their nation from one end to the other, is of a serious disadvantage to the nation; that serious misunderstandings and disputes frequently take place, as well as frauds, which are often practiced on the ignorant and uninformed of the nation, therefore it is agreed by the commissioners on the part of the government, and the chiefs of the nation, that no more licenses shall be granted by the agent of the Chickasaws to entitle any person or traffic merchandise in said nation; and that any person or persons, whomsoever, of the white people, who shall bring goods and sell them in the nation, contrary to this article, shall forfeit the whole of his or their goods, one half to the nation and the other half to the government of the United States; in all cases where this article is violated, and the goods are taken or seized, they shall be delivered up to the agent, who shall hear the testimony and judge accordingly." This article was presented to the commissioners by the chiefs and warriors of the Chickasaw Nation, and by their particular solicitation embraced in this treaty.

In testimony whereof, the said commissioners and undersigned chiefs and warriors have set their hands and seals. Done at the Chickasaw council house, this twentieth day of September, in the year of our Lord one thousand eight hundred and sixteen.

Andrew Jackson, [L. S.]
D. Meriwether, [L. S.]
J. Franklin, [L. S.]
Chinnubby, King, his x mark, [L. S.]
Tishshomingo, his x mark, [L. S.]
William McGillivray, his x mark, [L. S.]
Arpasarhtubby, his x mark, [L. S.]
Samuel Seeley, his x mark, [L. S.]
James Brown, his x mark, [L. S.]
Levi Colbert, his x mark, [L. S.]
Ickaryoucuttaha, his x mark, [L. S.]
George Pettygrove, his x mark, [L. S.]
Immartarharmicco, his x mark, [L. S.]
Major General William Colbert, his x mark, [L. S.]
Major William Glover, his x mark, [L. S.]
Major George Colbert, his x mark, [L. S.]

Captain Rabbit, his x mark, [L. S.]
Hopoyeahoummar, his x mark, [L. S.]
Immouklusharhopoyea, his x mark, [L. S.]
Hopoyeahoullarter, his x mark, [L. S.]
Tushkarhopoyea, his x mark, [L. S.]
Hopoyeahoummar, jr., his x mark, [L. S.]
Immouklusharhopyea, his x mark, [L. S.]
James Colbert, his x mark, [L. S.]
Coweamarthtar, his x mark, [L. S.]
Illachonwarhopoyea, his x mark, [L. S.]
Witness:
James Gadsden, secretary,
William Cocke,
John Rhea,
Malcolm McGee,
James Colbert, interpreter

1818—The 1818 treaty is known as the Great Chickasaw Cession; the treaty gave up claims to a large tract of land in west Tennessee and Kentucky between the Tennessee River and the Mississippi River. The Chickasaws were paid $300,000.00 over fifteen years for the land; William Colbert's debt of $1,115.00 was paid to John Gordon, and David Smith was paid $2,000.00 for providing 45 soldiers to the Chickasaws. The Chickasaws got claims to a four square mile tract of land containing a salt lick near the Sandy branch of the Tennessee River. Several Chickasaws got compensation; James Colbert got paid $1,089.00 as an interpreter, Levi Colbert and others got $150.00, George and James Colbert along with others got $100.00. William, Levi, George, and James Colbert signed the treaty.

Treaty with the Chickasaw, 1818

October 19, 1818. 7 Stat., 192. | Proclamation, Jan. 7, 1819.

Treaty with the Chickasaws, to settle all territorial controversies, and to remove all ground of complaint or dissatisfaction, that might arise to interrupt the peace and harmony which have so long and so happily existed between the United States of America and the Chickasaw Nation of Indians, James Monroe, President of the said United States, by Isaac Shelby and Andrew Jackson, of the one part, and the whole Chickasaw Nation, by their chiefs, head men, and warriors, in full council assembled, of the other part, have agreed on the following articles; which, when ratified by the President and Senate of the United States of America, shall form a treaty binding on all parties.

ARTICLE 1

Peace and friendship are hereby firmly established and made perpetual, between the United States of America and the Chickasaw Nation of Indians.

ARTICLE 2

To obtain the object of the foregoing article, the Chickasaw Nation of Indians cede to the United States of America, (with the exception of such reservation as shall be hereafter mentioned,) all claim or title which the said nation has to the land lying north of the south boundary of the State of Tennessee, which is bounded south by the thirty-fifth degree of north latitude, and which lands, hereby ceded, lies within the following boundary, viz: Beginning on the Tennessee river, about thirty-five miles, by water, below **Colonel George Colbert's** ferry, where the thirty-fifth degree of north latitude strikes the same; thence, due west, with said degree of north latitude, to where it cuts the Mississippi River at or near the Chickasaw Bluffs; thence, up the said Mississippi River, to the mouth of the Ohio; thence, up the Ohio River, to the mouth of Tennessee River; thence, up the Tennessee River, to the place of beginning.

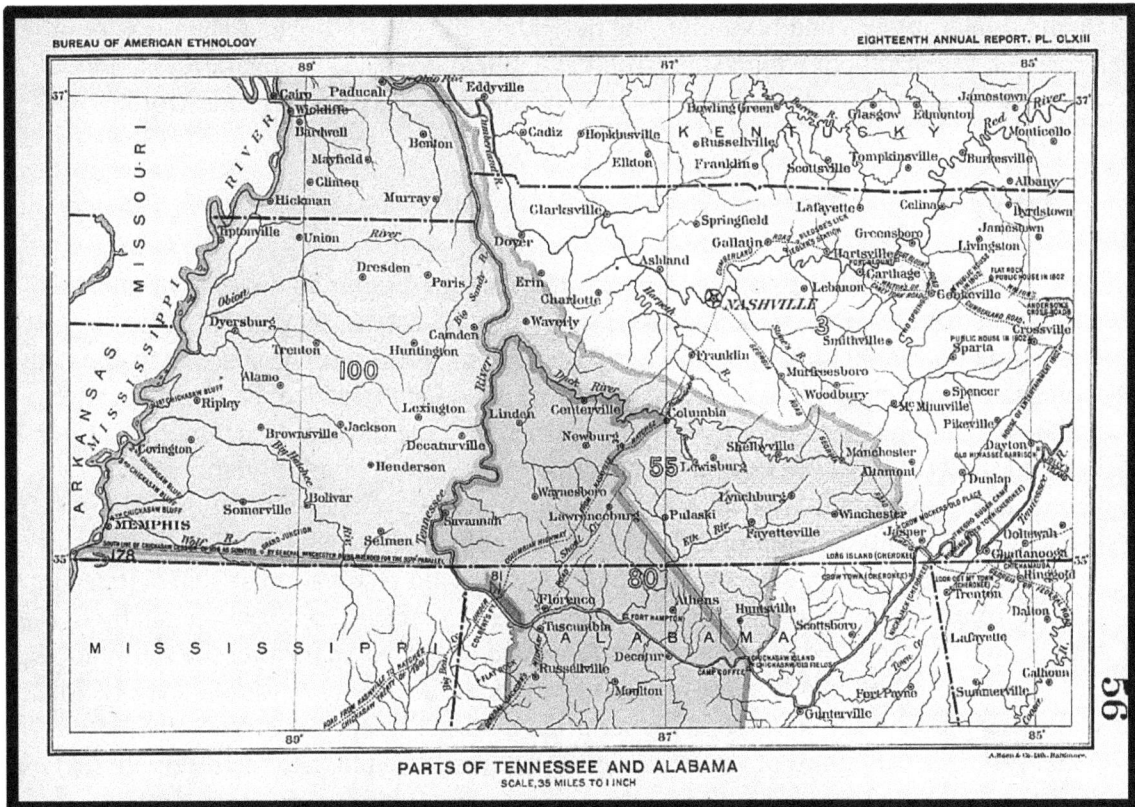

PARTS OF TENNESSEE AND ALABAMA
SCALE, 35 MILES TO 1 INCH

100-The Great Chickasaw Cession of 1818
80-The Turkey Town Cession of 1816
55-The Cotton Gin Treaty Cession of 1805

ARTICLE 3

In consideration of the relinquishment of claim and cession of lands in the preceding article, and to perpetuate the happiness of the Chickasaw Nation of Indians, the commissioners of the United States, before named, agree to allow the said nation the sum of twenty thousand dollars per annum, for fifteen successive years, to be paid annually; and, as a farther consideration for the objects aforesaid, and at the request of the chiefs of the said nation, the commissioners agree to pay captain John Gordon, of Tennessee, the sum of one thousand one hundred and fifteen dollars, it being a debt due by **General William Colbert**, of said nation, to the aforesaid Gordon; and the further sum of two thousand dollars, due by said nation of Indians, to captain David Smith, now of Kentucky, for that sum by him expended, in supplying himself and forty-five soldiers from Tennessee, in the year one thousand seven hundred and ninety-five, when assisting

191

them (at their request and invitation,) in defending their towns against the invasion of the Creek Indians; both which sums, (on the application of the said nation,) is to be paid, within sixty days after the ratification of this treaty, to the aforesaid Gordon and Smith.

ARTICLE 4

The commissioners agree, on the further and particular application of the chiefs, and for the benefit of the poor and warriors of the said nation, that a tract of land, containing four miles square, to include a salt lick or springs, on or near the river Sandy, a branch of the Tennessee River, and within the land hereby ceded, be reserved, and to be laid off in a square or oblong, so as to include the best timber, at the option of their beloved **Chief Levi Colbert**, and Major James Brown, or either of them; who are hereby made agents and trustees for the nation, to lease the said salt lick or springs, on the following express conditions, viz: For the benefit of this reservation, as before recited, the trustees or agents are bound to lease the said reservation to some citizen or citizens of the United States, for a reasonable quantity of salt, to be paid annually to the said nation, for the use thereof; and that, from and after two years after the ratification of this treaty, no salt, made at the works to be erected on this reservation, shall be sold within the limits of the same for a higher price than one dollar per bushel of fifty pounds weight; on failure of which the lease shall be forfeited, and the reservation revert to the United States.

ARTICLE 5

The commissioners agree, that there shall be paid to Oppassantubby, a principal chief of the Chickasaw Nation, within sixty days after the ratification of this treaty, the sum of five hundred dollars, as a full compensation for the reservation of two miles square, on the north side of Tennessee River, secured to him and his heirs by the treaty held, with the said Chickasaw Nation, on the twentieth day of September, 1816; and the further sum of twenty-five dollars to John Lewis, a half breed, for a saddle he lost while in the service of the United States; and, to show the regard the President of the United States has for the said Chickasaw Nation, at the request of the chiefs of the said nation, the commissioners agree that the sum of one thousand and eighty-nine dollars shall be paid to **Major James Colbert**, interpreter, within the period stated in the first part of this article, it being the amount of a sum of money taken from his pocket, in the month of June, 1816, at the theatre in Baltimore: And the said commissioners, as a further regard for said nation, do agree that the reservations made to **George Colbert** and **Levi Colbert**, in the treaty; held at the council house of said nation, on the twenty-sixth [twentieth] day of September, 1816, the first to **Colonel George Colbert**, on the north side of Tennessee River, and those to **Major Levi Colbert**, on the east side of the Tombigbee river, shall enure to the sole use of the said **Colonel George Colbert**, and **Major Levi Colbert**, their heirs and assigns, forever, with their butts and bounds, as defined by said treaty, and agreeable to the marks and boundaries as laid off and marked by the surveyor of the United States, where that is the case, and where the reservations has not been laid off and marked by a surveyor of the United States, the same shall be so done as soon after the ratification of this treaty as practicable, on the application of the reservees, or their legally appointed agent under them, and agreeably to the definition in the before recited treaty. This agreement is made on the following express conditions: that the said land, and those living on it, shall be subject to the laws of the United States, and all legal taxation that may be imposed on the land or citizens of the United States inhabiting the territory where said land is situate. The commissioners further agree, that the reservation secured to John McCleish, on the north side of Tennessee River, by the before recited treaty, in consequence of his having been raised in the State of Tennessee, and marrying a white woman, shall enure to the sole use of the said John McCleish, his heirs and assigns, forever, on the same conditions attached to the lands of **Colonel George Colbert** and **Major Levi Colbert**, in this article.

ARTICLE 6

The two contracting parties covenant and agree, that the line of the south boundary of the State of Tennessee, as described in the second article of this treaty, shall be ascertained and marked by commissioners appointed by the President of the United States; that the marks shall be bold; the trees to be blazed on both sides of the line, and the fore and aft trees marked U. S.; and that the commissioners shall be attended by two persons, to be designated by the Chickasaw Nation; and the said nation shall have due and seasonable notice when said operation is to be commenced. It is further agreed by the commissioners, that all improvements actually made by individuals of the Chickasaw Nation, which shall be found within the lands ceded by this treaty, that a fair and reasonable compensation shall be paid therefore, to the respective individuals having made or owned the same.

ARTICLE 7

In consideration of the friendly and conciliatory disposition evinced during the negotiation of this treaty, by the Chickasaw chiefs and warriors, but more particularly, as a manifestation of the friendship and liberality of the President of the United States, the commissioners agree to give, on the ratification of this treaty, to Chinnubby, King of the Chickasaw Nation, to Teshuamingo, William McGilvery, Anpassantubby, Samuel Seely, James Brown, **Levi Colbert**, Ickaryoucuttaha, George Pettygrove, Immartarharmicco, Chickasaw chiefs, and to Malcolm McGee, interpreter to this treaty, each, one hundred and fifty dollars, in cash; and to Major William Glover, **Colonel George Colbert**, Hopoyeahanmmar, Immauklusharhopoyea, Tushkarhopoye, Hopoyeahaummar, jun. Immauklusharhopoyea, **James Colbert**, Coweamartblar, Illachouwarhopoyea, military leaders, one hundred dollars each; and do further agree, that any annuity heretofore secured to the Chickasaw Nation of Indians, by treaty, to be paid in goods, shall hereafter be paid in cash.

In testimony whereof the said commissioners, and undersigned chiefs and warriors, have set their hands and seals. Done at the treaty ground east of Old Town, this nineteenth day of October, in the year of our Lord one thousand eight hundred and eighteen.

Isaac Shelby, [L. S.]
Andrew Jackson, [L. S.]
***Levi Colbert**, his x mark, [L. S.]*
Samuel Seely, his x mark, [L. S.]
Chinnubby, King, his x mark, [L. S.]
Teshuamingo, his x mark, [L. S.]
William McGilvery, his x mark, [L. S.]
Arpasheushtubby, his x mark, [L. S.]
James Brown, his x mark, [L. S.]
Ickaryaucuttaha, his x mark, [L. S.]
George Pettygrove, his x mark, [L. S.]
Immartaharmico, his x mark, [L. S.]
***Major General Wm. Colbert**, his mark, [L. S.]*

Major William Glover, his x mark, [L. S.]
Hopayahaummar, his x mark, [L. S.]
Immouklusharhopoyea, his x mark, [L. S.]
Tuskaehopoyea, his x mark, [L. S.]
Hopoyahaummar, jun. his x mark, [L. S.]
Immaaklusharhopoyea, his x mark, [L. S.]
***James Colbert**, [L. S.]*
Cowemarthlar, his x mark, [L. S.]
Illackanwarhopoyes, his x mark, [L. S.]
***Col. George Colbert**, his x mark, [L. S.]*

In the presence of *Robert Butler, adjutant-general and secretary, Th. J. Sherburne, agent for the Chickasaw Nation of Indians, Malcolm McGee, interpreter, his x mark, Martin Colbert, J. C. Bronaugh, assistant inspector-general S. D., Thos. H. Shelby, of Kentucky, R. K. Call, Captain U. S. Army, Benjamin Smith, of Kentucky, Richard I. Easter, A. D. Q. M. General. Ms. B. Winchester, W. B. Lewis.*

1830—The treaty of 1830 cedes all Chickasaw land east of the Mississippi River; in return, the Chickasaws get land west of the Mississippi River. The Chickasaw

Nation will be paid $300,000.00 over twenty years; each Chickasaw family will get half a section of land and individuals get half that amount. Levi, George, and James Colbert were granted reservations; Levi and George Colbert were permitted to have some of their sons and grandsons educated under the direction and care of the President of the United States. Levi, George, and James Colbert signed the treaty of 1830; the main treaty also included a supplementary treaty that was signed by the three Colbert brothers.

Treaty with the Chickasaw, 1830

August 31, 1830. Unratified. | Indian Office, box 1, Treaties, 1802-1853.

Articles of a treaty, entered into at Franklin, Tennessee, this 31st day of August, 1830, by John H. Eaton, Secretary of War, and General John Coffee, commissioners appointed by the President, on the part of the United States, and the chiefs and head men of the Chickasaw Nation of Indians, duly authorized, by the whole nation, to conclude a treaty.

ARTICLE 1

The Chickasaw Nation hereby cede to the United States all the lands owned and possessed by them, on the East side of the Mississippi River, where they at present reside, and which lie north of the following boundary, viz: beginning at the mouth of the Oacktibbyhaw (or Tibbee) Creek; thence, up the same, to a point, being a marked tree, on the old Natchez Road, about one mile Southwardly from Wall's old place; thence, with the Choctaw boundary, and along it, westwardly, through the Tunicha old fields, to a point on the Mississippi River, about twenty-eight miles, by water, below where the St. Francis river enters said stream, on the West side. All the lands North, and North-East of said boundary, to latitude thirty-five North the South boundary of the State of Tennessee, being owned by the Chickasaws, are hereby ceded to the United States.

ARTICLE 2

In consideration of said cession, the United States agree to furnish to the Chickasaw Nation of Indians, a country, West of the territory of Arkansas, to lie South of latitude thirty-six degrees and a half, and of equal extent with the one ceded; and in all respects as to timber, water and soil, it shall be suited to the wants and condition of said Chickasaw people. It is agreed further, that the United States will send one or more commissioners to examine and select a country of the description stated, who shall be accompanied by an interpreter and not more than twelve persons of the Chickasaws, to be chosen by the nation, to examine said country; and who, for their expenses and services, shall be allowed two dollars a day each, while so engaged.

If, after proper examination, a country suitable to their wants and condition cannot be found; then, it is stipulated and agreed, that this treaty, and all its provisions, shall be considered null and void. But, if a country shall be found and approved, the President of the United States shall cause a grant in fee simple to be made out, to be signed by him as other grants are usually signed, conveying the country to the Chickasaw people, and to their children, so long as they shall continue to exist as a nation, and shall reside upon the same.

ARTICLE 3

The Chickasaws being a weak tribe, it is stipulated that the United States will, at all times, extend to them their protection and care against enemies of every description, but it is, at the same time, agreed, that they shall act peaceably, and never make war, nor resort to arms, except with the consent and approval of the President, unless in cases where they may be invaded by some hostile power or tribe.

ARTICLE 4

As further consideration, the United States agree, that each warrior and widow having a family, and each white man, having an Indian family, shall be entitled to a half section of land, and if they have no family, to half that quantity. The delegation present, having full knowledge of the population of their country, stipulate, that the first class of cases (those with families), shall not exceed five hundred, and that the other class shall not exceed one hundred persons.

The reservations secured under this article, shall be granted in fee simple, to those who choose to remain, and become subject to the laws of the whites; and who, having recorded such intention with the agent, before the time of the first removal, shall continue to reside upon, and cultivate the same, for five years; at the expiration of which time, a grant shall be issued. But should they prefer to remove, and actually remove, then the United States, in lieu of such reservations will pay for the same, at the rate of one dollar and a half per acre; the same to be paid in ten equal, annual installments, to commence after the period of the ratification of this treaty, if, at that time, they shall have removed.

ARTICLE 5

It is agreed, that the United States, as further consideration, will pay to said Nation of Indians, fifteen thousand dollars annually, for twenty years; the first payment to be made after their removal shall take place, and they be settled at their new homes, West of the Mississippi.

ARTICLE 6

Whereas **Levi Colbert**, **George Colbert**, Tessemingo, William McGillivray and Samuel Seeley Senr, have been long known, as faithful and steady friends of the United States, and regardless of the interest of their own people; to afford them an earnest of our good feeling, now that they are about to seek a new home; the commissioners, of their own accord, and without any thing of solicitation or request, on the part of said persons, have proposed, and do agree, that they have reservations of four sections each, to include their present improvements, as nearly as may be; or, if they have improvements at any other place than one, then, equally to divide said reservations, so that two sections may be laid off at one place of improvement, and two at another; or, the whole at one place, as the party entitled may choose. They shall be entitled to the same in fee simple, to be resided upon; or, if they prefer it, they may, with the consent of the President, sell and convey the same, in fee. And it is further agreed, that upon the same terms and conditions, a reservation of two sections, to be surveyed together, and to include the improvements of the party entitled, shall and the same is hereby declared to be, secured to Capt. James Brown, **James Colbert**, John McLish & Isaac Alberson.

ARTICLE 7

The delegation having selected the following persons, as worthy their regard and confidence, to wit;—Ish to yo to pe, To pul ka, Ish te ke yo ka tubbe, Ish te ke cha, E le paum be, Pis te la tubbe, Ish tim mo lat ka, Pis ta tubbe, Im mo hoal te tubbe, Ba ka tubbe, Ish to ye tubbe, Ah to ko wa, Pak la na ya ubbe. In hie yo che tubbe, Thomas Sealy, Tum ma sheck ah, Im mo la subbe, Am le mi ya tubbe; Benjamin Love and Malcolm McGee;—it is consented that each of said persons shall be entitled to a reservation of one section of land to be located in a body, to include their present improvement, and upon which, intending to become resident citizens of the country, they may continue, and at the end of five years, shall receive a grant for the same; or, should they prefer to remove, they shall be entitled, in lieu thereof, to receive from the United States, one dollar and twenty-five cents per acre for the same, to be paid in two equal, annual installments, to commence after the ratification of this treaty, and after the nation shall have removed.

ARTICLE 8

No person receiving a special reservation shall be entitled to claim any further reservation, under the provisions of the fourth article of this treaty.

ARTICLE 9

At the request of the delegation, it is agreed that **Levi Colbert** shall have an additional section of land, to that granted him in the 6th article, to be located where he may prefer, and subject to the conditions contained in said sixth article.

ARTICLE 10

All the reservations made by this treaty, shall be in sections, half sections, or quarter sections, agreeably to the legal surveys made, and shall include the present houses and improvements of the reserves, as nearly as may be.

ARTICLE 11

It is agreed that the Chickasaw people, in removing to their new homes, shall go there at the expense of the United States; and that when they shall have arrived at their new homes, the United States will furnish to each one, for the space of one year, meat and corn rations, for himself and his family; that thereby, time may be afforded to clear the ground, and prepare a crop.

And the better to affect this object, it is agreed that one-half the nation shall remove in the fall of 1831, and the other half the following fall. The supplies to be furnished by the United States, are to be delivered at one or two places in the nation, which shall be as convenient to the body of the people as may be practicable; having regard to the position or places, where the supplies may be had or deposited, with the greatest convenience, and least expense to the United States.

ARTICLE 12

The United States, at the time of the removal of each portion of the nation, at the valuation of some respectable person, to be appointed by the President, agree to purchase all the stock they may desire to part with, (except horses), and to pay them therefore, at their new homes, as early as practicable after the ratification of this treaty. Also, to receive their agricultural and farming utensils, and to furnish them, at the West, with axes, hoes and ploughs, suited to their wants respectively. Also, to furnish each family with a spinning wheel and cards, and a loom to every six families.

ARTICLE 13

A council house, and two houses of public worship, which may be used for the purposes of schools, shall be built by the United States; and the sum of four thousand dollars shall be appropriated for that purpose. Also, one blacksmith, and no more, shall be employed at the expense of the government, for twenty years, for the use of the Indians; and a mill-wright for five years, to aid them in erecting their saw and grist-mills.

ARTICLE 14

The sum of two thousand dollars a year shall be paid for ten years, for the purpose of employing suitable teachers of the Christian religion, and superintending common schools in the nation. And it is further consented, that twenty Chickasaw boys of promise, from time to time, for the period of twenty years, shall be selected from the nation by the chiefs, to be educated within the States at the expense of the United States, under the direction of the Secretary of War.

ARTICLE 15

A desire having been expressed by **Levi Colbert**, that two of his younger sons, Abijah Jackson Colbert, and Andrew Morgan Colbert, aged seven and five years, might be educated under the direction and care of the President of the United States;—and **George Colber**t having also expressed— a wish that his grand-son, Andrew J. Frazier, aged about twelve years, might have a similar attention: It is consented, that at a proper age, as far as they may be found to have capacity, they shall receive a liberal education, at the expense of the United States, under the direction and control of the President.

ARTICLE 16

The United States shall have authority, after the ratification of this treaty by the Senate, to survey and prepare the country for sale; but no sale shall take place before the fall of 1832, or until they shall remove. And that every clause and article herein contained may be strictfully fulfilled;—it is stipulated and agreed, that the lands herein ceded shall be, and the same are hereby pledged, for the payment of the several sums which are secured and directed to be paid, under the several provisions of this treaty.

ARTICLE 17

The United States, and the Chickasaw Nation of Indians herein stipulate, that perpetual peace, and unaltered and lasting friendship, shall be maintained between them. It is agreed, that the President of the United States will use his good offices, and kind mediation, and make a request of the governor and legislature of the State of Mississippi, not to extend their laws over the Chickasaws; or to suspend their operation, until they shall have time to remove, as limited in this treaty.

In witness of all and everything herein determined, between the United States, and the delegation representing the whole Chickasaw Nation, the parties heave hereunto set their hands and seals, at Franklin, Tennessee, within the United States, this thirty-first day of August, one thousand eight hundred and thirty.

Jn H Eaton,
Secr. of War.
Jno. Coffee.
Levi Colbert, *his x mark.*
George Colbert, *his x mark.*
James Colbert, *his x mark.*
Wm. McGillivray, his x mark.
James Brown, his x mark.
Isaac Alberson, his x mark.
To pul ka, his x mark.
Ish te ke yo ka tubbe, his x mark.
Ish te ke cha, his x mark.
Im me houl te tubbe, his x mark.
In ha yo chet tubbe, his x mark.
Ish te ya tubbe, his x mark.
Ah to ko wa, his x mark.

Ook la na ya ubbe, his x mark.
Im mo la subbe, his x mark.
Hush ta ta be, his x mark.
In no wa ke che, his x mark.
Oh he cubbe, his x mark.
Kin hi che, his x mark.
J. W. Lish.
Signed in presence of us,
Preston Hay, Secretary.
Benj. Reynolds, U. S. agent.
Benjamin Love, interpreter.
R. M. Gavock.
R. P. Currin.
Lemuel Smith.
Leml. Donelson.
Jos. H. Fry.

James H. Wilson.   *J. R. Davis*

Articles, supplementary to a treaty this day entered into, between John H. Eaton and John Coffee, on the part of the United States, and the Chiefs of the Chickasaw Nation.

ARTICLE 1

It is agreed that the United States will furnish the Chickasaw Nation, to be distributed by the agent, under the direction of the chiefs, at or before the time of their removal west of the Mississippi River, three hundred rifles, with moulds and wipers; also, three hundred pounds of good powder, and twelve hundred pounds of lead. They will also furnish as aforesaid, three hundred copper or brass kettles, and six hundred blankets. Likewise three thousand weight of leaf tobacco.

ARTICLE 2

Colbert's Island, in the Tennessee River, just below the mouth of Caney Creek, supposed to contain five hundred acres, has always been in the use and occupancy of **George Colbert**, and has been admitted by the nation, to be his individual property. It is agreed now, that he shall be recognized, as having a title to the same, and that he shall receive from the United States, in consideration of it, one thousand dollars, to be paid in one year after the Chickasaws shall remove to their new homes.

ARTICLE 3

James Colbert has represented, that he has a claim of thirteen hundred dollars, of money due from a citizen of the United States, that he has become insolvent, and is unable to pay it. It is further represented, that by the rule of the Chickasaw people, where an Indian cannot pay a debt due to a white man, the nation assumes it. Also, **Levi Colbert** shows, that some time since, he purchased of a white citizen, a horse which was stolen, and proven and taken out of his possession, as stolen property, for which he has not, and cannot, obtain remuneration. Being now about to leave their ancient homes, for a new one, too distant to attend to their business here;—it is agreed that a section of land may be located and reserved, to be bound by sectional lines; which land, with the consent of the President, they may sell.

ARTICLE 4

The Chickasaw delegation request, that a reservation of land may be made in favor of their excellent agent, Col. Benjamin Reynolds, who, since he has been among them, has acted uprightly and faithfully, and of their sub-agent, Major John L. Allen, who also, has been of much service:—The commissioners accordingly consent thereto; and it is stipulated that Col. Reynolds shall have a reservation of five quarter sections of land, to be bounded by sectional lines, or quarter sectional lines, and to lie together, in a body; and in further consideration, it is stipulated, with the consent of said Reynolds, that his pension of two hundred and forty dollars a year, granted to him by the United States, shall thereafter cease and determine. The application in favor of the sub-agent, Maj. Allen, is also recognized, and a reservation of a quarter section is admitted to his wife, to whom and for whose benefit a grant shall issue. But said reservations shall not be located, so as to interfere with other claims to reservations, secured under this treaty, nor shall this treaty be affected if this article is not ratified.

ARTICLE 5

The 4th article of the treaty of 19th October 1818, which reserves a salt lick, and authorizes **Levi Colbert** and James Brown to lease the same for a reasonable quantity of salt, is hereby changed;—And with the consent of the commissioners present, the following agreement, made by Robert P. Currin, for himself and William B. Lewis, is entered as part of this treaty, to wit;

Whereas a lease of land, of four miles square, was secured under the fourth article of a treaty, concluded on the 19th day of October 1818, between the United States and the Chickasaw Nation of Indians; and **Levi Colbert** and James Brown, under the same treaty, were appointed agents and trustees by the Chickasaw nation to make said lease. And whereas William B. Lewis, a citizen of the United States afterwards procured from said trustees, Colbert and Brown, a lease for the same, on condition of his paying annually, a certain amount of salt to said nation, provided he should succeed in finding salt water. And whereas the said William B. Lewis and Robert P. Currin, who subsequently became interested with him, have, as is shown, expended about the sum of three thousand dollars, in endeavoring to find salt water, but without success. And the Indians, who are about to leave their ancient country, being desirous to have this land and lease placed in such a condition, as that some benefit may result to their nation, They do hereby agree with said Robert P. Currin, a citizen of the United States, for himself, and as the agent and attorney in fact of the said William B. Lewis (John H. Eaton and John Coffee, the United States commissioners, to treat with said Chickasaw nation being present and assenting thereto); that the lease heretofore made, be so changed, that the rent therein agreed to be paid is entirely released and discharged, from the date of said lease, together with all claim arising on account of the same.

And it is now agreed, that said lease shall remain, as heretofore made, with this alteration: that two thousand dollars shall be paid to said Colbert and Brown, trustees as aforesaid, for the Chickasaw Nation: to wit: five hundred dollars now in hand; five hundred dollars on the first day of October one thousand eight hundred and thirty-one; and one thousand dollars on the first day of October one thousand eight hundred and thirty-two. And it is further agreed, in consideration of said alteration of said original contract and lease, herein made and agreed upon; and the said Robert P. Currin, for himself and the said William B. Lewis, for each and for both, he having full authority to act in the premises, will annually pay to said trustees, four bushels of salt, or the value thereof, as they and the nation may agree to and direct.

In testimony whereof, and in the presence of the commissioners, appointed to treat with the Chickasaw Nation of people, on the part of the United States, the parties respectively have hereto set their hands and affixed their seals, this first day of September, one thousand eight hundred and thirty.

Jn. H. Eaton, Secty. of War.
Jno. Coffee.
Levi Colbert, *his x mark.*
George Colbert, *his x mark.*
James Colbert, *his x mark.*
Wm. McGilvery, his x mark.
Isaac Alberson, his x mark.
James Bown, his x mark.
To pul ka, his x mark.
Ish te ki yo ka tubbe, his x mark.
Ish te he cha, his x mark.
Im me houl te tubbe, his x mark.
In hei yo chit tubbe, his x mark.
Ish te ya tubbe, his x mark.
Ah to ko wa, his x mark.
Ook la na ya ubbe, his x mark.
Im mo la tubbe, his x mark.

Hush ta ta be, his x mark.
In no wa ke che, his x mark.
On he cubbe, his x mark.
Kin hu che, his x mark.
J. W. Lish.
Signed in presence of us,
Preston Hay, secretary.
Benj. Reynolds, U. S. agent.
Benjamin Love, as interpreter.
R. M. Gavock.
Leml. Donelson.
Leml. Smith.
R. P. Currin.
Jos. H. Fry.
James H. Wilson.
J. R. Davis.

1832—On October 20, 1832, the Chickasaws signed the Pontotoc Creek Treaty which gave up all land claims east of the Mississippi River; in return, the United States will sell the land at public auction and reimburse the Chickasaws except for expenses. George and Levi Colbert signed the Pontotoc Creek Treaty of 1832 and a supplementary treaty of 1832; these treaties identified the mechanisms for the sale of all Chickasaw lands east of the Mississippi River

Treaty with the Chickasaw, 1832

Oct. 20, 1832. 7 Stat., 381 | Proclamation Mar. 1, 1833.

Articles of a treaty made and entered into between Genl. John Coffee, being duly authorized thereto, by the President of the United States, and the whole Chickasaw Nation, in General Council assembled, at the council House, on Pontitock Creek on the twentieth day of October, 1832.

The Chickasaw Nation find themselves oppressed in their present situation; by being made subject to the laws of the States in which they reside. Being ignorant of the language and laws of the white man, they cannot understand or obey them. Rather than submit to this great evil, they prefer to seek a home in the west, where they may live and be governed by their own laws. And believing that they can procure for themselves a home, in a country suited to their wants and condition, provided they had the means to contract and pay for the same, they have determined to sell their country and hunt a new home. The President has heard the complaints of the Chickasaws, and like them believes they cannot be happy, and prosper as a nation, in their present situation and condition, and being desirous to relieve them from the great calamity that seems to await them, if they remain as they are—He has sent his Commissioner Genl. John Coffee, who has met the whole Chickasaw Nation in Council, and after mature deliberation, they have entered into the following articles, which shall be binding on both parties, when the same shall be ratified by the President of the United States by and with the advice and consent of the Senate.

ARTICLE 1

For the consideration hereinafter expressed, the Chickasaw Nation does hereby cede, to the United States, all the land which they own on the east side of the Mississippi River, including all the country where they at present live and occupy.

PONTOTOC CREEK TREATY

S.E. about 7 miles is site of council house where on October 20, 1832, treaty was signed providing for cession of over 6 million acres to U.S. and removal of Chickasaws to West.

ARTICLE 2

The United States agree to have the whole country thus ceded, surveyed, as soon as it can be conveniently done, in the same manner that the public lands of the United

States are surveyed in the States of Mississippi and Alabama, and as soon thereafter as may be practicable, to have the same prepared for sale. The President of the United States will then offer the land for sale at public auction, in the same manner and on the same terms and conditions as the other public lands, and such of the land as may not sell at the public sales shall be offered at private sale, in the same manner that other private sales are made of the United States lands.

ARTICLE 3

As a full compensation to the Chickasaw Nation, for the country thus ceded, the United States agree to pay over to the Chickasaw Nation, all the money arising from the sale of the land which may be received from time to time, after deducting therefrom the whole cost and expenses of surveying and selling the land, including every expense attending the same.

ARTICLE 4

The President being determined that the Chickasaw people shall not deprive themselves of a comfortable home, in the country where they now are, until they shall have provided a country in the west to remove to, and settle on, with fair prospects of future comfort and happiness—It is therefore agreed to, by the Chickasaw Nation, that they will endeavor as soon as it may be in their power, after the ratification of this treaty, to hunt out and procure a home for their people, west of the Mississippi River, suited to their wants and condition; and they will continue to do so during the progress of the survey of their present country, as is provided for in the second article of this treaty. But should they fail to procure such a country to remove to and settle on, previous to the first public sale of their country here then and in that event, they are to select out of the surveys, a comfortable settlement for every family in the Chickasaw Nation, to include their present improvements, if the land is good for cultivation, and if not they may take it in any other place in the nation, which is unoccupied by any other person. Such settlement must be taken by sections. And there shall be allotted to each family as follows (to wit): To a single man who is twenty-one years of age, one section—to each family of five and under that number two sections—to each family of six and not exceeding ten, three sections, and to each family over ten in number, four sections—and to families who own slaves, there shall be allowed, one section to those who own ten or upwards and such as own under ten, there shall be allowed half a section. If any person shall now occupy two places and wish to retain both, they may do so, by taking a part at one place, and a part at the other, and where two or more persons are now living on the same section, the oldest occupant will be entitled to remain, and the others must move off to some other place if so required by the oldest occupant. All of which tracts of land, so selected and retained, shall be held, and occupied by the Chickasaw people, uninterrupted until they shall find and obtain a country suited to their wants and condition. And the United States will guaranty to the Chickasaw Nation, the quiet possession and uninterrupted use of the said reserved tracts of land, so long as they may live on and occupy the same. And when they shall determine to remove from said tracts of land, the Chickasaw Nation will notify the President of the United States of their determination to remove, and thereupon as soon as the Chickasaw people shall remove, the President will proclaim the said reserved tracts of land for sale at public auction and at private sale, on the same terms and conditions, as is provided for in the second article of this treaty, to sell the same, and the net proceeds thereof, to be paid to the Chickasaw Nation, as is provided for in the third article of this treaty.

ARTICLE 5

If any of the Chickasaw families shall have made valuable improvements on the places where they lived and removed from, on the reservation tracts, the same shall be valued by some discreet person to be appointed by the President, who shall assess the real cash value of all such improvements, and also the real cash value of all the land within their improvements, which they may have cleared and actually cultivated, at least one year in good farming order and condition. And such valuation of the improvements and the value of the cultivated lands as before mentioned shall be paid to the person who shall have made the same. To be paid out of the proceeds of the sales of the ceded lands. The person who shall value such land and improvements, shall give to the owner thereof, a certificate of the valuation, which shall be a good voucher for them to draw the money on, from the proper person, who shall be appointed to pay the same, and the money shall be paid, as soon as may be convenient, after the valuation, to enable the owner thereof to provide for their families on their journey to their new homes. The provisions of this article are intended to encourage industry and to enable the Chickasaws to move comfortably. But least the good intended may be abused, by designing persons, by hiring hands and clearing more land, than they otherwise would do for the benefit of their families—It is determined that no payment shall be made for improved lands, over and above one-eighth part of the tract allowed and reserved for such person to live on and occupy.

ARTICLE 6

The Chickasaw Nation cannot receive any part of the payment for their land until it shall be surveyed and sold; therefore, in order to the greater facilitate, in surveying and preparing the land for sale, and for keeping the business of the nation separate and apart from the business and accounts of the United States, it is proposed by the Chickasaws, and agreed to, that a Surveyor General be appointed by the President, by and with the advice and consent of the Senate, to superintend alone the surveying of this ceded country or so much thereof as the President may direct, who shall appoint a sufficient number of deputy surveyors, as may be necessary to complete the survey, in as short a time as may be reasonable and expedient. That the said Surveyor General be allowed one good clerk, and one good draftsman to aid and assist him in the business of his office, in preparing the lands for sale. It is also agreed that one land office be established for the sale of the lands, to have one Register and one Receiver of monies, to be appointed by the President, by and with the advice and consent of the senate, and each Register and Receiver to have one good clerk to aid and assist them in the duties of their office. The Surveyor's office, and the office of the Register and Receiver of money, shall be kept somewhere central in the nation, at such place as the President of the United States may direct. As the before mentioned officers, and clerks, are to be employed entirely in business of the nation, appertaining to preparing and selling the land, they will of course be paid out of the proceeds of the sales of the ceded lands. That the Chickasaws, may now understand as near as may be, the expenses that will be incurred in the transacting of this business—It is proposed and agreed to, that the salary of the Surveyor General be fifteen hundred dollars a year, and that the Register and Receiver of monies, be allowed twelve hundred dollars a year each, as a full compensation for their services, and all expenses, except stationary and postages on their official business, and that each of the clerks and draftsman be allowed seven hundred and fifty dollars a year, for their services and all expenses.

ARTICLE 7

It is expressly agreed that the United States shall not grant any right of preference, to any person, or right of occupancy in any manner whatsoever, but in all cases, of either public or private sale, they are to sell the land to the highest bidder, and also that none of the lands be sold in smaller tracts than quarter sections or fractional sections of the same size as near as may be, until the Chickasaw Nation may require the President to sell in smaller tracts. The Chiefs of the nation have heard that at some of the sales of the United States lands, the people there present, entered into combinations, and united in purchasing much of the land, at reduced prices, for their own benefit, to the great prejudice of the Government, and they express fears, that attempts will be made to cheat them, in the same manner when their lands shall be offered at public auction. It is therefore agreed that the President will use his best endeavors to prevent such combinations, or any other plan or state of things which may tend to prevent the land selling for its full value.

ARTICLE 8

As the Chickasaws have determined to sell their country, it is desirable that the nation realize the greatest possible sum for their lands, which can be obtained. It is therefore proposed and agreed to that after the President shall have offered their lands for sale and shall have sold all that will sell for the Government price, then the price shall be reduced, so as to induce purchasers to buy, who would not take the land at the Government minimum price;—and it is believed, that five years from and after the date of the first sale, will dispose of all the lands, that will sell at the Government price. If then at the expiration of five years, as before mentioned, the Chickasaw nation may request the President to sell at such reduced price as the nation may then propose, it shall be the duty of the President to comply with their request, by first offering it at public and afterwards at private sale, as in all other cases of selling public lands.

ARTICLE 9

The Chickasaw Nation expresses their ignorance and incapacity to live, and be happy under the State laws, they cannot read and understand them, and therefore they will always need a friend to advise and direct them. And fearing at someday the Government of the United States may withdraw from them, the agent under whose instructions they have lived so long and happy—They therefore request that the agent may be continued with them, while here, and wherever they may remove to and settle. It is the earnest wish of the United States Government to see the Chickasaw Nation prosper and be happy, and so far as is consistent they will contribute all in their power to render them so—therefore their request is granted. There shall be an agent kept with the Chickasaws as heretofore, so long as they live within the jurisdiction of the United States as a nation, either within the limits of the States where they now reside, or at any other place. And whenever the office of agent shall be vacant, and an agent to be appointed, the President will pay due respect to the wishes of the nation in selecting a man in all respects qualified to discharge the responsible duties of that office.

ARTICLE 10

Whenever the Chickasaw Nation shall determine to remove from, and leave their present country, they will give the President of the United States timely notice of such intention, and the President will furnish them the necessary funds, and means for their transportation and journey, and for one year provisions, after they reach their new homes, in such quantity as the nation may require, and the full amount of such funds, transportation and provisions, is to be paid for, out of the proceeds of the sales of the ceded lands. And should the Chickasaw Nation remove, from their present country, before they receive money, from the sale of the lands, hereby ceded; then and in that case, the United States shall furnish them any reasonable sum of money for national purposes, which may be deemed proper by the President of the United States, which sum shall also be refunded out of the sales of the ceded lands.

ARTICLE 11

The Chickasaw Nation has determined to create a perpetual fund, for the use of the nation forever, out of the proceeds of the country now ceded away. And for that purpose they propose to invest a large proportion of the money arising from the sale of the land, in some safe and valuable stocks which will bring them in an annual interest or dividend, to be used for all national purposes, leaving the principal untouched, intending to use the interest alone. It is therefore proposed by the Chickasaws, and agreed to, that the sum to be laid out in stocks as above mentioned, shall be left with the government of the United States, until it can be laid out under the direction of the President of the United States, by and with the advice and consent of the Senate, in such safe and valuable stock as he may approve of, for the use and benefit of the Chickasaw Nation. The sum thus to be invested, shall be equal to, at least three-fourths of the whole net proceeds of the sales of the lands; and as much more, as the nation may determine, if there shall be a surplus after supplying all the national wants. But it is hereby provided, that if the reasonable wants of the nation shall require more than one fourth of the proceeds of the sales of the land, then they may, by the consent of the President and Senate, draw from the government such sum as may be thought reasonable, for valuable national purposes, out of the three-fourths reserved to be laid out in stocks. But if any of the monies shall be thus drawn out of the sum first proposed, to be laid out on interest, the sum shall be replaced, out of the first monies of the nation, which may come into the possession of the United States government, from the sale of the ceded lands, over and above the reasonable wants of the nation. At the expiration of fifty years from this date, if the Chickasaw Nation shall have improved in education and civilization, and become so enlightened, as to be capable of managing so large a sum of money to advantage, and with safety, for the benefit of the nation, and the President of the United States, with the Senate, shall be satisfied thereof, at that time, and shall give their consent thereto, the Chickasaw Nation may then withdraw the whole, or any part of the fund now set apart, to be laid out in stocks, or at interest, and dispose of the same, in any manner that they may think proper at that time, for the use and benefit of the whole nation; but no part of said fund shall ever be used for any other purpose, than the benefit of the whole Chickasaw Nation. In order to facilitate the survey and sale of the lands now ceded, and to raise the money therefrom as soon as possible, for the foregoing purpose, the President of the United States is authorized to commence the survey of the land as soon as may be practicable, after the ratification of this treaty.

ARTICLE 12

The Chickasaws feel grateful to their old chiefs for their long and faithful services, in attending to the business of the nation. They believe it a duty, to keep them from want in their old and declining age—with those feelings, they have looked upon their old and beloved chief Tish-o-mingo, who is now grown old, and is poor and not able to live, in that comfort, which his valuable life and great merit deserve. It is therefore determined to give him out of the national funds, one hundred dollars a year during the balance of his life, and the nation request him to receive it, as a token of their kind feelings for him, on account of his long and valuable services.

Our old and beloved Queen Puc-caun-la, is now very old and very poor. Justice says the nation ought not to let her suffer in her old age; it is therefore determined to give her out of the national funds, fifty dollars a year during her life, the money to be put in the hands of the agent to be laid out for her support, under his direction, with the advice of the chiefs.

ARTICLE 13

The boundary line between the lands of the Chickasaws and Choctaws, has never been run, or properly defined, and as the Choctaws have sold their country to the United States, they now have no interest in the decision of that question. It is therefore agreed to call on the old Choctaw chiefs, to determine the line to be run, between the Chickasaws and their former country. The Chickasaws, by a treaty made with the United States at Franklin in Tennessee, in August 31, 1830, declared their line to run as follows, to wit: Beginning at the mouth of Oak tibby-haw and running up said stream to a point, being a marked tree, on the old Natchez Road, one mile southwardly from Wall's old place.

Thence with the Choctaw boundary, and along it, westwardly through the Tunicha old fields, to a point on the Mississippi River, about twenty-eight miles by water below where the St. Francis River enter said stream on the west side.

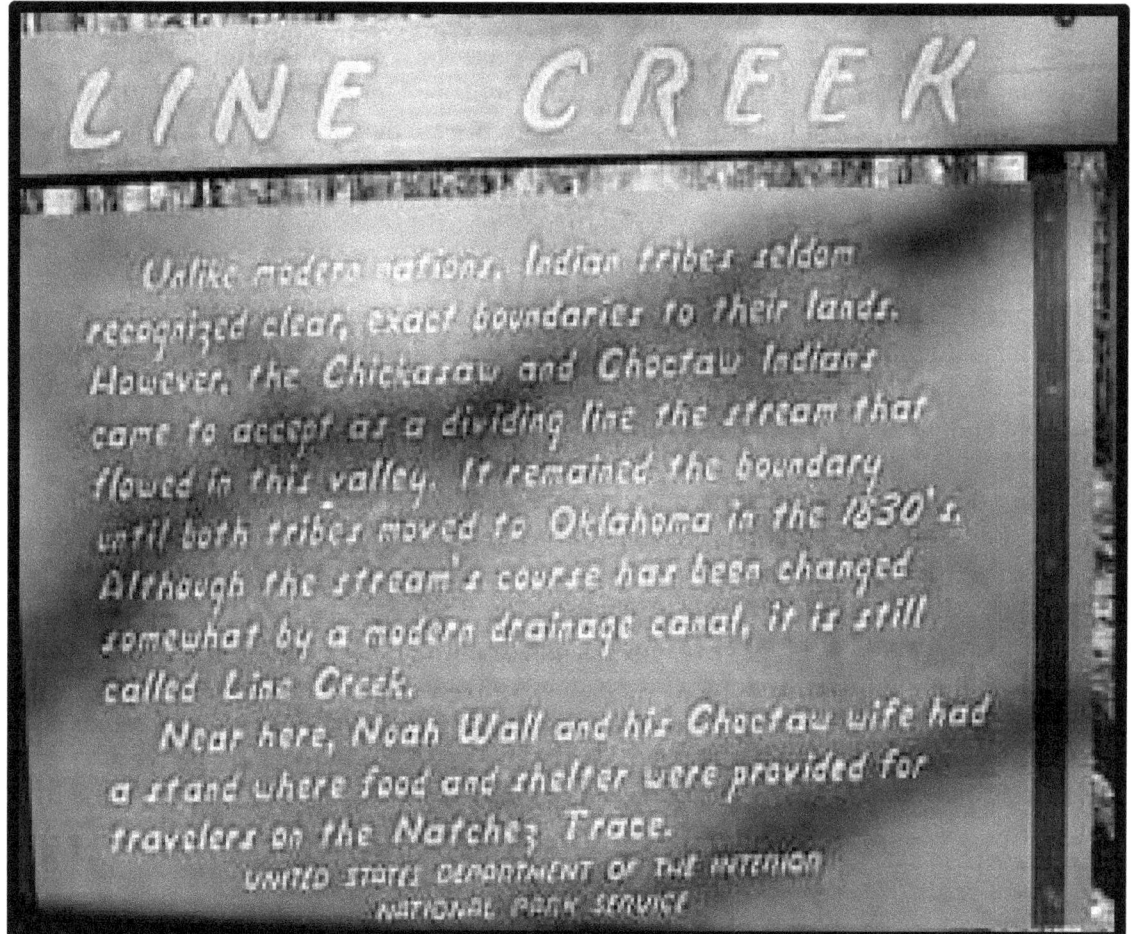

LINE CREEK

Unlike modern nations, Indian tribes seldom recognized clear, exact boundaries to their lands. However, the Chickasaw and Choctaw Indians came to accept as a dividing line the stream that flowed in this valley. It remained the boundary until both tribes moved to Oklahoma in the 1830's. Although the stream's course has been changed somewhat by a modern drainage canal, it is still called Line Creek.

Near here, Noah Wall and his Choctaw wife had a stand where food and shelter were provided for travelers on the Natchez Trace.

UNITED STATES DEPARTMENT OF THE INTERIOR
NATIONAL PARK SERVICE

Chickasaw-Choctaw Boundary Historic Marker at Noah Wall's Stand

It is now agreed, that the surveys of the Choctaw country which are now in progress, shall not cross the line until the true line shall be decided and determined; which shall be done as follows, the agent of the Choctaws on the west side of the Mississippi shall call on the old and intelligent chiefs of that nation, and lay before them the line as claimed by the Chickasaws at the Franklin treaty, and if the Choctaws shall determine that line to be correct, then it shall be established and made the permanent line, but if the Choctaws say the line strikes the Mississippi River higher up said stream, then the best evidence which can be had from both nations, shall be taken by the agents of both nations, and submitted to the President of the United States for his decision, and on such evidence, the President will determine the true line on principles of strict justice.

ARTICLE 14

As soon as the surveys are made, it shall be the duty of the chiefs, with the advice and assistance of the agent to cause a correct list to be made out of all and every tract of land, which shall be reserved, for the use and benefit of the Chickasaw people, for their residence, as is provided for in the fourth article of this treaty, which list, will designate the sections of land, which are set apart for each family or individual in the nation, showing the precise tracts which shall belong to each and every one of them, which list shall be returned to the register of the land office, and he shall make a record of the same, in his office, to prevent him from offering any of said tracts of land for sale, and also as evidence of each person's lands. All the residue of the lands will be offered by the President for sale.

ARTICLE 15

The Chickasaws request that no persons be permitted to move in and settle on their country before the land is sold. It is therefore agreed, that no person, whatsoever, who is not Chickasaw or connected with the Chickasaws by marriage, shall be permitted to come into the country and settle on any part of the ceded lands until they shall be offered for sale, and then there shall not be any person permitted to settle on any of the land, which has not been sold, at the time of such settlement, and in all cases of a person settling on any of the ceded lands contrary to this express understanding, they will be intruders, and must be treated as such, and put off of the lands of the nation.

In witness of all and everything herein determined, between the United States and the whole Chickasaw Nation in general council assembled, the parties have hereunto set their hands and seals, at the council-house, on Pontotock Creek, in the Chickasaw Nation, on the twentieth day of October, one thousand eight hundred and thirty-two.

John Coffee, [L. S.]
Ish-te-ho-to-pa, [king,] his x mark, [L. S.]
Tish-o-min-go, his x mark, [L. S.]
Levi Colbert, *his x mark, [L. S.]*
George Colbert, *his x mark, [L. S.]*
William M'Gilvery, his x mark, [L. S.]
Samuel Sely, his x mark, [L. S.]
To-pul-kah, his x mark, [L. S.]
Isaac Albertson, his x mark, [L. S.]
Em-ub-by, his x mark, [L. S.]
Pis-tah-lah-tubbe, his x mark, [L. S.]
Ish-tim-o-lut-ka, his x mark, [L. S.]
James Brown, his x mark, [L. S.]
Im-mah-hoo-lo-tubbe, his x mark, [L. S.]
Ish-ta-ha-chah, his x mark,[L. S.]
Lah-fin-hubbe, his x mark, [L. S.]
Shop-pow-me, his x mark, [L. S.]
Nin-uck-ah-umba, his x mark, [L. S.]
Im-mah-hoo-la-tubbe, his x mark, [L. S.]

Illup-pah-umba, his x mark, [L. S.]
Pitman Colbert, [L. S.]
Con-mush-ka-ish-kah, his x mark, [L. S.]
James Wolfe, [L. S.]
Bah-ha-kah-tubbe, his x mark, [L. S.]
E. Bah-kah-tubbe, his x mark, [L. S.]
Captain Thompson, his x mark, [L. S.]
New-berry, kis x mark, [L. S.]
Bah-ma-hah-tubbe, his x mark, [L. S.]
John Lewis, his x mark, [L. S.]
I-yah-hou-tubbe, his x mark, [L. S.]
Tok-holth-la-chah, his x mark, [L. S.]
Oke-lah-nah-nubbe, his x mark, [L. S.]
Im-me-tubbe, his x mark, [L. S.]
In-kah-yea, his x mark, [L. S.]
Ah-sha-cubbe, his x mark, [L. S.]
Im-moh-ho-bah, his x mark, [L. S.]
Fit-chah-pla, his x mark, [L. S.]
Unte-mi-ah-tubbe, his x mark, [L. S.]
Oke-lah-hin-lubbe, his x mark, [L. S.]
John Glover, his x mark, [L. S.]

Bah-me-hubbe, his x mark, [L. S.]
Hush-tah-tah-ubbe, his x mark, [L. S.]
Un-ti-ha-kah-tubbe, his x mark, [L. S.]
Yum-mo-tubbe, his x mark, [L. S.]
Oh-ha-cubbe, his x mark, [L. S.]
Ah-fah-mah, his x mark, [L. S.]
Ah-ta-kin-tubbe, his x mark, [L. S.]
Ah-to-ko-wah, his x mark, [L. S.]
Tah-ha-cubbe, his x mark, [L. S.]
Kin-hoi-cha, his x mark, [L. S.]
Ish-te-ah-tubbe, his x mark, [L. S.]
Chick-ah-shah-nan-ubbe, his x mark,
[L. S.]
Che-wut-ta-ha, his x mark, [L. S.]
Fo-lut-ta-chah, his x mark, [L. S.]
No-wo-ko, his x mark, [L. S.]
Win-in-a-pa, his x mark, [L. S.]
Oke-lah-shah-cubbe, his x mark, [L. S.]
Ish-ta-ki-yu-ka-tabbe, his x mark, [L.
S.]
Mah-te-ko-shubbe, his x mark, [L. S.]

Tom-chick-ah, his x mark, [L. S.]
Ei-o-che-tubbe, his x mark, [L. S.]
Nuck-sho-pubbe, his x mark, [L. S.]
Fah-lah-mo-tubbe, his x mark, [L. S.]
Co-chub-be, his x mark, [L. S.]
Thomas Sely, his x mark, [L. S.]
Oke-lah-sha-pi-a, his x mark, [L. S.]
Signed and sealed in the presence of—
Ben. Reynolds, Indian agent,
John L. Allen, subagent,
Nath. Anderson, secretary to the
commissioner,
Benj. Love, United States interpreter,
Robert Gordon, Mississippi,
George Wightman, of Mississippi,
John Donley, Tennessee,
D. S. Parrish, Tennessee,
S. Daggett, Mississippi,
Wm. A. Clurm,
G. W. Long.

Supplementary Treaty with the Chickasaw, 1832

October 22, 1832. 7 Stat., 388.

Articles supplementary to, and explanatory of, a treaty which was entered into on the 20th instant, between General John Coffee on the part of the United States, and the whole Chickasaw Nation in General Council assembled.

The fourth article of the treaty to which this is a supplement, provides that each Chickasaw family, shall have a tract of land, reserved for the use of the family, to live on and occupy, so long as the nation resides in the country where they now are. And the fifth article of the treaty provides that each family or individual shall be paid for their improvements, and the value of their cleared lands, when the nation shall determine to remove and leave the said reserved tracts of land. It is now proposed and agreed to, that no family or person of the Chickasaw Nation, who shall or may have tracts of land, reserved for their residence while here, shall ever be permitted to lease any of said land, to any person whatsoever, nor shall they be permitted to rent any of said land, to any person, either white, red, or black, or mixed blood of either. As the great object of the nation is to preserve the land, and timber, for the benefit of posterity, provided the nation shall continue to live here, and if they shall at any time determine to remove and sell the land, it will be more valuable, and will sell for more money, for the benefit of the nation, if the land and timber be preserved.

It is also expressly declared by the nation, that, whenever the nation shall determine to remove from their present country, that every tract of land so reserved in the nation, shall be given up and sold for the benefit of the nation. And no individual or family shall have any right to retain any of such reserved tracts of land, for their own use, any longer than the nation may remain in the country where they now are.

As the reserve tracts of land above alluded to, will be the first choice of land in the nation, it is determined that the minimum price of all the reserved tracts, shall be three dollars an acre, until the nation may determine to reduce the price, and then they will notify the President, of their wishes, and the price to which they desire to reduce it.

The Chiefs still express fears that combinations may be formed at the public sales, where their reserved tracts of land shall be offered for sale, and that they may not be sold so high as they might be sold, by judicious agents at private sale. They therefore suggest the propriety of the President determining on some judicious mode of selling the reserves at private sale.

It is therefore agreed that the suggestion be submitted to the President, and if he and the Chiefs can agree on a plan of a sale, different from the one proposed in the treaty, to which this is a supplement, and which shall be approved of by both parties, then they may enter into such agreement and the President shall then be governed by the same, in the sale of the reserved tracts of land, whenever they may be offered for sale.

In the provisions of the fourth article of the treaty to which this is a supplement, for reserves to young men who have no families, it expresses that each young man, who is twenty-one years of age, shall have a reserve. But as the Indians mature earlier than white men, and generally marry younger, it is determined to extend a reserve, to each young man who is seventeen years of age. And as there are some orphan girls in the nation or whose families do not provide for them, and also some widows in the same situation, it is determined to allow to each of them a reservation of one section, on the same terms and conditions in all respects, with the other reservations for the nation generally, and to be allowed to the same ages, as to young men.

Colbert Moore and family have always lived in the Chickasaw Nation, and he requests the liberty to continue with the nation. The Chiefs and nation agree to his request, and they also agree to allow him and his family a reserve tract of land to live on and occupy in the same manner, and on the same terms and conditions as is provided for the Chickasaw families, in the nation generally, during his good behavior.

The Chiefs of the nation represent that they in behalf of the nation gave a bond to **James Colbert** for a debt due to him, of eighteen hundred and eleven dollars, ninety-three and three fourth cents principal, that **James Colbert** transferred said note to Robert Gordon and that said note, and the interest thereon is yet due and unpaid, and the said Robert Gordon has proposed to take a section of land for said note, and interest up to this date. It is therefore agreed by the nation to grant him a section of land, to be taken anywhere in the nation, so as not to interfere with any reserve which has been provided as a residence for the Chickasaws, which shall be in full for said note and interest.

The Treaty, to which this is a supplement provides that there shall be offices kept some where central in the nation, at such place as the President shall determine, for transacting the business of the nation in selling their lands &c. It is now agreed to by the nation, that the President may select a section of land, or four quarter sections adjoining, at such place as he may determine agreeably to that provision of the Treaty, to establish the said offices on, and for all the necessary uses thereto attached, and he is permitted to improve the said tract of land in any manner, whatsoever, but when it shall cease to be used for the purposes, for which it is set apart—for offices &c.—then the same shall be sold under the direction of the President—and the proceeds thereof shall be paid to the Chickasaw Nation, after deducting therefrom the value of all the improvements on the land, which value shall be assessed by the President, and in no case shall it exceed one half the sale of the land.

The Chickasaw Nation request the government to grant them a cross mail route through the nation as follows, one to pass from Tuscumbia in Alabama, by the Agency, and by the place to be selected for the offices to be kept and to Rankin in Mississippi on horseback, once a week each way. The other to run from Memphis in Tennessee, by the offices and to the Cotton Gin in Mississippi—to pass once a week each way. They conceive these mails would be useful to the nation, and indispensable to the carrying on the business of the nation when the offices are established, but they would respectfully solicit the mails to be started as soon as possible, to open the avenues of information into their country.

John Donley has long been known in this nation as a mail carrier; he rode on the mails through our nation when a boy and for many years after he was grown; we think he understands that business as well, if not better than any other man—and we should prefer him to carry our mails to any other person—and if he is given the contract, the nation will set apart a section of land for his use while we remain here in this country, which section he may select with the advice of the Chiefs anywhere that suits him best, so as not to interfere with any of the reserves, and he may use it in any manner to live on, or make such improvements as may be necessary for keeping his horses, or to raise forage for them. But when the nation shall move away and leave this country this tract of land must be sold for the benefit of the nation, in the same manner that the reserve tracts are sold &c. and he is not to claim of the nation any pay for improving said tract of land.

In witness of all and everything herein determined between the United States and the whole Chickasaw Nation, in general council assembled, the parties have hereunto set their hands and seals at the council house, on Pontotock Creek, in the Chickasaw Nation, on this twenty-second day of October one thousand eight hundred and thirty-two.

Jno. Coffee
Ish-te-ho-to-pa, his x mark, [L. S.]
Tish-o-min-go, his x mark, [L. S.]
Levi Colbert, *his x mark, [L. S.]*
George Colbert, *his x mark, [L. S.]*
William McGilvery, his x mark, [L. S.]
Samuel Sely, his x mark, [L. S.]
To-pul-kah, his x mark, [L. S.]
Isaac Albertson, his x mark, [L. S.]
Im-mubbe, his x mark, [L. S.]
Pis-ta-la-tubbe, his x mark, [L. S.]
Ish-tim-o-lut-ka, his x mark, [L. S.]
James Brown, his x mark, [L. S.]
Im-ma-hoo-lo-tubbe, his x mark, [L. S.]
Ish-ta-ha-cha, his x mark, [L. S.]
Lah-fin-hubbe, his x mark, [L. S.]
Shop-pow-we, his x mark, [L. S.]
Nin-uck-ah-umba, his x mark, [L. S.]
Im-mah-hoo-lo-tubbe, his x mark, [L. S.]

Il-lup-pah-umba, his x mark, [L. S.]
Pitman Colbert, [L. S.]
Con-nush-koish-kah, his x mark, [L. S.]
James Wolf, [L. S.]
Bah-ha-kah-tubbe, his x mark, [L. S.]
E-bah-kah-tubbe, his x mark, [L. S.]
Captain Thompson, his x mark, [L. S.]
New-berry, his x mark, [L. S.]
Bah-me-hah-tubbe, his x mark,[L. S.]
John Lewis, his x mark, [L. S.]
I-yah-hou-tubbe, his mark, [L. S.]
Tok-holth-la-chah, his x mark, [L. S.]
Oke-lah-nah-nubbe, his x mark, [L. S.]
Im-me-tubbe, his x mark, [L. S.]
In-kah-yea, his x mark, [L. S.]
Ah-shah-cubbe, his x mark, [L. S.]
Im-mah-ho-bah, his x mark, [L. S.]
Fit-chah-ple, his x mark, [L. S.]
Unte-mi-ah-tubbe, his x mark, [L. S.]
Oke-lah-hin-lubbe, his x mark, [L. S.]

John Glover, his x mark, [L. S.]
Bah-me-hubbe, his x mark, [L. S.]
Ah-to-ko-wah, his x mark, [L. S.]
Hush-tah-tah-hubbe, his x mark, [L. S.]
Un-ti-ha-kah-tubbe, his x mark, [L. S.]
Yum-me-tubbe, his x mark, [L. S.]
Oh-ha-cubbe, his x mark, [L. S.]
Ah-fah-mah, his x mark, [L. S.]
Ah-take-in-tubbe, his x mark, [L. S.]
Tah-ha-cubbe, his x mark, [L. S.]
Kin-hoi-cha, his x mark, [L. S.]
Ish-te-ah-tubbe, his x mark, [L. S.]
Chick-ah-shah-nan-ubbe, his x mark,
[L. S.]
Chee-wut-ta-ha, his x mark, [L. S.]
Fo-lut-ta-chah, his x mark, [L. S.]
No-wo-ko, his x mark, [L. S.]
Win-in-a-pa, his x mark, [L. S.]
Oke-lah-shah-cubbe, his x mark, [L. S.]
Ish-ta-ki-yu-ka-tubbe, his x mark, [L.
S.]
Mah-ta-ko-shubbe, his x mark, [L. S.]
Tom-ah-chich-ah, his x mark, [L. S.]

Ehi-o-che-tubbe, his x mark, [L. S.]
Nuck-sho-pubbe, his x mark, [L. S.]
Fah-lah-mo-tubbe, his x mark, [L. S.]
Co-chub-be, his x mark, [L. S.]
Thomas Sely, his x mark, [L. S.]
Oke-lah-sha-pi-a, his x mark, [L. S.]
Signed and sealed in presence of—
Ben. Reynolds, Indian agent,
John L. Allen, subagent,
Nath. Anderson, secretary to
commissioner,
Benjamin Love, United States
interpreter,
Robt. Gordon, of Mississippi,
George Wightman,
John Donley,
D. S. Parrish,
S. Daggett, of Mississippi,
Wm. A. Clurm, of Mississippi,
G. W. Long,
W. D. King,
John H. McKennie.

1834—The treaty of 1834 set aside a reservation for George Colbert to include land sixty yards beyond his dwelling house at Colbert's Ferry on the Natchez Trace where his wife Tuskiahooto Doublehead was buried. George Colbert is the only son of James Logan Colbert who signs this treaty. The treaty identifies the mechanisms for the division of property among the Chickasaws and reservations provided by the United States.

Treaty with the Chickasaw, 1834

May 24, 1834. 7 Stat., 450. | Proclamation, July 1, 1834.

Articles of convention and agreement proposed by the Commissioners on the part of the United States, in pursuance of the request made, by the Delegation representing the Chickasaw Nation of Indians, and which have been agreed to.

ARTICLE 1

It is agreed that perpetual amity, peace and friendship, shall exist between the United States, and the Chickasaw Nation of Indians.

ARTICLE 2

The Chickasaws are about to abandon their homes, which they have long cherished and loved; and though hitherto unsuccessful, they still hope to find a country, adequate to the wants and support of their people, somewhere west of the Mississippi and within the territorial limits of the United States; should they do so, the Government of the United States, hereby consent to protect and defend them against the inroads of any other tribe of Indians, and from the whites; and agree to keep them without the limits of any State or Territory.

The Chickasaws pledge themselves never to make war upon any Indian people, or upon the whites, unless they are so authorized by the United States. But if war be made upon them, they will be permitted to defend themselves, until assistance, be given to them by the United States, as shall be the case.

ARTICLE 3

The Chickasaws are not acquainted with the laws of the whites, which are extended over them and the many intruders which break into their country, interrupting their rights and disturbing their repose, leave no alternative whereby restraint can be afforded, other than an appeal to the military force of the country, which they are unwilling to ask for, or see resorted to; and therefore they agree to forbear such a request, for prevention of this great evil, with the understanding, which is admitted, that the agent of the United States, upon the application of the chiefs of the nation, will resort to every legal civil remedy, (at the expense of the United States,) to prevent intrusions upon the ceded country; and to restrain and remove trespassers from any selected reservations, upon application of the owner of the same.

And it is also agreed, that the United States, will continue some discreet person as agent, such as they now have, to whom they can look for redress of wrongs and injuries which may be attempted against them; and it is consented, that if any of their property, he taken by persons of the United States, covertly or forcibly, the agent on satisfactory and just complaint being made, shall pursue all lawful civil means, which the laws of the State permit, in which the wrong is done, to regain the same, or to obtain a just remuneration; and on failure or inability to procure redress, for the offended, against the offending party; payment for the loss sustained, on production of the record, and certificate of the facts, by the agent, shall be made by the United States; but in all such cases, satisfactory proof, for the establishing of the claim, shall be offered.

ARTICLE 4

The Chickasaws desire to have within their own direction and control, the means of taking care of themselves. Many of their people are quite competent to manage their affairs, though some are not capable, and might be imposed upon by designing persons; it is therefore agreed that the reservations hereinafter admitted, shall not be permitted to be sold, leased, or disposed of unless it appear by the certificate of at least two of the following persons, to wit: Ish-ta-ho-ta-pa the King, **Levi Colbert**, **George Colbert**, Martin Colbert, Isaac Alberson, Henry Love, and Benj. Love, of which five have affixed their names to this treaty, that the party owning or claiming the same, is capable to manage, and to take care of his or her affairs; which fact, to the best of his knowledge and information, shall be certified by the agent; and furthermore that a fair consideration has been paid; and thereupon, the deed of conveyance shall be valid provided the President of the United States, or such other person as he may designate shall approve of the same, and endorse it on the deed; which said deed and approval, shall be registered, at the place, and within the time, required by the laws of the State, in which the land may be situated; otherwise to be void. And where such certificate is not obtained; upon the recommendation of a majority of the Delegation, and the approval of the agent, at the discretion of the President of the United States, the same may be sold; but the consideration thereof, shall remain as part of the general Chickasaw fund in the hands of the Government, until such time as the chiefs in council shall think it advisable to pay it to the claimant or to those, who may rightfully claim under said claimant, and shall so recommend it. And as the King, **Levi Colbert**, and the Delegation, who have signed this agreement, and to whom certain important and interesting duties pertaining to the nation, are assigned, may die, resign, or remove, so that their people may be without the benefit of their services, it is stipulated, that as often as any vacancy happens, by death, resignation, or otherwise, the chiefs shall select some discrete person of their nation to till the occurring vacancy, who, upon a certificate of qualification, discretion and capability, by the agent, shall be appointed by the Secretary of War; whereupon, he shall possess all the authority granted to those who are here named and the nation will make to the person so appointed, such reasonable compensation, as they with the assent of the agent and the Secretary of War, may think right, proper and reasonable to be allowed.

ARTICLE 5

It is agreed that the fourth article of the "Treaty of Pontotock," be so changed, that the following reservations be granted in fee:—To heads of families, being Indians, or having Indian families, consisting of ten persons, and upwards, four sections of land are reserved. To those who have five and less than ten persons, three sections. Those who have less than five, two sections. Also those who own more than ten slaves shall be entitled to one additional section; and those owning ten and less than ten to half a section. These reservations shall be confined, to the sections or fractional sections on which the party claiming lives, or to such as are contiguous or adjoining to the sections resided upon, subject to the following restrictions and conditions:—*Firstly*. In cases where there are interferences arising, the oldest occupant or settler, shall have the preference, or, *Secondly*. Where the land is adjudged unfit for cultivation, by the Agent, and three of the seven persons, named in the fourth article above the party entitled, shall be, and is, hereby authorized, to locate his claim upon other lands, which may be unappropriated, and not subject to any other claim; and where two or more persons, insist upon the entry of the same unappropriated section or fractional section, the priority of right shall be determined by lot; and where a fractional section is taken leaving a balance greater or less than the surveyed subdivision of a section, then the deficiency shall be made up, by connecting all the deficiencies so arising: and the Register and Receiver thereupon, shall locate full or fractional sections, fit for cultivation, in the names respectively of the different persons claiming which shall be held by them as tenants in common, according to the respective interests of those who are concerned; and the proceeds when sold by the parties claiming, shall be divided according to the interests, which each may have in said section or fractional section, so located, or the same may be divided agreeably to quality or quantity.

ARTICLE 6

Also reservations of a section to each, shall be granted to persons male and female, not being heads of families, who are of the age of twenty-one years, and upwards, a list of whom, within a reasonable time shall be made out by the seven persons herein before mentioned, and filed with the Agent, upon whose certificate of its believed accuracy, the Register and Receiver, shall cause said reservations to be located upon lands fit for cultivation, but not to interfere with the settlement rights of others. The persons thus entitled, are to be excluded from the estimated numbers contained in any family enumeration, as is provided for in the fifth article preceding: and as to the sale, lease, or disposition of their reserves, they are to be subject to the conditions and restrictions, set forth in the fourth article. In these and in all other reserves where the party owning or entitled, shall die, the interest in the same shall belong to his wife, or the wife and children, or to the husband, or to the husband and children, if there be any; and in cases of death, where there is neither husband wife, nor children left, the same shall be disposed of for the general benefit; and the proceeds go into the general Chickasaw fund. But where the estate as is prescribed in this article comes to the children, and having so come, either of them dies, the survivor or survivors of them, shall be entitled to the same. But this rule shall not endure longer than for five years nor beyond the period when the Chickasaws may leave their present for a new home.

ARTICLE 7

Where any white man, before the date hereof has married an Indian woman, the reservation he may be entitled to under this treaty, she being alive, shall be in her name, and no right of alienation of the same shall purtain to the husband unless he divest her of the title, after the mode and manner that feme coverts, usually divest themselves of title to real estate, that is, by the acknowledgment of the wife which may be taken before the Agent, and certified by him, that she consents to the sale freely, and without compulsion from her husband, who shall at the same time certify that the head of such family is prudent, and competent to care of and manage his affairs; otherwise the proceeds of said sale shall be subject to the provisions and restrictions contained in the fourth article of this agreement. Rights to reservations as are herein, and in other articles of this agreement secured, will purtain to those who have heretofore intermarried with the Chickasaws and are residents of the nation.

ARTICLE 8

Males and females below the age of twenty-one years, whose father being dead, the mother again has married, or who have neither father nor mother, shall each be entitled to half a section of land, but shall not be computed as parts of families under the fifth article, the same to be located under the direction of the Agent, and under the supervision of the Secretary of War, so as not to interfere with any settlement right. These lands may be sold upon a recommendation of a majority of the seven persons, heretofore named in this agreement, setting forth that it will prove advantageous to the parties interested; subject however, to the approval of the President, or such other person as he shall designate. If sold, the funds arising shall be retained, in the possession of the Government, or if the President deem it advisable they shall be invested in stocks for the benefit of the parties interested, if there be a sufficient sum to be invested, (and it can be invested,) until said persons marry or come of age, when the amount shall be paid over to those who are entitled to receive it provided a majority of the seven persons, with the Agent, shall certify, that in their opinion, it will be to their interest and advantage,then, and in that case, the proceeds shall be paid over to the party or parties entitled to receive them.

ARTICLE 9

But, in running the sectional lines, in some cases it will happen, that the spring and the dwelling house, or the spring and the cleared land or the cleared land and the dwelling house of settlers, may be separated by sectional lines, whereby manifest inconvenience and injury will be occasioned; it is agreed, that when any of these occurrences arise, the party shall be entitled as parts and portions of his reservations, to the adjoining section or fraction, as the case may be, unless there be some older occupant, claiming a preference; and in that event, the right of the party shall extend no farther than to give to the person, thus affected and injured, so much of his separated property, as will secure the spring; also, where a sectional line shall separate any improvement, dwelling house, kitchen or stable, so much of the section, which contains them, shall be added into the occupied section, as will secure them to their original owner; and then and in that case, the older occupant being deprived of preference, shall have his deficiency thus occasioned, made up to him by some fractional section, or after the mode pointed out in the latter part of the fifth article of this treaty.

ARTICLE 10

Reservations are admitted to the following persons, in addition to those which may be claimed under the fifth article of this Treaty to wit:-Four sections to their beloved and faithful old **Chief Levi Colb**ert; To **George Colbert**, Martin Colbert, Isaac Alberson, Henry Love and Benj. Love, in consideration of the trouble they have had in coming to Washington, and of the farther trouble hereafter to be encountered in taking care of the interests of their people, under the provisions of this treaty, one section of land to each. Also there is a fractional section, between the residence of **George Colbert**, and the Tennessee River, upon which he has a ferry, it is therefore consented, that said **George Colbert**, shall own and have so much of said fraction, as may be contained in the following lines, to wit.-beginning near Smith's Ferry at the point where the base meridian line and the Tennessee river come in contact,-thence south so far as to pass the dwelling-house, (and sixty yards beyond it,) within which is interred the body of his wife,-thence east of the river and down the same to the point of beginning. Also there shall be reserved to him an island, in said river, nearly opposite to this fraction, commonly called Colberts Island. A reservation also of two sections is admitted to Ish-ta-ho-ta-pa the King of the Chickasaw Nation. And to Min-ta-ho-yea the mother of Charles Colbert one section of land. Also one section, each, to the following persons: Im-mub-bee, Ish-tim-o-lut-ka, Ah-to-ho-woh, Pis-tah-lah-tubbe, Capt. Samuel Seley and William McGilvery. To Col. Benj. Reynolds their long tried and faithful Agent, who has guarded their interests and twice travelled with their people far west, beyond the Mississippi, to aid them in seeking and finding a home, there is granted two sections of land. Jointly to William Cooper and John Davis, lawyers of Mississippi who have been faithful to the Indians, in giving them professional advice, and legal assistance, and who are to continue to do so, within the States of Tennessee, Alabama and Mississippi, while the Chickasaw people remain in said States, one section is granted. To Mrs. Margt. Allen wife of the subagent in her own right, half a section. These reservations to Benj. Reynolds, William Cooper, James Davis and Margt. Allen, are to be located so as not to interfere with the Indian reservations.

Death of Colonel Benjamin Reynolds-*The Franklin (Ala.) Democrat announces the death of Colonel BENJAMIN REYNOLDS, late Chickasaw Agent, which took place at his residence in north Alabama on the 20th September 1843 Ult. Colonel REYNOLDS was in the 60th year of his age.*

ARTICLE 11

After the reservations are taken and located, which shall be the case as speedily as may be after the surveys are completed, of which the Register and Receiver shall give notice, the residue of the Chickasaw country shall be sold, as public lands of the United States are sold, with this difference; The lands as surveyed shall be offered at public sale at a price not less than one dollar and a quarter per acre; and thereafter for one year those which are unsold, and which shall have been previously offered at public sale shall be liable to private entry and sale at that price; Thereafter, and for one year longer they shall be subject to entry and private sale, at one dollar per acre; Thereafter and during the third year, they shall be subject to sale and entry, at fifty cents per acre; Thereafter, and during the fourth year, at twenty-five cents per acre; and afterwards at twelve and a half cents per acre. But as it may happen, in the fourth and after years, that the expenses may prove greater than the receipts, it is agreed, that at any time after the third year, the Chickasaws may declare the residue of their lands abandoned to the United States, and if so, they shall be thenceforth acquitted of all and every expense on account of the sale of the same.

And that they may be advised of these matters it is stipulated, that the Government of the United States, within six months after any public sale takes place, shall advise them of the receipts and expenditures, and of balances in their favor; and also at regular intervals of six months, after the first report is made, will afford them information of the proceeds of all entries and sales. The funds thence resulting, after the necessary expenses of surveying and selling, and other advances which may be made, are repaid to the United States, shall from time to time be invested in some secure stocks, redeemable within a period of not more than twenty years; and the United States will cause the interest arising therefrom, annually to be paid to the Chickasaws.

ARTICLE 12

When any portion of the country is fully surveyed, the President may order the same to be sold, but will allow six months, from the date of the first notice to the first sale; and three months' notice of any subsequent intended public sale, within which periods of time, those who can claim reservations, in the offered ranges of country, shall file their applications and entries with the Register and Receiver; that the name of the owner or claimant of the same, may be entered and marked on the general plat, at the office, whereby mistakes in the sales may be avoided, and injuries be prevented.

ARTICLE 13

If the Chickasaws shall be so fortunate as to procure a home, within the limits of the United States, it is agreed, that with the consent of the President and Senate so much of their invested stocks, as may be necessary to the purchase of a country for them to settle in, shall be permitted to them to be sold, or the United States will advance the necessary amount, upon a guarantee and pledge of an equal amount of their stocks; also, as much of them may be sold, with the consent of the President and Senate, as shall be adjudged necessary for establishing schools, mills, blacksmiths shops; and for the education of their children; and for any other needful purpose, which their situation and condition, may make, and by the President and Senate be considered, necessary; and on the happening of such a contingency and information thereof being given of an intention of the whole of any portion of the nation to remove; the United States will furnish competent persons, safely to conduct them to their future destination, and also supplies necessary to the same, and for one year after their arrival at the west, provided the Indians shall desire supplies, to be furnished for so long a period; the supplies so afforded, to be chargeable to the general Chickasaw account, provided the funds of said nation shall be found adequate to the expenses which under this and other articles of this agreement may be required.

ARTICLE 14

It is understood and agreed, that articles twelve and thirteen of the "Treaty of Pontotock," of the twentieth day of October one thousand, eight hundred and thirty-two, and which was concluded with Genl. John Coffee shall be retained; all the other articles of said treaty, inconsistent in any respect with the provisions of this, are declared to be revoked. Also so much of the supplemental treaty as relates to Colbert Moore; to the bond of **James Colbert** transferred to Robert Gordon; to the central position of the Land Office; to the establishment of mail routes through the Chickasaw country; and as it respects the privilege given to John Donely; be, and the same are declared to be in full force.

ARTICLE 15

By the sixth article of a treaty made with the Chickasaw nation, by Andrew Jackson and Isaac Shelby, on the nineteenth day of October, one thousand eight hundred and eighteen, it was provided that a Commissioner should be appointed, to mark the southern boundary of said cession; now it is agreed that the line which was run and marked by the Commissioner on the part of the United States, in pursuance of said treaty, shall be considered the true line to the extent that the rights and interests of the Chickasaws are concerned, and no farther.

ARTICLE 16

The United States agree that the appropriation made by Congress, in the year one thousand eight hundred and thirty-three, for carrying into effect "the treaty with the Chickasaws," shall be applicable to this; to be reimbursed by them: and their agent may receive and be charged with the same, from time to time, as in the opinion of the Secretary of War, any portion may be wanted for national purposes, by the Chickasaws; of which nature and character, shall be considered their present visit to Washington City.

Done at the city of Washington, on the 24th day of May, one thousand eight hundred and thirty-four.

Jn. H. Eaton, commissioner on the part of the United States.	*Ben. Reynolds, Indian agent,*
	G. W. Long,
George Colbert, *his x mark,*	*James Standefer,*
Isaac Albertson, his x mark,	*Thomas S. Smith,*
Martin Colbert, *[L. S.]*	*Saml. Swartwout,*
Henry Love, [L. S.]	*Wm. Gordon,*
Benjamin Love, [L. S.]	*F. W. Armstrong, c. agent,*
Witnesses—	*John M. Millard.*
Charles F. Little, secretary to commissioner,	

The undersigned, appointed by the Chickasaw Nation of Indians in the two-fold capacity of a delegate and interpreter, hereby declares that in all that is set forth in the above articles of convention and agreement, have been by him fully and accurately interpreted and explained, and that the same has been approved by the entire delegation. May 24, 1834.

Benjamin Love, delegate and interpreter.
Charles F. Little, secretary to commissioner.
Ben. Reynolds, Indian agent.

Articles supplementary to those concluded and signed, by the United States Commissioner, and the Chickasaw delegation on the 24th day of May, one thousand eight hundred and thirty-four which being agreed to by the President and, Senate of the United States, are to stand as part of said treaty.

May 24, 1834. | 7 Stat., 456.

ARTICLE 1

It is represented that the old chiefs **Levi Colbert** and Isaac Alberson, who have rendered many and valuable services to their nation, desire on account of their health, to visit some watering place during the present year, for recovery and restoration; it is agreed that there be paid to the agent for these purposes' and to discharge some debts which are due and owing from the nation, the sum of three thousand dollars, out of the appropriation of one thousand eight hundred and thirty-three, for carrying into effect the "Treaty of Pontotock," which said sum so far as used is to be hereafter reimbursed to the nation, by said **Levi Colbert** and Isaac Alberson, and by the nation to the United States, as other advances are to be reimbursed, from the sale of their lands.

ARTICLE 2

The Chickasaw people express a desire that the Government shall at the expense of the United States, educate some of their children, and they urge the justice of their application, on the ground, that they have ever been faithful and friendly to the people of this country, that they have never raised the tomahawk, to shed the blood of an American, and have given up heretofore to their white brothers, extensive and valuable portions of their country, at a price wholly inconsiderable and inadequate; and from which the United States have derived great wealth and important advantages; therefore, with the advice and consent of the President and Senate of the United States, it is consented, that three thousand dollars for fifteen years, be appropriated and applied under the direction of the Secretary of War, for the education and instruction within the United States, of such children male and female or either, as the seven persons named in the treaty to which this is a supplement, and their successors, with the approval of the agent, from time to time may select and recommend.

ARTICLE 3

The Chickasaw Nation desire to close finally, all the business they have on the east side of the Mississippi, that their Great Father, may be no more troubled with their complaints and to this end, they ask the Government to receive from them a tract of land, of four miles square, heretofore reserved under the 4th article of their "Treaty of

1818," and to pay them within three months, from the date of this arrangement, the Government price of one dollar and a quarter per acre, for said reserve; and accordingly the same is agreed to, provided a satisfactory relinquishment of title from the parties interested, be filed with the Secretary of War, previous to said payment being made.

ARTICLE 4

Benj. Reynolds, agent at the time of paying their last annuity, had stolen from him by a negro slave of the Chickasaws, a box containing one thousand dollars; the chiefs of the Chickasaw people satisfied of the fact, and hence unwilling to receive the lost amount from their agent, ask, and it is agreed, that the sum so stolen and lost shall be passed to the credit of their nation by the United States, to be drawn on hereafter for their national purposes.

ARTICLE 5

The Chickasaw people are aware that one clerk is insufficient to the bringing of their lands early into market; and rather than encounter the delay which must ensue, they prefer the increased expense of an additional one. It is therefore stipulated that the President shall appoint another clerk, at the same annual compensation, agreed upon by the "Treaty of Pontotock;" who shall be paid after the manner prescribed therein. But whenever the President shall be of opinion that the services of any officer employed under this treaty, for the sale of lands can be dispensed with; he will in justice to the Chickasaws, and to save them from unnecessary expenses, discontinue the whole, or such as can be dispensed with.
Signed the 24th of May, 1834.

Jn. H. Eaton, commissioner on the part of the United States.
George Colbert, *his x mark,*
Isaac Albertson, his x mark,
Martin Colbert, *[L. S.]*
Henry Love, [L. S.]
Benjamin Love, [L. S.]
Witnesses:

Charles F. Little, secretary to commissioner,
Ben. Reynolds, Indian agent,
G. W. Long,
Thomas S. Smith,
Saml. Swartwout,
Wm. Gordon,
F. W. Armstrong, C. agent,
John M. Millard.

Chickasaw Removal

Indian removal was one of the darkest blots of American history because of the total disregard for native Indian people who had called this area home for thousands of years. The Chickasaws were the first tribe in the Tennessee Valley to make peace and ally with the United States Government. The Colbert brothers, especially George Colbert, served with the United States military in several campaigns against other rebellious Indian tribes; and, the brothers were promoted as officers because of their contributions during several conflicts. George's older half-brother William Colbert was promoted to the rank of General. The Chickasaws had fought the French, Spanish, and finally the British while serving under General Andrew Jackson.

Since the Chickasaw Colbert boys had served with General Andrew Jackson in various military campaigns, they held Jackson in high esteem. Even though the Chickasaws trusted and admired Jackson, he would ultimately be responsible for their removal to the west of the Mississippi River by 1837. One motivating factor for the removal of the Chickasaws and other Indian people was the greed of Andrew Jackson for their lands. Andrew Jackson became one of the first white land owners in Lawrence County, Alabama. Even though the Chickasaws owned the land by treaty, Andrew Jackson got David Melton, a Cherokee mixed-blood and nephew of Doublehead, to deed him the Melton's Bluff Plantation and some 60 black slaves on November 22, 1816, prior to the Turkey Town Treaty being ratified in July 1817. It is obvious that Jackson speculated on Indian lands and forced his control and ownership of large tracts of Indian property. Jackson had a vested interest in the removal of Indian people even though they had served him faithfully.

According to Francis P. Prucha (1975) in her book, _Documents on United States Indian Policy_, Andrew Jackson seems to justify the taking of Indian lands for his personal benefit as seen in a speech by Jackson on December 8, 1829. The statements he makes incriminate his actions and attempt to excuse his land grabbing scheme as follows: _"The Southern tribes, having mingled much with the whites and made some progress in the arts of civilized life, have lately attempted to erect an independent government within the limits of Georgia and Alabama. These States, claiming to be the only sovereigns within their territories, extended their laws over the Indians, which induced the latter to call upon the United States for protections."_ Jackson went on the say, _"It seems to me visionary to suppose that in this state of things claims can be allowed on tracts of country on which they have neither dwelt nor made improvements, merely because they have seen them from the mountain or passed them in the chase."_

Jackson was elected President of the United States in 1828; and this great Indian fighter of the Southeast, believed in the spoils of the system, *"To the victor belong the spoils of war."* Even though Indian people in the southeast were a defeated people and were living at peace with the United States, Jackson's greed for all Indian lands was displayed to the public by his passage of Indian Removal Act in 1830. After the removal act was passed, President Andrew Jackson continued his efforts in securing title to all Indian lands and the removal of all Indian people from the Southeastern United States which was finally accomplished by 1840. As he had earlier stolen land from Indian people in the Tennessee Valley prior to the time that any legal land claims could be made, President Andrew Jackson had no reservations about eliminating all Indian lands east of the Mississippi River after becoming President of the United States.

According to Foreman (1989), *"The major part of the Choctaw tribe had emigrated west by the end of 1833 and it was planned to remove the Chickasaw Indians and cause them to be united on the same domain and under one tribal government. The efforts to affect a union of these tribes were responsible for much dissatisfaction on the part of the Chickasaw people and delayed their removal. Thus it was not until 1837 that their emigration began, but it was practically completed within a year"* (Foreman, 1989).

The Chickasaw tribe was the smallest group of Indians to be removed from the Tennessee and Tombigbee River Valley areas of the Southeastern United States. In 1830 before removing to Indian Territory west of the Mississippi River, the Chickasaw tribe sent a group to inspect the land of the proposed relocation. The group of Chickasaws inspected the area bound by the Arkansas and Canadian rivers to which they were to settle and rejected the proposed land for suitability to the tribe. Ratification of the 1830 Treaty of Franklin depended on the results of the trip. A few months after their trip one of the tribal leaders, Levi Colbert, wrote a letter to President Andrew Jackson, saying the Chickasaws had found the land unsuitable. The rejection by the Chickasaw Nation effectively voided the treaty and delayed removal to the west. In 1833 another delegation of Chickasaws came through the area on their way to Indian Territory to look for land under provisions of the 1832 Treaty of Pontotoc. This area was also rejected by the Chickasaw Nation. After other inspections of land in the west during 1835 and 1836, the same result reoccurred with the Chickasaws rejecting the proposed area. The exploring party of 1836 reached an agreement with the Choctaws at Doaksville, Indian Territory, whereby the Chickasaws could purchase a part of the western portion of the Choctaw domain as a permanent home. At the time, the Chickasaws numbered about 4,914 and 1,156 slaves. Finally in January of 1837 a treaty was approved by the Chickasaw Nation. Eventually in 1837, the Chickasaw leaders met with the Choctaw leaders near Fort Towson in Indian Territory and agreed to pay the Choctaw for the part of the Choctaws' region in their southern Indian Territory.

Once the treaty was agreed upon and signed, arrangements were made for Chickasaw removal to begin in the summer 1837 under the supervision of A. A. M. Upshaw. Following the usual method for removal, each party would be assigned the following: a conductor to lead the group; a physician to take care of the group and determined how far to travel each day; and, a disbursing officer to distribute rations. The Chickasaw tribe was divided into several groups for the removal west of the Mississippi River. The leaders of the different groups included: Colonel A.M.M. Upshaw, Supervisor of Chickasaw Removal; John M. Millard; Captain Joe A. Phillips; Dr. C.G. Keenan; W.R. Guy; Chief Ishtehopa; Kin-hi-cha; and Chief Sealy with Lieutenant Governor Morris and Daniel McCurtain an interpreter. Some of the removal groups of Chickasaws took the overland route and while other groups chose a water route. The Chickasaws being removed arrived at Memphis, Tennessee in November 1837; and, from Memphis many took steamships under the direction of Captain Simeon Buckner to Fort Coffee. Some Chickasaws traveled by land directed by John M. Millard and other removal leaders.

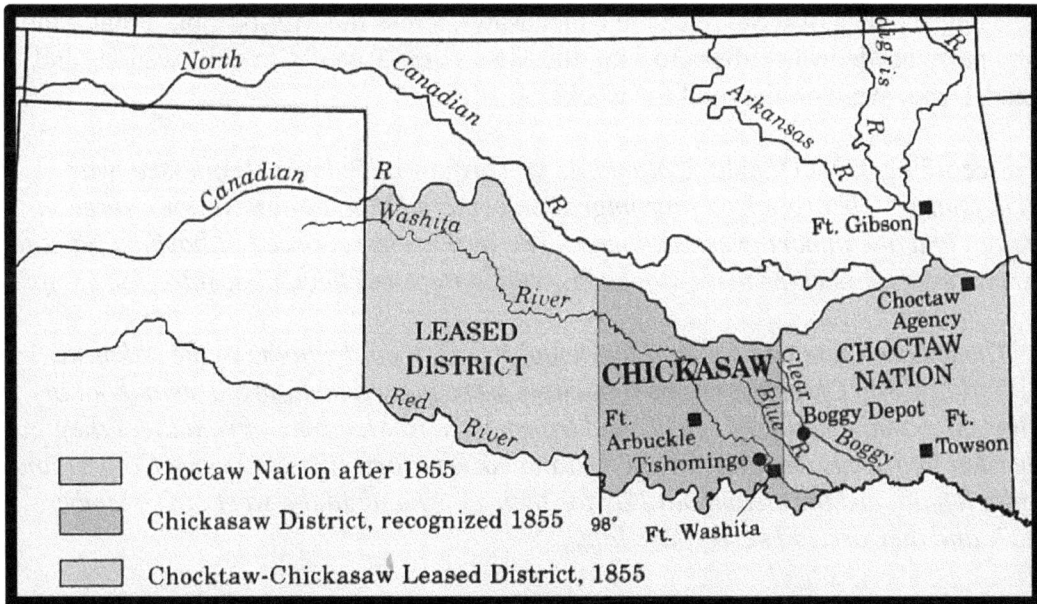

The first overland group of 450 Chickasaws was led by conductor John M. Millard and disbursing agent Captain Joseph A. Phillips. The group marched with their personal belongings, slaves, and livestock to Memphis, Tennessee and crossed the Mississippi River on July 4, 1837. The Mississippi Swamp with their wagons was a difficult task because of heavy rains. Millard said, "We traveled boggy roads and through mud and water, frequently up to the axletrees of the wagons and made about eight miles a day."

During the summer and fall of 1837, some 4,000 Chickasaws enrolled for removal and began the trip west of the Mississippi River. In four groups they marched to Memphis and began establishing their camps on November 9, 1837. Colonel A. M. Upshaw contracted with Kentuckian Simeon Buckner to transport the Chickasaws by boat from Memphis to Fort Coffee, using six steamboats: Kentuckian, Cinderella, DeKalb, Fox, Cavalier, and the Itasca. These boats would be pulling flatboats and keelboats to carry the Chickasaws' property. Five contingents of Chickasaws had left by water; thus, four boats left Memphis on November 25, 1837. The steamboats carrying the Chickasaws reached Fort Coffee in eight to ten days.

However, about a thousand Chickasaws decided to avoid the boats and would drive their livestock overland. Since supplies were not set up for overland removal, Phillips and Upshaw had to hire additional teams and drivers for the overland parties. In addition, M.B. Winchester, Simeon Buckner, and J. McMahon were hired to ferry horses, oxen, supplies, wagons, and the Chickasaws across the Mississippi. Finally the overland party headed west after crossing the Mississippi River with their wagons and horses; and, they were on the road for weeks.

According to McDonald, *Colonel A. M. Upshaw of Pulaski, Tennessee, was placed in charge. He organized four migration centers in the Indian Nation: three in Mississippi and one in northwest Alabama. The Indians were forced at bayonet point to leave their homes and enter these stockades, which were in effect, concentration camps.*

Their main route was by land to Memphis and, then, by boats to the Arkansas River. Initially, 300 Chickasaws and Choctaws were placed on board a steamboat at Waterloo, Alabama on July 13, 1837, and transported to Memphis. From there they were herded into boats destined for the Oklahoma Territory. Chief George Colbert and his family left aboard the steamboat Fox for their new home in the west on November 14, 1837, and they arrived seven days later.

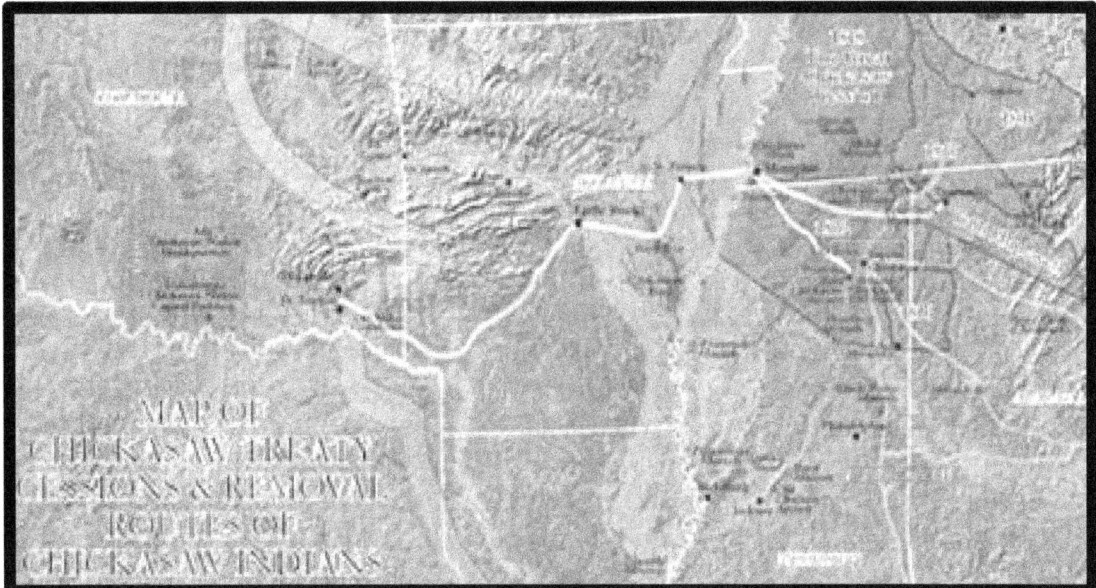

Map of Chickasaw Treaty Cession and Removal Routes of Chickasaw Indians

Before leaving for his new home along the Red River, George Colbert presented his colorful sash and cap used during times of ceremony to a neighbor as a token of the friendship they had enjoyed. The sash was later donated by a descendant of this neighbor to the Indian Mound Museum at Florence. She presented Chief Colbert's cap to the Helen Keller Library at Tuscumbia. Chief Colbert also left behind a silver medal that had been presented to him by the President of the United States in 1801. Colbert gave this medal to Lewis Alsobrook whose family had settled in a small valley near the Alsobrook community in west Colbert County. Alsobrook, an employee of Chief Colbert, had been engaged to marry one of the old chief's beautiful daughters. It was said that she broke the engagement because she did not want to be left behind when her family was removed to the Oklahoma Territory. Although the Chickasaws endured better than the Cherokees, it was not uncommon for the long trains of horses and wagons to stop and bury their dead as often as four or five miles in a single day. Their worst treatment was at the hands of white contractors who fed them spoiled meat and other deteriorated rations. When the Chickasaws reached Oklahoma Territory they were scattered into five relocation camps, some over one hundred miles apart. This, according to Colonel Upshaw, was due to the threat of smallpox among the Arkansas and Canadian River settlements (McDonald, 2007).

Bowes Reed McIlvaine, a Louisville merchant, crossed the Mississippi with the land party and described the Chickasaws as they marched to the river. *"I do not think that I have ever been a witness of so remarkable a scene as was formed by this immense column of moving Indians, several thousand, with the train of Government wagons, the multitude of horses; it is said three to each Indian and beside at least six dogs and cats to an Indian. They were all most comfortably clad—the men in complete Indian dress with showy shawls tied in turban fashion round their heads—dashing about on their horses, like Arabs, many of them presenting the finest countenances and figures that I ever saw. The women also very decently clothed like white women, in calico gowns— but much tidier and better put on than common white-people--and how beautifully they managed their horses, how proud and calm and erect, they sat in full gallop. The young women have remarkably mild and soft countenances and are singularly decorous in their dress and deportment. There were some white women, wives of Indians and they were decidedly the least neat of the party.*

I shall never forget the singular picture the whole party presented, when all were got across the Mississippi River--and in one mass covered the whole open ground on the bank. It was a scene to paint, not describe with words—civilized society is as uniform and tame in the dress and manner and equipage that a crowd has no life in it. Here however no one man was like another, no horse caparisoned like another. Their clothing was of all the bright colors of the rainbow and arranged with every possible variety of form & taste—but all flowing and fantastic and untailored like. I wish I could have sketched that scene, as they stood each above the other from the water's edge to the top of the ascending ground. They seemed grouped there, to present one grand display of barbaric pomp. Only the poorest of the squaws carried burdens—nearly all had ponies for that purpose, which they led, riding other horses on good side saddles. The fondness for dogs was the most prevalent and amusing. One old woman who had lost her pony was carrying a heavy load on her back with a belt across her forehead— to balance which, she had a basket in front suspended round her neck in which were nine fine puppies; the respectable mother of which, trotted contentedly—though doggedly behind, to see that none were dropped by the way. Some had their cats and litters of kittens—others their favorite chickens, ducks, and turkeys."

McIlavine also described the camps at night as follows: *"It was a striking scene at night—when the multitudes of fires kindled, showed to advantage the whole face of the country covered with the white tents and white covered wagons, with all the interstices . . .filled with a dense mass of animal life in the shape of savages, uncouth looking white hunters, the picturesque looking Indian Negroes, with dress belonging to no country but partaking of all, and these changing and mingling with the hundreds of horses hobbled and turned out to feed and the troops of dogs chasing about in search of food--and then you would hear the whoops of Indians calling their family party together to receive their rations, from another quarter a wild song from the Negroes preparing the corn, with the strange chorus that the rest would join in--and then the fires would catch tall dead trees and rushing to the tops throw a strong glare over all this moving scene, deepening the savage traits of the men, and softening the features of the women. It was my delight to wander at will, wherever anything strange led me, going into the tents—making friends with the men by shaking hands and with the women by playing with the little fat naked wild children—dividing apples among them, to their great satisfaction. Great pains were taken by the agents to keep liquor from the men, and few were drunk—the women neither drink nor smoke—but mostly were seated on skins sewing or doing some kind of work—singularly calm and composed—and contrasted with the incessant galloping about of the men."*

The last official contingent of Chickasaws to be removed west of the Mississippi River began gathering at Memphis, Tennessee in late October of 1838. This last group numbering some 300 Chickasaws began crossing the river in November, 1838. The crossing was problematic at that time because low water levels made ferrying across the river extremely difficult. Some historians claim that small groups of Chickasaws continue to head west through 1850; but, finally, the removal of the Chickasaw Nation from their ancestral homelands was complete. Most of the Chickasaws that were removed west remained in the vicinity of Boggy Depot and Fort Townson until the military post at Fort Washita was established in 1842, and some protection from the plains Indians could be afforded them.

Fort Washita--*Fort Washita was established in 1842 in the Choctaw Nation, Indian Territory, as the southwestern-most military post of the United States. The mission of the soldiers was to protect the recently immigrated Choctaw and Chickasaw Indians. The Southern Plains Indians to the west and non-Indian intruders posed threats to the peace and stability of the region.*

Troops stationed at Fort Washita on a rotational basis during the 1840s...to the beginning of the Civil War in 1861...After the war the Chickasaw Nation received the old post grounds and buildings from the federal government. **The prominent Chickasaw Colbert family owned the property until it was acquired in 1962 by the Oklahoma Historical Society.** *The site is on the National Register of Historic Places and designated as a National Historic Landmark* (Oklahoma Historical Society Publication, 2010).

Fort Washita, Oklahoma remains of South Barracks

According to McDonald, *"The once brave Chickasaws, who were feared by all other Indians, were afraid to occupy their western lands. They obtained permission from their old enemies, the Choctaws, to use part of their holdings until the Federal Government could send troops to protect them from the Kickapoos and other wild western tribes. They eventually moved to their own lands. However, only about three-fourths of the tribe actually occupied the territory that had been set aside for them. Mingling with the Choctaws caused them to lose much of their identity as the once proud Chickasaws.*

The Chickasaws received over three million dollars from surplus land sales they had vacated in Alabama and Mississippi. This amount provided annual interest payments from $60,000 to $70,000, an average income of $75 to $100 for each family. As a result these once proud people became idle, with some braves living in tents for the remainder of their days. Recognizing what was happening their agent, Colonel

Upshaw, led them into a partial Renaissance that resulted in the Chickasaws becoming productive farmers in the Red River Valley of Oklahoma.

The Colberts, along with the other wealthy mixed bloods, came to the western lands early in the removal period. They selected choice locations on the open tracts along the Red River, putting their slaves to work planting cotton and corn. They regularly returned to Mississippi and Alabama to look after their gins, mercantile operations, and homesteads until they finally were forced to cut all ties, and to permanently relocate in their western lands. Chief George Colbert settled near Doaksville in the fall of 1838 after returning for a time to his former lands in Mississippi. No individual worked harder than George Colbert to prevent his people from being uprooted and sent to the Oklahoma Territory. One of his final efforts was made on the streets of Tuscumbia where he gave a passionate speech on the behalf of the Chickasaw Nation (McDonald, 2007).

Death of George Colbert

George Colbert was the "Half Blood Prince" of his beloved Chickasaw people; he loved his Alabama and Mississippi homelands and did all in his power to remain in the land were his dead lay buried. He left his eastern home on November 14, 1837, and on November 7, 1839, was laid to rest near Fort Towson in the Choctaw Nation of Indian Territory. During his life, George Colbert conducted himself in a noble and honorable manner; he had a distinguished military career, rose to the rank of chief among the Chickasaws, and negotiated on behalf of his people with Presidents of the United States. After only two years in Indian Territory, George Colbert died a long way from his place of birth in a new land that did not belong to his Chickasaw people.

According to Grant Foreman (1989), *a number of wealthier half-breeds settled on the rich bottom lands near Fort Towson where they engaged on a large scale in raising cotton and other farm products. One of them Colonel George Colbert, the first year after his arrival prepared to plant from three to five hundred acres of cotton with the labor of his 150 slaves.*

For many years George Colbert had been conspicuous and valuable member of the Chickasaw Tribe. He lived to see his people through their great crisis, and then died in their new home, honored by all who knew him. The following account is from an army officer: "Fort Towson, November 7th, 1839. We this day buried with the honors of war, General George Colbert, the head chief of the Chickasaw Nation, a man of superior intelligence, the greatest of warriors, and the white man's friend. He was a revolutionary veteran; he served under General Washington in our struggle for independence, from which he received a commission of Major of Militia in the United States Service, and a sword

He served under General Wayne, and also under General Jackson in the Florida War against the Seminoles; for his bravery General Jackson presented him with a Colonel's commission, and afterwards a sword, when President of the United States. He gained the entire confidence of the officers he served under for his integrity and valor; he was physically and mentally a great man; although 95 years of age, he walked upright as a man of 25.

The commanding officer, on having received and read the commissions, ordered and escort from the fort, of three officers, a captain and sub-alternates; also all the men doing military duty, to escort his corpse to its last resting place with reversed arms and buried with the customary salute due his rank; he was interred with his saddle and bridle, the sword presented to him by Generals Washington and Jackson, and a United States flag. He was of great importance to the cause of civilization among his people by his examples of industry; he was a planter, his fields of cotton whitened the hills and dales near the fort. He educated his sons and located them on plantations among his people, and worked moral influence among them; he was looked up to as a father, and exercised a father's influence over his people.

Further information is given by the press of Tennessee: "He was born in the Chickasaw country, now north Mississippi, near the Tennessee River, and was a half-breed. Early becoming attached to the whites, he united himself and nation to their interests and was regularly commissioned a Colonel by President Washington. At St. Clair's defeat he was taken prisoner and after his release, accompanied General Wayne to the western frontier. He was with Jackson in all his campaigns; and in all situations on all occasions, proved himself the devoted friend, the sagacious counselor, the gallant soldier, uniting in a happy combination, the ennobling qualities of the Indian and white man. His unwavering amiable frankness, were proverbial with all who knew him. He was survived by three daughters and an adopted son (Foreman, 1989). It should be noted that George and Saleecie Doublehead Colbert's children were one quarter Scots, one eighth German, one quarter Chickasaw, and three eighths Cherokee.

George Colbert never made it to the promise land that would become the new Chickasaw Nation in the west because of threats from the western wild Indians. He died in the Choctaw Nation near Fort Towson after having two successful farming seasons with his cotton and corn. The location of George Colbert's grave site at Fort

Towson has been lost with the passing of time; but, the stories of his life will live forever. George Colbert and his family's namesake of Colbert County, Alabama will forever be a reminder of these Celtic Indian people that left their legacy on our historical landscape.

Last home of Chickasaw Chief George Colbert
Map showing Doaksville and Fort Towson

References

Britton, Morris L., *Colbert's Ferry*, Oklahoma Historical Society, "Colbert's Ferry" marker at Colbert homestead, 1978.

Bryan, Hob, *Mound Site Dates to 600 B.C.,* Tupelo Daily Journal, August 13, 1971.

Buggey, L. JoAnne, and others, *America! America!*, Scott, Foresman, and Company, Illinois, 1980.

Colbert, Richard A., *James Logan Colbert of the Chickasaws: The Man and the Myth*, The North Carolina Genealogical Society Journal, Volume XX, Number 2, May 1994.

Cushman, Horatio Bardwell, *History of the Choctaw, Chickasaw and Natchez Indians*, Headlight Printing House, University of California, 1899.

Daniels, Jonathan, *The Devil's Backbone: The Story of the Natchez Trace*, Pelican Publishing, 1985.

Davis, Cornelius, *The New York Missionary Magazine and Repository of Religious Intelligence*, Volume 1, University of Michigan, 1800.

Dow, Lorenzo, *History of Cosmopolite: or, the four volumes of Lorenzo's journal concentrated into one: containing his experience & travels, from childhood to 1814, being upwards of thirty-six years*, Printed and sold by John C. Totten, No.9 Bowery-Lane, Princeton University, 1814.

Durham, Walter T., *Isaac Bledsoe (1735-1793)*, Tennessee Encyclopedia of History and Culture, Gallatin, Tennessee, December 25, 2009.

Elliott, Jack D., Jr. *"The Buried City: A Meditation on History and Place"*, *Journal of Mississippi History* 66, Number 2, Summer 2004

Foreman, Carolyn Thomas, *Alexander McGillivray, Emperor of the Creeks*, Chronicles of Oklahoma, Volume 7, Number 1, March 1929.

Foreman, Grant, *The Five Civilized Tribes—Cherokee, Chickasaw, Choctaw, Creek, Seminole*, University of Oklahoma Press, 1989.

Garrett, William Robertson, John M. Bass, Albert Virgil Goodpasture, Editors, *American Historical Magazine*, Volume 5, Peabody Normal College, Tennessee Historical Society, University Press, Harvard University, 1900.

Gibson, Arrell, *The Chickasaws*, University of Oklahoma Press, Norman, Oklahoma, 1971.

Goodpasture, Albert V., *Indian Wars and Warriors of the Old Southwest, 1730-1807*, Tennessee Historical Magazine, Volume 4, Number 1, March 1918.

Green, Richard, *Chickasaws Visit President Washington* (1794), published by The Chickasaw Times, July 2009, printed in ushistory.org

Hunter, Clark, *The Life and Letters of Alexander Wilson*, Philadelphia: American Philosophical Society, 1983.

Kappler, Charles J., *Indian Affairs: Laws and Treaties*, Volume II, Government Printing Office, Washington, D.C., 1904.

Leftwich, Nina, *Two Hundred Years at Muscle Shoals*, The American Southern Publishing Company, Northport, Alabama, 1935.

Malone, James Henry, *The Chickasaw Nation: A Short Sketch of a Noble People*, Louisville, Kentucky, John P. Morton & Company, University of Michigan, 1922.

Martini, Don, *Southeastern Indian Notebook*, Ripley Printing, Ripley, Mississippi, 1986.

Meserve, John Bartlett, *Governor Cyrus Harris*, Chronicles of Oklahoma, Volume 15, Number 4, Oklahoma Historical Society, Oklahoma City, Oklahoma, December, 1937.

Mississippi Historical Society, *Publications of the Mississippi Historical Society*, Volume 7, Published by The Society, Harvard University, 1903.

Nicholson, Charles P., *Alexander Wilson's Travels in Tennessee*, The Migrant, Published by the Tennessee Ornithological Society, Volume 57, Number 1, March 1986.

Oklahoma Historical Society Publication, *Fort Washita*, Durant, Oklahoma, 2010.

Owen, Thomas McAdory and Marie Bankhead Owen, *History of Alabama and Dictionary of Alabama Biography*, Volume 1, The S. J. Clarke Publishing Company, Harvard University, 1921.

Parton, James, *Life of Andrew Jackson*, Volume 1, Mason Brothers Publishers, University of California, 1859.

Pickett, Albert James, *History of Alabama*, 1851.

Prucha, Francis Paul. *Documents of United States Indian Policy*, University of Nebraska Press, Lincoln, Nebraska, 1975.

Smith, Z. F., *History of Kentucky: From the earliest discoveries and settlements to the year 1891*, Courier-Journal Job Printing Company, 1891.

Stutzenberger, Fred, *The Natchez Trace Part III*, Muzzle Blasts Online, Volume 3, Number 6, January 1999.

Thayer, Bill, *Colonel John Montgomery*, Tennessee Historical Magazine, published by Tennessee Historical Society, May 11, 2009.

Warren, Harry, *Some Chickasaw Chiefs and Prominent Men*, Published by Mississippi Historical Society, Franklin Lafayette Riley, Editor, University of Virginia, 1904.

Warren, Harry Warren, *Chickasaw Traditions, Customs, etc.*,"Mississippi Historical Society Publications, VIII, Oxford, Mississippi (1898-1914), 1908.

Warren, Harry, "*Missions, Missionaries, Frontier Characters and Schools*", E. T. Winston, "Father" Stuart and the Monroe Mission, Meridian, Mississippi, 1927.

Wikipedia: *The Free Encyclopedia*, wikipedia.org, 2012.

Index

247

251

Rickey Butch Walker is a lifelong native son of the Warrior Mountains. He descends from Cherokee, Creek, and Celtic (Scots-Irish) people who migrated into the hills and coves of the mountainous region of north Alabama some 250 years ago. He, as was his father, is a member of the Echota Cherokee Tribe of Alabama. His Indian name is Fish Bird in honor of his fifth, fourth, and third great grandmothers-Catherine Kingfisher, Experience Fish, and Elizabeth Bird.

The kingfisher and fish bird (osprey) love to fish and so does Butch. In addition, the osprey is of contrasting colors of black and white which identify Butch's character. Things that rule his life are true or false, yes or no, and black or white with virtually no gray areas; therefore, he lives his life somewhat as an open book. Also, according to Indian legend, the birds of prey soar high in the sky and carry the prayers of the earthly creatures to the great spirit. Fish Bird (Butch) has his entire adult life been an advocate to preserve and protect the environment for all the earthly creatures that are unable to speak for themselves.

As a young boy, Butch was born and raised in the shadows of the Warrior Mountains where he was taught by his grandpa the ways of the wild. He squirrel hunted on Brushy Mountain, trapped in Sugar Camp Hollow, searched for ginseng in Indian Tomb Hollow, and fished in West Flint Creek. He walked with his grandparents on old Indian trails including Black Warriors' Path, Sipsie Trail, and many others. He explored the deep canyons, rolling hills, steep bluff lines, and vast hollows containing beautiful waterfalls where he would stand in the spray to cool off on a hot day. He was nourished by the subsistence of West Flint Creek and surrounding hardwood bottoms, and molded from traveling the trails and paths his people once trod. He grew up with a fierce love for the Warrior Mountains in which his ancestors lived, died, and are buried

In 1966, because of the love of his mountainous homeland, Butch became an advocate to stop the clear cutting of old growth woodlands that he roamed and hunted as a youngster. He worked to help establish the Sipsey Wilderness Area which was dedicated in 1975 and wrote weekly articles about the forest for the Moulton Advertiser.

In 1992, Butch teamed up with Lamar Marshall and helped begin the Bankhead Monitor to fight the clear cutting and destructive practices by the United States Forest Service taking place in the sacred Indian Tomb Hollow. The Monitor became Wild Alabama and later Wild South. Butch served as Chairman of the Board of Directors until Wild South merged with the Southern Appalachain Biodiversity Project in 2006

Rickey Butch Walker retired after some 35 years with the Lawrence County Board of Education during which he earned post graduate degrees in science, education, and supervision. He taught high school science for 11 years and served as Director of Lawrence County Schools' Indian Education Program and Oakville Indian Mounds Education Center until his retirement in 2009. In addition to his Masters Thesis, he has written several books including *High Town Path, Warrior Mountains Folklore, Indians of the Warrior Mountains, Indian Trails of the Warrior Mountains, Warrior Mountains Indian Heritage, Warrior Mountains Indian HeritageStudent Edition, Chickasaw Chief George Colbert: His Family and His Country,* and *Indians of the Warrior Mountains and Southeast.*

You can find Butch's book at Amazon.com or www.Historicaltruth101.com.

You can also subscribe to his weekly blog at www.RickeyButchWalker.com or

http://rickeybutchwalker.blogspot.com to receive Butch's weekly updates on the historical research he is currently writing.

Bluewater Publications is a multi-faceted publishing company capable of meeting all of your reading and publishing needs. Our two-fold aim is to:

1) Provide the market with educationally enlightening and inspiring research and reading materials.
2) Make the opportunity of being published available to any author and or researcher who desire to be published.

We are passionate about preserving history; whether through the re-publishing of an out-of-print classic, or by publishing the research of historians and genealogists. Bluewater Publications is the *Peoples' Choice Publisher*.

For company information or information about how you can be published through Bluewater Publications, please visit:

www.BluewaterPublications.com

Also check Amazon.com to purchase any of the books that we publish.

Confidently Preserving Our Past,
Bluewater Publications.com

www.ingramcontent.com/pod-product-compliance
Lightning Source LLC
Chambersburg PA
CBHW080542110426
42813CB00006B/1185